Forensic Apocalyptic Theology

Forensic Apocalyptic Theology

Karl Barth and the Doctrine of Justification

Shannon Nicole Smythe

Fortress Press
Minneapolis

FORENSIC APOCALYPTIC THEOLOGY

Karl Barth and the Doctrine of Justification

Cover design: Alisha Lofgren

Library of Congress Cataloging-in-Publication Data

Print ISBN: 978-1-5064-1055-5

eBook ISBN 978-1-5064-1029-6

The paper used in this publication meets the minimum requirements of American National Standard for Information Sciences — Permanence of Paper for Printed Library Materials, ANSI Z329.48-1984.

Manufactured in the U.S.A.

This book was produced using Pressbooks.com, and PDF rendering was done by PrinceXML.

Contents

Acknowledgments

In a myriad of ways, it has been the camaraderie of a handful of my female colleagues that has carried me along through each stage of my work in the doctoral program, but most especially as I brought this project to its completion during the first year of my son's life. I am a better scholar-wife-mother because of the solidarity of Katie Douglass, Laura Holmes, Elaine James, Christina Busman-Jost, Cambria Kaltwasser, Nicole Kirk, Sarah Stewart-Kroeker, Kara Lyons-Pardue, Lisa Powell, Anna Kate Shurley, Jennifer Thweatt, Melanie Webb, and Brittany Wilson.

This work testifies to the extraordinary education I received from the faculty of Princeton Theological Seminary during my time in the master of divinity and doctoral programs. I am grateful for the ways Professor George Hunsinger sharpened my interest in Reformed theology, Karl Barth, and the doctrine of justification during the MDiv program. I sincerely thank the members of my dissertation committee: Professors Bruce McCormack, Beverly Gaventa, and Darrell Guder. Professor McCormack has been my theological mentor for more than a decade. Being advised by him has been a profound honor. I am indebted to him for all the ways his scholarship and feedback on my work have shaped this project. Professor Gaventa's contribution to my work has been enormous. She not only introduced me to Pauline apocalyptic theology through her teaching and scholarship and provided invaluable insights to this project from the perspective of Pauline studies, but also she has promoted a real openness to deeper dialogue between Paul and Karl. Professor Guder taught me how to attend carefully both to the original German text of Barth's writings and to Barth's underlying missional impulse. Thanks are due to Professors Nancy Duff and Daniel Migliore for their important contributions to my formation as a scholar and teacher.

My formal theological training began at Seattle Pacific University. I was a most grateful recipient of that most cherished combination of teaching and mentorship provided so superbly by the faculty in the School of Theology. The passion for theology in Professor Kerry Dearborn first led me to consider a vocation in theology, and it was she who introduced me to Karl Barth. Professors Rob Wall and Frank Spina were also instrumental in nurturing in me a commitment to theological interpretation of Christian Scripture. Professors Jack Levison and Priscilla Pope-Levison have for many years wisely counseled me in my scholarly pursuits.

It is my family, however, in whom I found my first theological dialogue partners. Even from a young age, I enjoyed theological discussions with my father. My mother first taught me how to study the Bible and urged me to "seize the day" when I confided in her my desire to pursue a doctorate in theology. Finally, the faithful love of my husband, Kevin, along with our always thought-provoking conversations on topics theological and otherwise, have proved a continual inspiration. I am blessed to share life with him. As much of this project came together during the first year of life of our son, Micah, it is to him that I dedicate this book.

Abbreviations

AB	Anchor Bible
CD	Karl Barth, *The Church Dogmatics*. Edited by Geoffrey W. Bromiley and Thomas F. Torrance. Translated by Geoffrey W. Bromiley et al. 5 vols. in 14 parts. Edinburgh: T&T Clark, 1936–77
KD	Karl Barth, *Die kirchliche Dogmatik*. 5 vols. in 14 parts. Zollikon-Zürich: Evangelischer Verlag, 1932–70
SR	Karl Barth, *Kurze Erklärung Des Römerbriefes*. München: Chr. Kaiser, 1956. Eng. trans., Karl Barth, *A Shorter Commentary on Romans*. Edited by Maico Michielin. Translated by D. H. van Daleen. Aldershot, UK: Ashgate, 2007
WUNT	Wissenschaftliche Untersuchungen zum Neuen Testament

1

Introduction

> He does not project theological speculations out of his own mind; he is not concerned about a system; he is and he remains a student and teacher of Holy Scriptures. Whoever tries to understand him as other than this will not understand him at all.
>
> —Eduard Thurneysen, "Die Anfänge"

> What delights *me* most is . . . *Paul! That's what it is!* Next to him all dogmatics is slime, and ethics too.
>
> —Karl Barth to Eduard Thurneysen, May 18, 1924

Bringing an Old Outsider into a Perennial Debate

When it first hit the scene almost a century ago, Karl Barth's interpretation of Paul's theology in both the first and second editions of his *Römerbrief* was the subject of much critique, debate, and mostly dismissal by the New Testament guild.[1] As Richard Burnett points out,

1. This is not to say that his Romans commentary, in the first and second editions, was entirely ignored or failed to bring Barth any accolades. On the contrary, the first edition earned him an honorary professorship at the University of Göttingen, and the second edition quickly made him one of the most influential theologians of his day. As Ernst Käsemann observes, "Barth's *Epistle to the Romans* brought 'thoroughgoing eschatology' back out of its existence among the shades and made it into the keynote of New Testament interpretation in Germany." See Ernst Käsemann, "On the Subject of Primitive Christian Apocalyptic," in *New Testament Questions of Today*, trans. W. J. Montague (London: SCM Press, 1969), 109n2. Similarly, Rudolf Bultmann comments that "Barth

the most common allegation against Barth was that his exegesis had little to do with the actual content of Paul's letter to the church in Rome but was instead a reading of his own theology into Paul's letter.[2] Sadly, the legacy of the critiques leveled against Barth by his first reviewers still lives on in some quarters. Far too often, Barth's theological exegesis remains untapped by biblical scholars and theologians alike.[3]

Today there are old debates raging with new fire within Pauline studies—debates not unknown to Barth and his contemporaries. In particular, in discussions about the theology of the apostle, a frequent question surfaces as to the extent to which Paul even has a concept of justification by grace through faith, a concept so crucial to the Reformation and much Protestant theology that followed after.[4] While the Reformers found fodder for this doctrine in their reading of Paul's letters, the "Lutheran" conception of justification by faith alone has, since the twentieth century, been under constant fire in various works within Pauline scholarship. This recurrent trend was inaugurated, to a great extent, by the work of four scholars.

First on the scene were William Wrede and Albert Schweitzer, each of whom, in his own way, argued that justification is entirely peripheral to Paul's thought. For Wrede, justification is Paul's polemical doctrine.[5] For Schweitzer, it is merely a "subsidiary crater."[6] A seminal essay by Krister Stendahl in 1963, warning of the danger in reading Paul through Luther, has had a lasting effect on Pauline

has grasped Paul's view . . . in its depths . . . through his exegesis many details have become more alive." See Rudolf Bultmann, "Karl Barth's *Epistle to the Romans* in Its Second Edition," in *The Beginnings of Dialectic Theology*, ed. James M. Robinson, trans. Keith R. Crim (Richmond, VA: John Knox, 1962), 1:119.

2. Richard E. Burnett, *Karl Barth's Theological Exegesis: The Hermeneutical Principles of the Römerbrief Period* (Grand Rapids: Eerdmans, 2004), 17.
3. However, Barth's contribution to New Testament studies was officially recognized in 1925 through an appointment at Münster to a chair in dogmatics and New Testament exegesis.
4. For a survey of some of the important works in the twentieth-century debates in New Testament studies regarding the study of Paul and understanding his teaching on justification, see David E. Aune, "Recent Readings of Paul Relating to Justification by Faith," in *Rereading Paul Together: Protestant and Catholic Perspectives on Justification*, ed. David E. Aune (Grand Rapids: Baker Academic, 2006), 188–245.
5. Willliam Wrede, *Paul*, trans. Edward Lummis (repr., Eugene, OR: Wipf & Stock, 2001).
6. Albert Schweitzer, *The Mysticism of Paul the Apostle*, trans. William Montgomery (Baltimore: Johns Hopkins University Press, 1998), 225.

studies.[7] The fourth scholar credited with pummeling the doctrine of justification is E. P. Sanders, whose 1977 groundbreaking work, *Paul and Palestinian Judaism*, not only attacks a "Lutheran" understanding of Paul's Jewish context but also argues that distorted and limited views on Judaism in Paul's day have resulted in distortions of Paul's writings.[8] The conclusions of these scholars have been further developed with the advent of the so-called New Perspective[9] on Paul, such that many today doubt the validity of any sort of "Reformational" reading of Paul, finding it to be highly anachronistic, overly psychologized, and/or inappropriately focused on the role of the individual's faith in salvation.[10]

To be fair, it must be said that the scholars debating justification in Paul are not the sole actors in the current movement within the

7. Krister Stendahl, "The Apostle Paul and the Introspective Conscience of the West," *Harvard Theological Review* 56 (1963): 199–215; repr. in *The Writings of St. Paul: Annotated Text and Criticism*, ed. W. A. Meeks, Norton Critical Editions in the History of Ideas (New York: W. W. Norton, 1972).
8. I absolutely grant that the great benefit of the work of Sanders and many after him is the improved view of Second Temple Judaism it has afforded us, especially given the relatively negative view of Judaism during the Reformation, resulting from Luther's tendency to conflate the Jews with the scholastic theologians against whom he was reacting.
9. The phrase itself comes from an essay by James D. G. Dunn, "The New Perspective on Paul," *Bulletin of the John Rylands Library* 65 (1983): 95–122; repr. with an additional note in *Jesus, Paul, and the Law: Studies in Mark and Galatians* (Louisville: Westminster John Knox, 1990), 183–214. While there are many scholars whose work can be classified within the New Perspective on Paul category, Dunn has been one of the most energetic. For a sampling on Dunn's reexamination of justification, particularly in Romans and Galatians, see James D. G. Dunn, *The Theology of Paul the Apostle* (Grand Rapids: Eerdmans, 1998); *The Epistle to the Galatians* (Peabody, MA: Hendrickson, 1993); *Romans 1–8*, Word Biblical Commentary 38A (Waco: Word Books, 1988); *Romans 9–16*, Word Biblical Commentary 38B (Waco: Word Books, 1988). It should be noted, however, that Dunn argues that the New Perspective on Paul is not opposed to the classical Reformation doctrine of justification, even agreeing that it is *articulus stantis et cadentis ecclesiae*; see "The New Perspective: Whence and Whither?" in *The New Perspective on Paul*, WUNT 185 (Tübingen: Mohr Siebeck, 2005), 17–22, esp. 21, 33.

   Right beside him is N. T. Wright, who followed immediately after Sanders's *Paul and Palestinian Judaism* with his own important essay in 1978 on Paul's relationship to Judaism, arguing that "the tradition of Pauline interpretation has manufactured a false Paul by manufacturing a false Judaism for him to oppose." See N. T. Wright, "The Paul of History and the Apostle of Faith," *Tyndale Bulletin* 29 (1978): 78. Other New Perspective on Paul contributions by Wright include "Justification: The Biblical Basis and Its Relevance for Contemporary Evangelicalism," in *The Great Acquittal: Justification by Faith in Current Christian Thought*, ed. Gavin Reid (London: Collins, 1980), 13–37; *The Climax of the Covenant: Christ and the Law in Pauline Theology* (Minneapolis: Fortress Press, 1991); "Romans and the Theology of Paul," in *Pauline Theology*, vol. 3, *Romans*, ed. D. M. Hay and E. E. Johnson (Minneapolis: Fortress Press, 1992), 30–67; *The New Testament and the People of God* (Minneapolis: Fortress Press, 1992); *What Saint Paul Really Said: Was Paul of Tarsus the Real Founder of Christianity?* (Grand Rapids: Eerdmans, 1997).
10. For a helpful overview of the history and representatives of the New Perspective, see Stephen Westerholm, *Perspectives Old and New on Paul: The "Lutheran" Paul and His Critics* (Grand Rapids: Eerdmans, 2004), 101–200, 249–60.

academy to call into question the validity of the Protestant doctrine of justification. To their ranks, the following must be added: (1) the trend in ecumenical discussions to focus on the themes of union with Christ and deification, notwithstanding the advances made in 1999 with Lutheran and Roman Catholic churches in signing the "Joint Declaration in the Doctrine of Justification;" (2) the ambiguity among Protestant laypersons and scholars about their theological identity; and (3) recent scholarship on the Reformation that aims at downplaying the Reformers' commitment to a judicial framework (forensicism).[11] One regrettable outcome is that Protestant theology, and most especially the doctrine of justification, has fallen into disrepute and been subjected to caricatures of its key tenets. Yet, for the Reformers, justification was not simply one doctrine among many. The doctrine of justification *was* the Reformation, full stop. Justification is *the* hallmark doctrine that makes Protestant churches and theology Protestant. For Martin Luther, the stakes were always high: justification was the doctrine by which the church stands or falls. But John Calvin, too, called justification "the main hinge on which religion turns. . . . For unless you first of all grasp what your relationship to God is, and the nature of his judgment concerning you, you have neither a foundation on which to establish your salvation nor one on which to build piety toward God."[12] It is with full awareness of the seriousness of what is being called into question that this book seeks to lessen the widening chasm between Paul and Reformation theology by offering a thorough analysis of Karl Barth's Pauline theology of justification.

Throughout the debates over the relationship of the doctrine of justification to Pauline theology, Karl Barth's later exegesis and

11. For a brief sampling see J. Todd Billings, *Calvin, Participation and the Gift: The Activity of Believers in Union with Christ* (Oxford: Oxford University Press, 2007); Julie Canlis, *Calvin's Ladder: A Spiritual Theology of Ascent and Ascension* (Grand Rapids: Eerdmans, 2010); The Lutheran World Federation and the Roman Catholic Church, *Joint Declaration on the Doctrine of Justification*, English language ed. (Grand Rapids: Eerdmans, 2000); Tuomo Mannermaa, *Christ Present in Faith: Luther's View of Justification* (Minneapolis: Fortress Press, 2005); and Veli-Matti Kärkkäinen, *One with God: Salvation as Deification and Justification* (Collegeville, MN: Liturgical, 2004).

12. John Calvin, *Institutes of the Christian Religion*, ed. John T. McNeill, trans. Ford Lewis Battles, 2 vols., Library of Christian Classics, reissued ed. (Louisville: Westminster John Knox, 2006), 726.

theology have remained virtually unknown and untapped.[13] John Webster has noted the "surprising and regrettable" fact that there is a lack of any thorough study of Barth's work as a commentator on Holy Scripture.[14] This lacuna is strange indeed when we consider (1) the sheer amount of exegetical work in the Pauline corpus done throughout Barth's career; (2) the decidedly Pauline shape of his doctrine of reconciliation, which stresses that the apocalypse of God has already taken place in the death and resurrection of Jesus Christ; and (3) his fundamentally Reformed doctrine of justification. While there have been numerous studies on the theologies of the atonement and justification in Augustine, Luther, Calvin, and John Wesley, as well as studies of contemporary Lutheran understandings of justification,[15] an appraisal of Barth's later work, in relationship to this debate, has been almost inexplicably absent.[16]

This book seeks to fill in this gap in theological and biblical scholarship by investigating Barth's interpretation of Pauline

13. The exceptions to this trend are one essay by Douglas Harink, "Justification: Beyond Protestantism," in *Paul among the Postliberals: Pauline Theology beyond Christendom and Modernity* (Grand Rapids: Brazos, 2003), 23–65; and one essay by Benjamin Myers, "From Faithfulness to Faith in the Theology of Karl Barth," in *The Faith of Jesus Christ: Exegetical, Biblical and Theological Studies*, ed. Michael F. Bird and Preston M. Sprinkle (Carlisle, UK: Paternoster, 2009), 291–308.

14. John Webster, "Karl Barth," in *Reading Romans through the Centuries: From the Early Church to Karl Barth*, ed. Jeffrey P. Greenman and Timothy Larsen (Grand Rapids: Brazos, 2005), 208. Webster comments that a "beginning is made in David P. Henry's comparison of Barth's practices as commentator in the two editions of *Der Römerbrief* against the background of some standard German commentators from the early twentieth century; but, quite apart from its restricted focus on only a portion of Romans 5, Henry's work suffers from some mischaracterizations of both Barth's exegetical practice and his theological commitments" (n9). See David P. Henry, *The Early Development of the Hermeneutic of Karl Barth as Evidenced by His Appropriation of Romans 5.12–21* (Macon, GA: Mercer University Press, 1985).

15. Mark C. Mattes, *The Role of Justification in Contemporary Theology* (Grand Rapids: Eerdmans, 2004), 3–20; Robert Kolb, "Contemporary Lutheran Understandings of the Doctrine of Justification," in *Justification: What's at Stake in the Current Debates?*, ed. Mark Husbands and Daniel J. Treier (Downers Grove, IL: InterVarsity Press, 2004), 153–76.

16. Westerholm, *Perspectives Old and New on Paul*, 3–97, 201–25; Husbands and Treier, *Justification*; Charles E. Hill and Frank A. James III, eds., *The Glory of the Atonement: Biblical, Historical and Practical Perspectives* (Downers Grove, IL: InterVarsity Press, 2004); Bruce L. McCormack, ed., *Justification in Perspective: Historical Developments and Contemporary Challenges* (Grand Rapids: Baker Academic, 2006); and Oswald Bayer, *Living by Faith: Justification and Sanctification* (Grand Rapids: Eerdmans, 2003).

The few treatments of Barth's relationship to the Reformation and Pauline theology, especially on the doctrines of atonement and justification, can be found in the following essays by Bruce McCormack: "*Justitia aliena*: Karl Barth in Conversation with the Evangelical Doctrine of Imputed Righteousness," in *Justification in Perspective*, 167–96; "The Ontological Presuppositions of Barth's Doctrine of Atonement," in *Glory of the Atonement*; 346–66; and "What's at Stake in Current Debates over Justification?" in Husbands and Treier, *Justification*, 81–117.

justification in Romans. With the field of theological interpretation of Scripture burgeoning, Barth's work as both commentator and theologian has the potential to narrow the divide that often exists between the fields of systematic theology and biblical studies. Furthermore, such a study would enable students of Barth to look more closely at his work with Scripture and from this to consider "what may be learned about the overall character of Barth's theological commitments from the fact that he expended much labor on biblical commentary."[17]

Seeking Allies: Scholars of Pauline Apocalyptic Eschatology

It goes without saying that there are a myriad of ways to interpret the central theological concerns in Paul's letter to the church in Rome. For instance, with respect to the way salvation is described in Romans, there are readings ranging from the individual-spiritual to the sociopolitical, from the salvation-historical to the salvation from Roman tyranny. One rather recent strand of interpretation within Pauline studies reads Paul with an eye to his apocalyptic eschatology. The exegetical-theological reading of Paul done by these scholars places a high premium on the way that Paul draws out the radical in-breaking of God into this world, the full and inclusive judgment of God on humanity, and the nature of the relationship of God to the powers of sin and death.[18]

While Weiss and Schweitzer were the first to produce historical scholarship on apocalyptic, it was the scholarship of Ernst Käsemann that was instrumental in reviving interest in apocalyptic and its creative role within the New Testament. Most notably, he claimed, in a series of essays from the 1960s, that Paul's thinking is defined by

17. Webster, "Karl Barth," 208.

18. While Barry Matlock has noted that the term "apocalyptic" itself can denote a variety of things, thus lending it an air of ambiguity with such frequent usage, it is important to state at the outset that the Pauline interpreters who undertake an apocalyptic interpretation of Paul's texts do so with a more focused agenda. First, they are defining themselves in relation to different basic approaches to Paul. Second, they are most often influenced by the seminal work of Käsemann and, more recently, J. Louis Martyn. See Barry Matlock, *Unveiling the Apocalyptic Paul: Paul's Interpreters and the Rhetoric of Criticism* (Sheffield: Sheffield Academic Press, 1996), 258–63.

apocalyptic eschatology.[19] Against what he saw as Rudolf Bultmann's existentialist interpretation of Paul, Käsemann attempted instead to recover Paul's apocalyptic focus.[20] Initially he argued that Paul's perpetual focus on the return of Christ is the defining feature of his apocalyptic eschatology.[21] Yet in Käsemann's later work, he also understood Christ's death and resurrection as the event of God's invasion of a world imprisoned by cosmic powers.[22] Paul's theology, in his mind, asks the "the apocalyptic question": "'To whom does the sovereignty of the world belong?' To God or the evil powers?"[23] Another scholar of Pauline apocalyptic eschatology, J. Christiaan Beker, defines Paul's gospel as apocalyptic for the way it anticipates the

19. Käsemann's essays can be found in *New Testament Questions of Today*, trans. W. J. Montague (Philadelphia: Fortress Press, 1969), and include: "The Beginnings of Christian Theology," 82–107; "'The Righteousness of God' in Paul," 168–82; "On the Subject of Primitive Christian Apocalyptic," 108–37; and "Paul and Early Catholicism," 236–51.

20. While the debates between Käsemann and his teacher, Bultmann, are well known, what is not well known is that in his later years Käsemann ended up affirming and extending "Bultmann's program of demythologizing in a way that reveals the surprising continuity between Bultmann and apocalyptic theology. . . . Despite his debates with Bultmann in his younger years, Käsemann later proved himself to be one of Bultmann's most faithful students." See David W. Congdon, "Eschatologizing Apocalyptic: An Assessment of the Present Conversation on Pauline Apocalyptic," in *Apocalyptic and the Future of Theology: With and beyond J. Louis Martyn*, edited by Joshua B. Davis and Douglas Harink (Eugene, OR: Cascade Books, 2012), 126n29. See also Ernst Käsemann, *On Being a Disciple of the Crucified Nazarene: Unpublished Lectures and Sermons*, ed. Rudolf Landau and Wolfgang Kraus, trans. Roy A. Harrisville (Grand Rapids: Eerdmans, 2010), 100–101, 177, 199–200. For a full defense of Bultmann as himself an apocalyptic theologian, see Congdon's *The Mission of Demythologizing: Rudolf Bultmann's Dialectical Theology* (Minneapolis: Fortress Press, 2015).

21. Käsemann, "'Righteousness of God' in Paul," 181; "On the Subject of Primitive Christian Apocalyptic," 109n1, 131; and "Paul and Early Catholicism," 241.

22. Ernst Käsemann, *Commentary on Romans*, ed. and trans. Geoffrey W. Bromiley (Grand Rapids: Eerdmans, 1980), 134.

In an effort to bring greater precision to the increasingly divergent scholarship on apocalyptic, whether biblical or theological, Congdon has suggested a schematic of "Apocalyptic A" and "Apocalyptic B." See "Eschatologizing Apocalyptic: An Assessment." In Apocalyptic A are scholars such as Käsemann and Beker, who view the apocalyptic event "as something literal, immanent, and directly observable" (132). In Apocalyptic B are scholars such as Martyn and Christopher Morse, who view "the apocalyptic event as something nonliteral, transcendent, and indirectly or paradoxically present" (132). Congdon clarifies that the mature theological work of Käsemann fits better within Apocalyptic B (126n29). However, I would add that his work as a Pauline scholar, as evidenced in his *Commentary on Romans*, also demonstrates that he fits in Apocalyptic B. This will become clear throughout this book. While Congdon cites nothing from Beker to defend his claim for putting him in camp B, in another essay he names Beker's misinformed critiques and dismissals of Barth's and Bultmann's projects. See Congdon, "Bonhoeffer and Bultmann: Toward an Apocalyptic Rapprochement," *International Journal of Systematic Theology* 15, no. 2 (2013): 172–95. While Congdon's insights into Beker's misreading of Barth and Bultmann are on target, my work with Beker, in chap. 2, will show that he does not neatly fit in Congdon's camp B category.

23. Käsemann, "On the Subject of Primitive Christian Apocalyptic," 135–36.

final triumph of God in Christ over all the powers that oppose God's redemptive plans.[24] Thus, according to Beker, the center of the gospel for Paul is the unwavering certainty that the divine invasion of Christ's death and resurrection into our world have made possible both a new future and a new creation. More recently, J. Louis Martyn, Leander Keck, Beverly Gaventa, and others have highlighted Paul's passionate conviction that God has invaded our world to set it right—not by anything humans can do, but by God's sovereign "rectification."[25] Martinus de Boer's work focuses on bringing out the elements in Paul's apocalyptic eschatology that, like the Jewish apocalyptic eschatology that precedes it, make for a cosmic drama played out between divine and cosmic forces.[26] Above all, Martyn is credited with advancing even beyond Käsemann in defining apocalyptic in Paul, having argued convincingly that for Paul both apocalyptic and the heart of the gospel are concentrated in the cross and resurrection of Jesus Christ.[27] According to Martyn, Pauline apocalyptic eschatology centers on "God's liberating invasion of the cosmos,"[28] which is enacted "in

24. See J. Christiaan Beker, *Paul the Apostle: The Triumph of God in Life and Thought* (Philadelphia: Fortress Press, 1980); *The Triumph of God: The Essence of Paul's Thought* (Minneapolis: Fortress Press, 1990).

25. It should be noted that most current biblical scholars of Pauline apocalyptic eschatology prefer to use the term "rectification" instead of "justification" in order to highlight that the "subject Paul addresses is that of God's *making right what has gone wrong*" (250). As far as I can tell, Martyn and Keck were some of the first to do so. Käsemann, Bultmann, and Barth do not use this language, and scholars writing on apocalyptic theology, such as Morse, Nathan Kerr, and Congdon, use the language of justification.

Martyn's explanation of what is at stake in translating Paul in this way is instructive. He notes that the "thrust of the verb [*dikaioō*] and of the noun [*dikaiosyne*] is exceedingly difficult to grasp, and equally difficult to render in a modern language." Martyn goes on to clarify that while these words in Greek are linguistic cognates, this connection is often obscured when translating them in English as "to justify" and "righteousness." Compounding this linguistic difficulty is the more serious issue, according to Martyn, that the English translations put Paul's terms in linguistic realms in which he does not intend for them to be. For the verb, translated as "to justify," the realm is the law, with implications of "the existence of a definable legal norm." For the noun, the realm is religion and morality, with the implication of "a definable religious or moral norm." See J. Louis Martyn, *Galatians: A New Translation with Introduction and Commentary*, AB 33A (New York: Doubleday, 1997), 249–50; see also 263–75.

26. Martinus C. de Boer, *The Defeat of Death: Apocalyptic Eschatology in 1 Corinthians 15 and Romans 5* (Sheffield: JSOT, 1988); "Paul and Apocalyptic Eschatology," in *The Origins of Apocalypticism in Judaism and Christianity*, ed. John J. Collins, vol. 1 of *The Encyclopedia of Apocalypticism* (New York: Continuum, 1998), 345–83; and "Paul, Theologian of God's Apocalypse," *Interpretation* 56 (2002): 21–33.

27. Richard E. Sturm, "Defining the Word 'Apocalyptic': A Problem in Biblical Criticism," in *Apocalyptic and New Testament: Essays in Honor of J. Louis Martyn*, ed. Joel Marcus and Marion L. Soards, Journal for the Study of the New Testament Supplement Series 24 (Sheffield: JSOT, 1988), 39.

Christ" as old creation is crucified (including our enslavement to the cosmic powers of "Sin" and "Death") and then delivered, by the Spirit, into new creation, the in-breaking of which "is itself revelation, apocalypse."[29] He submits that Paul's apocalyptic perspective has three foci: Christ's future coming, Christ's past advent (his death and resurrection), and the present war against the powers of evil, inaugurated by his Spirit and taking place between these two events.[30] The present powers of evil are classified by Martyn as anti-God powers whose appearance on the scene fundamentally changes things and by this change indicates "what has really gone wrong and what is really involved in God's making right in the whole cosmos."[31] Moreover, he also emphasizes that God's liberating invasion causes an "epistemological crisis" for those whom it encounters, since it reveals their world in a wholly different light. Such an apocalyptic confrontation causes them to see "bifocally" "both the evil age and the new creation simultaneously."[32]

It is Pauline apocalyptic eschatology with which I will put Barth's own work in conversation. Before adducing why this is so, it will be helpful to articulate what is meant by the use of the term "apocalyptic." Generally speaking, Pauline scholarship that falls within this strand of interpretation can be characterized as emphasizing these four notions in Paul's work: (1) the sovereign, unconditional action of God in the world to set right what has gone wrong; (2) an emphasis on divine revelation that discloses a new reality and age; (3) a christological understanding that the old age was characterized by humanity's oppression by evil powers; and (4) an eschatological construal of the cosmic horizons of Christ's death and resurrection expressed in Paul's account of the gospel.[33]

28. J. Louis Martyn, "The Apocalyptic Gospel in Galatians," *Interpretation* 54, no. 3 (2000): 244–66 (on 254).
29. Martyn, *Galatians*, 104.
30. Ibid., 105.
31. Ibid., 272–73.
32. Ibid., 104.
33. Fleming Rutledge has defined the following dimensions as crucial to the approach: "divine agency is central . . . ; Sin and Death are Powers who have invaded the world and established their dominion; the human condition is genuinely tragic because humanly speaking, there is no escape

There are three reasons for choosing scholars of Pauline apocalyptic eschatology as allies with Barth. The first reason is that, albeit at times indirectly, their work fundamentally challenges some of the key "New Perspective" conclusions that aim to distance the Reformation's doctrine of justification as at all connected to Paul's own notion of justification. Westerholm's judicious observation throws the situation into sharp relief: "if central to the new perspective is the claim that Paul's rejection of the works of the law had nothing to do with opposition to a role for human activity in justification, then ... [scholars of Paul's apocalyptic eschatology] ... must be reckoned among its most forceful critics."[34] This being the case, the work of these scholars maintains a certain commitment, along with Barth, to the view that it is God and God alone who effects justification/rectification in Christ and that human response and/or decision contributes nothing to the achievement of redemption within Paul's theology. Insofar as Barth's exegetical work and doctrine of reconciliation might strike similar chords within the spectrum of Pauline interpretation with these scholars, Barth's work can be seen as an ally and resource for the debates over Pauline justification today.

The second reason these scholars are appropriate allies with Barth is that many of the scholars of Pauline apocalyptic eschatology see ties between their own work and Barth's.[35] As Douglas Harink has, to a large

from bondage to the Powers; the earthly human world is subject to incursion from the divine world—'cosmic breaking and entering' (Martyn)—in Jesus Christ, the end of the ages has come upon us ... ; the divine apocalypse is less a disclosure than it is an invasion; justification (*dikaiosune*) is understood less as individual salvation, more as rectification constituting a new world ... ; there are *three* parties in the apocalyptic drama, not two: God, enslaved humanity, and the Powers of Sin and Death ... ; Jesus Christ waged apocalyptic warfare against these demonic forces ... ; the apocalypse of Jesus Christ means the end of conventional warfare, because the line between good and evil runs through each person ... ; apocalyptic metaphor is God's poetry (Martyn), telling us the truth about our condition and our hope; the New Creation dawns even now, in the Church's participation in the Cross and Resurrection; and cruciform Christian witness is anchored by secure confidence in God's triumph at the ultimate End, the Last Day when God puts an end to Sin, Death, and the devil, establishing the Kingdom of God in its eternal, victorious completeness." See Fleming Rutledge, "A Modest Proposal: Apocalyptic Theology," *Generous Orthodoxy Blog*, October 23, 2009, http://ruminations.generousorthodoxy.org/2009/10/modest-proposal-apocalyptic-theology.htm.

34. Westerholm, *Perspectives Old and New on Paul*, 240.

35. Martyn has remarked that "Barth was an exegete as well as a systematic theologian; for over a considerable period of time he correctly emphasized that Paul saw Adam in the light of Christ, sin in the light of grace, and so on." See J. Louis Martyn, "God's Way of Making Right What Is Wrong,"

degree, correctly observed, Barth's work in the second edition of his *Römerbrief* has a "powerful *apocalyptic* tone and message."[36] Yet what is interesting is that Harink then goes on to argue that Barth's work, both in the *Römerbrief* and *Church Dogmatics* IV/1, has anticipated the "discoveries" of recent Pauline scholarship regarding a more "genuine Pauline theology of justification,"[37] a theology that, according to his classification, is quite antithetical to the "usual Protestant story of justification and faith."[38]

Harink's argument demands further attention for several reasons. First, he wants not only to distance his apocalyptic reading of Paul's theology of justification from the "usual" Protestant doctrine of justification but also to enlist the aid of Karl Barth in so doing. Second, insofar as Harink pits a Protestant conception of justification against what he calls a more "genuine Pauline theology of justification,"[39] his

in *Theological Issues in the Letters of Paul* (Nashville: Abingdon, 1997), 144n8. Martyn himself claims to follow after Barth in his own work in Paul. He also finds E. P. Sanders's famous observation that Paul thinks from solution to plight to have been anticipated in Barth's *Church Dogmatics*. See Martyn, *Galatians*, 95n43. Furthermore, Martyn sees something in the biblical work of Paul Meyer that cannot be otherwise accounted for except to note that he was Barth's student for a year. See Martyn, "A Personal Word," in *The Word in the World: Essays in New Testament Exegesis and Theology*, ed. Paul W. Meyer and John T. Carroll (Louisville: Westminster John Knox, 2004), xviii. Harink finds Barth's early commentaries on Romans and later volumes of the *Church Dogmatics* to be a thorough outworking of Harink's own portrayal of the Pauline theme of "'justification by the faithfulness of Jesus Christ.'" See Harink, *Paul among the Postliberals*, 45. Hays indicates that his appreciative reading of Barth while studying at Yale in the 1970s, together with his contact with David Kelsey's narrative interpretation of Barth and Hans Frei's project to retrieve from Barth the category of realistic narrative, were factors that influenced his book on the faith of Jesus. See Richard B. Hays, *The Faith of Jesus Christ: The Narrative Substructure of Galatians 3:1–4:11*, 2nd ed. (Grand Rapids: Eerdmans, 2002), xxiii–xxiv. Gaventa regularly cotaught a course at Princeton Theological Seminary entitled "Paul and Karl," in which she shared with students the impact that reading Barth's second Romans commentary had on her during her graduate studies, as well as the similarity she finds in Barth between her own work on God "handing them over" in Rom. 1:24, 26, 28 and Barth's discussion of Judas being handed over in a small-print section of *CD* II/2. See Beverly Roberts Gaventa, "Interpreting the Death of Jesus Apocalyptically: Reconsidering Romans 8:32," in *Jesus and Paul Reconnected: Fresh Pathways into an Old Debate*, ed. Todd D. Still (Grand Rapids: Eerdmans, 2007), 131n12.

36. Harink, *Paul among the Postliberals*, 46. Harink is not the first to discover the apocalyptic tones in Barth's *Römerbrief*. Käsemann engages with Barth's *Römerbrief* throughout his own Romans commentary. Martyn, too, while referring occasionally in his scholarship to passages in Barth's *Church Dogmatics*, also seems familiar with the apocalypticism in Barth's reading of Paul in his *Römerbrief* because he used to assign it in his course on Romans at Union Seminary, New York. (Gaventa relayed this piece of information in her opening lecture for the Princeton Theological Seminary course she cotaught on "Paul and Karl." As she narrates it, Martyn's course on Romans was her first introduction to Barth's *Römerbrief*.)
37. Harink, *Paul among the Postliberals*, 46.
38. Ibid., 45.
39. Bruce McCormack argues that Harink, in *Paul among the Postliberals*, has polemicized against

work only recycles the same dismissal of the core theological insight of the Reformation first promulgated by Wrede and Schweitzer[40] and so propagates the widening gap between Paul and Reformation theology. Thus even as it has been recognized that scholars of Paul's apocalypticism pose a sure challenge to the New Perspective on Paul, it seems that, at times, they also want to distance Reformation theology from Paul's apocalyptic eschatology.[41] This is seen not only in Harink's essay but also in the decision to translate δικαιοσύνη as "rectification" rather than "justification," which, at the very least, does away with the linguistic connection between Paul and the doctrine of justification. Finally, Harink's use and understanding of Barth reveals that among those Pauline scholars who find an advocate in Barth's second Romans commentary, it is not always well known how Barth's doctrine of justification developed from its earlier roots in the second edition of his Romans commentary to his more mature theology in the fourth volume of the *Church Dogmatics*.[42]

This brings us to the final reason for choosing scholars of Paul's apocalyptic eschatology as allies. Though Barth never abandoned his actualistic account of revelation, set forth in the second edition of his Romans commentary, which does indeed line up well with apocalyptic readings of Paul, he nevertheless expands on and corrects his earlier

the Reformation by creating false either-or decisions for his readers. See Bruce McCormack, "*Justitia aliena*," 168. See Harink, *Paul among the Postliberals*, 25–26. Harink is not the only one, however. Richard Hays targets Luther. See Hays, *Faith of Jesus Christ*, 119–22. Meyer, too, classifies Reformation interpretations of Romans 7 as anachronistic understandings that inhibit the text from being read according to the original form and function Paul had in mind. See Paul W. Meyer, "The Worm at the Core of the Apple: Exegetical Reflections on Romans 7," in *The Conversation Continues: Studies in Paul and John in Honor of J. Louis Martyn*, ed. Robert T. Fortna and Beverly Roberts Gaventa (Nashville: Abingdon, 1990), 62–84.

40. See Harink, *Paul among the Postliberals*, 44–45. For a helpful summary of the scholarship of Wrede and Schweitzer on this issue, see Westerholm, *Perspectives Old and New on Paul*, 101–16.

41. As McCormack notes, "If there is a consensus that stretches across these rather diverse groupings where Paul's doctrine of justification is concerned, it is this: the so-called Lutheran Paul constitutes a serious distortion of Paul's teaching." See McCormack, "Can We Still Speak of 'Justification by Faith'?: An In-House Debate with Apocalyptic Readings of Paul," in *Galatians and Christian Theology: Justification, the Gospel, and Ethics in Paul's Letter*, ed. Mark W. Elliott, Scott J. Hafemann, N. T. Wright, and John Frederick (Grand Rapids: Baker Academic, 2014), 161.

42. Even Myers's essay "From Faithfulness to Faith in the Theology of Karl Barth," which is more nuanced in its understanding of Barth's theology, still only highlights the Pauline thread running through the second edition of Barth's Romans commentary to *CD* IV to the neglect of paying attention to the significant developments that occurred between them.

doctrine of justification in ways that nuance current apocalyptic readings of Paul and ultimately create heretofore unnoticed or underdeveloped ties between the work of scholars of Paul's apocalyptic eschatology and a Barthian revision of the Reformation's doctrine of justification. This project proceeds on the conviction that Barth's later theology and exegesis in *A Shorter Commentary on Romans* and the *Church Dogmatics* also need to be mined for ways that both challenge and contribute to the apocalyptic readings of Pauline theology. Yet this must be done without leaving behind the core insights of the second edition of Barth's Romans commentary. As Bruce McCormack has convincingly argued: "the gains made in *Romans* II[43] are everywhere presupposed throughout the *Church Dogmatics*; . . . the continuity in theological perspective between these two great works so greatly outweighs the discontinuity that those who wish to read the dogmatics without the benefit of the lens provided by *Romans* II will understand everything in the wrong light."[44]

The Significance of Barth's Genetic-Historic Development

A significant element of this study is the movement that will be made from the second edition of Barth's commentary on Romans (chap. 2) to his later exegesis of Romans, contained within *A Shorter Commentary on Romans*, and his doctrine of reconciliation in *CD* IV/1 (chaps. 4–8), plus three brief ventures into II/2, *Christ and Adam*,[45] and IV/3.1 in chapters 3, 6, and 8, respectively. Even more defining is the reason for this movement across texts. While it is true that a more comprehensive picture of the depth of Barth's Pauline-shaped doctrine of justification will be gained, there is a more fundamental impetus underlying the decision to seek after the fullness of Barth's thought. The impetus lies in the fact that the reading Barth gives to Paul in the second

43. This is McCormack's shorthand for the second edition of Barth's *Römerbrief*.
44. Bruce L. McCormack, *Karl Barth's Critically Realistic Dialectical Theology: Its Genesis and Development 1909–1936* (Oxford: Clarendon, 2004), 244–45.
45. Karl Barth, *Christus und Adam nach Römer 5* (Zollikon-Zurich: Evangelischer Verlag, 1952); Eng. trans., Karl Barth, *Christ and Adam: Man and Humanity in Romans 5*, trans. T. A. Smail (New York: Harper & Brothers, 1956).

edition of his Romans commentary, while honing in on several defining aspects of Pauline apocalyptic eschatology, gives only half the story. The second edition of the Romans commentary is one-sided in its understanding of the relationship of God to humanity set forth by Paul. This is because Barth was singularly focused on the problem of revelation: how God could reveal God's self to humanity in time and space without ceasing to be God. Barth's aim throughout his second commentary study was to look to Paul's letter to the church in Rome to answer the question of how the sovereign, high, and unknown God could be known. Barth's discovery, simply put, is that God can only be known in and through God's self-revelation in Jesus Christ. "Knowledge of God is possible only as a divine possibility (miracle!) and never as a human possibility."[46]

Barth's focus in the second edition of the Romans commentary is absorbed with the problem of how God can be known without then becoming something that humans can possess. The solution, Barth argues, is that God must only be known *indirectly*, by way of an intermediary. More importantly, the revelation of God through the intermediary must always remain distinct from the intermediary itself. In Jesus Christ, God veils God's self completely, in order that God may unveil God's self only to faith. Thus in the second edition of the Romans commentary, Jesus Christ is *not* the revelation of God but only the medium of God's self-revelation. While Jesus is the locus of revelation in his commentary, Barth's understanding of the incarnation, and its place in Pauline theology, is largely undeveloped.

Noting the one-sidedness of the second edition of the commentary, however, does not mean that Barth was not intent on listening to Paul's witness to the subject matter (*Sache*) to which all biblical texts point. In the preface to the second edition, Barth defines the *Sache* of the Bible as the "'infinite qualitative difference' between time and eternity, between God and the human. The relation—or, more accurately, the *relating*—of God to the human was understood to be a dialectical one, a dialectic of judgment and redemption."[47] McCormack points out that

46. McCormack, *Barth's Critically Realistic Dialectical Theology*, 248.

for Barth "[w]hat did change from time to time was his description of the one 'subject-matter' of which all biblical texts, with greater or lesser clarity, speak."[48] This is indeed what happens for Barth from the second edition of the Romans commentary to *A Shorter Commentary on Romans* and the *Church Dogmatics.*

While Barth's transition to his more mature Christology from *CD* II/2 onward was a gradual one, there were two decisive occurrences that affected Barth's theological thought. Both of these events occurred in the years after the second edition of the Romans commentary, and the transition in Barth's thinking, which these events help to bring on, directly affected his later readings of Paul and his further development of the doctrine of justification. The first of these occurrences came in May 1924, when Barth happened on the anhypostatic-enhypostatic christological dogma of the ancient church while reading post-Reformation theologians Heinrich Schmid's and Heinrich Heppe's textbooks on Reformed dogmatics.[49] The net effect of the discovery of this christological doctrine, in relationship to the doctrine of revelation set forth in the second edition of the commentary, was that it allowed Barth to shift away from the time-eternity dialectic, which was his chosen way of maintaining the primacy of God in his self-revelation, to achieving the same results through christological means. The anhypostatic/enhypostatic doctrine affirms that the second Person of the Trinity took on human nature completely and lived a human life in and through it. Outwardly, Jesus is a human just like any other, but inwardly the subject of the human Jesus is the second Person of the Trinity. Barth could now preserve the critical distance between God and humanity within his Christology and, at the same time, take into full account the doctrine of the incarnation, rather than reducing the location of revelation to the single point of the event

47. Bruce L. McCormack, "The Significance of Karl Barth's Theological Exegesis of Philippians," in *Orthodox and Modern: Studies in the Theology of Karl Barth* (Grand Rapids: Baker Academic, 2008), 98.
48. Ibid.
49. For a full narration and exploration of the significance of this discovery for Barth's theology, see chap. 8 of McCormack's *Karl Barth's Critically Realistic Dialectical Theology*. McCormack has, more recently, made a "modest correction" to his paradigm of Barth's development. See Bruce L. McCormack, "Seek God Where He May Be Found: A Response to Edwin Chr. Van Driel," *Scottish Journal of Theology* 60, no. 1 (2007): 63–64.

of the resurrection, as he did in the second edition of the Romans commentary.

The second occurrence that helped further Barth's theological thought came during the summer of 1936, when Barth heard a lecture given by Pierre Maury on the doctrine of election. Maury's lecture was given at a conference of Calvin scholars. His lecture was titled "Election and Faith," and the upshot of his argument was to reground election in Christology rather than treat it in abstraction from the person and work of Jesus Christ. In the first instance, the subject of election is God's Son, who chooses to be for humanity by taking the consequences of human sin against God onto himself. The effect of Maury's lecture on Barth's own thinking did not take long to sink in. Barth subsequently gave a series of lectures in Debrecen, Hungary, in September 1936 on "God's Gracious Election," which provided the basic structure of his full-length treatment of the doctrine election in *CD* II/2.[50] However, Barth's thinking in 1936 was still in development. Matthias Gockel has shown that in the Debrecen lectures, it was the "*eternal* God and thus also the eternal Son of God [who] is the *electing* God"[51] for Barth, as it was for Maury. Not until *CD* II/2, whose material Barth presented "prior to its publication in regular lecture-course at the University of Basel, . . . between the autumn of 1939 and the summer of 1941,"[52] does Barth arrive at the new conclusion, which is his alone, that the person of Jesus Christ is both the object *and* the subject of election. Additionally, it was Barth and/or Charlotte von Kirschbaum who introduced the idea of Jesus' "election for damnation" into Maury's lecture, which was translated into German in 1940 by Kirschbaum, in order to bring Maury's ideas more in line with Barth's own emerging thought at the time.[53] McCormack has argued that Barth's new foundation of Jesus Christ as both the object and subject of election had an all-encompassing impact for the whole of his subsequent theology.

50. McCormack, *Barth's Critically Realistic Dialectical Theology*, 458.
51. Matthias Gockel, *Barth and Schleiermacher on the Doctrine of Election: A Systematic-Theological Comparison* (Oxford: Oxford University Press, 2006), 161n8.
52. Ibid., 164.
53. Ibid., 162n14.

It is the key to his mature theology; it marks the difference between his earlier focus on revelation in the second edition of the Romans commentary and his christological concentration in volumes 2–4 of the *Church Dogmatics*. Incidentally, the incorporation of *A Shorter Commentary on Romans* into this study, in addition to providing further insight into Barth's exegesis of Romans, also gives the benefit of illuminating Barth's reading of Romans after he had been affected by Maury's lecture on election *and* after he had developed Maury's thinking about the subject of election in an even deeper way in *CD* II/2. The commentary was compiled from the manuscript of a course of lectures on Romans that Barth gave in Basel during the winter of 1940–41, which is concurrent with the time he was lecturing on the material presented within *CD* II/2.

The Argument

With the perennial debate over Pauline justification in mind, the interpretative allies identified, and the significance of Barth's genetic-historical development in view, what remains is to set forth the particular argument this study proposes. The aim of this study is to undertake a more sustained, accurate, and theologically complex reading of Barth's contribution to the question of a Pauline theology of justification. Furthermore, this study has the distinction of providing not only a broader treatment of Pauline apocalyptic eschatology in relationship to Barth but also of analyzing Barth's understanding of apocalyptic eschatology by taking closer account of the lines of continuity and discontinuity that run from his understanding of justification in the second edition of his commentary on Romans to his mature doctrine of justification in the fourth volume of the *Church Dogmatics*.

The main arc of this study is to sketch out the form and content of Barth's *forensic* apocalyptic understanding of justification, which emerges out of his mature Christology in his doctrine of reconciliation in *CD* IV and later readings of Paul both in the *Church Dogmatics* and *A Shorter Commentary on Romans*. It is the contention of this study that while Barth's understanding of Paul's apocalyptic eschatology in the second edition of his Romans commentary is wholly compatible with Pauline apocalyptic, significant theological development occurred for Barth after the publication of the second edition of the Romans commentary, which resulted in his moving beyond the earlier perspective of the second Romans commentary. When Barth composed the commentary on Romans, in its second edition, he did so with no real knowledge of the Reformation and its theology. All of that would change when he took up the post of honorary professor of Reformed theology in Göttingen—a post that he was awarded based on the first edition of the Romans commentary. His honorary chair carried the requirement that Barth teach "introduction to the Reformed confessions, Reformed doctrine and Reformed church life."[54] For such a task, Barth felt unqualified, remarking that he had not even read any of the Reformed confessional writings. He quickly set about to remedy that situation and soon was teaching various aspects of the Reformed theological tradition to his students. Through this process, Barth became well acquainted with the forensic (judicial) framework the Reformers gave to the doctrines of justification and atonement. This knowledge would later affect the unique forensic shape Barth gave to the whole of his soteriology in *CD* IV.

This study proposes that this development in Barth's knowledge and understanding of the Reformation, coupled with the revisions that he would make to his doctrine of election in *CD* II/2, created the necessary groundwork for him to adapt and intensify the forensic reading of Paul's theology of justification, which heretofore had been carried out by the Reformation. I will demonstrate that Barth's revision of forensicism, based as it is on the historicized theological ontology that comes to expression in his mature Christology, is apocalyptic in nature. Insofar as Barth's mature Christology is apocalyptic in nature, Barth's later reading of Romans takes up some of the same concerns as the cosmic apocalyptic readings of Paul, if on slightly different grounds.

54. Eberhard Busch, *Karl Barths Lebenslauf* (München: Christian Kaiser Verlag, 1975); Eng. trans., *Karl Barth: His Life from Letters and Autobiographical Texts*, trans. John Bowden (Philadelphia: Fortress Press, 1976), 128–29.

At the same time, because Barth revises Reformational forensicism according to Pauline apocalyptic eschatology, his doctrine of justification is not susceptible to the same criticisms commonly brought against forensicism, while his soteriology becomes more consistently forensic than that of the Reformation.

In choosing to use the term "forensic apocalyptic" to describe Barth's doctrine of justification, it needs to be clarified what this term does and does not mean. The term itself comes from the scholarship of de Boer. De Boer, himself a scholar of Paul's apocalyptic eschatology, has argued that there are two different patterns of Jewish apocalyptic theology present in Paul's letters. He clarifies first that "[a]pocalyptic eschatology is fundamentally concerned with God's active and visible rectification (putting right) of the created world (the 'cosmos'), which has somehow gone astray and become alienated from God."[55] De Boer further rehearses the important distinction, first made by Philipp Vielhauer,[56] that a defining characteristic of apocalyptic eschatology is its focus on an eschatological dualism between this age and the age to come. Out of this two-age dualism de Boer distinguishes two different patterns, within Jewish literature, of apocalyptic eschatology. The first pattern he names cosmic-apocalyptic. It is defined by the created world coming under the power of evil forces such that God's sovereignty is seized and the whole world is led into idolatry. The righteous remnant of God's people waits for the time when "God will invade the world under the dominion of the evil powers and defeat them in a cosmic war."[57] The second pattern, de Boer notes, is a modified version of the cosmic-apocalyptic pattern. This is the forensic version of apocalyptic eschatology and, most notably, with this pattern the notion of evil cosmic powers does not play a role. Rather, human free will and individual human decisions are stressed. Sin results from an individual choosing to reject God, and death is the punishment. The law is God's solution to humanity's sin, and the final judgment is

55. De Boer, "Paul and Apocalyptic Eschatology," 350.
56. See Philipp Vielhauer, "Introduction," in *New Testament Apocrypha*, ed. E. Hennecke and W. Schneemelcher (Philadelphia: Westminster, 1963–65), 2:581–607.
57. De Boer, "Paul and Apocalyptic Eschatology," 359.

not "a cosmic war but . . . a courtroom in which all humanity appears before the bar of the judge, God [who] will reward with eternal life those who have . . . chosen the law and observed its commandments (the righteous), while he will punish with eternal death those who have not (the wicked)."[58] De Boer notes that each of these two patterns of Jewish apocalyptic eschatology is present in Paul's letters, though "christologically adapted and modified."[59] While the patterns appear, in Jewish literature, to be alternatives to each other, with Paul as our example, this certainly need not be the case in Christian theology. However, de Boer argues that even though each of the patterns are christologically adapted in Romans, it is the cosmic-apocalyptic pattern that largely circumscribes and overtakes the forensic motifs. The language and perspectives of forensic apocalyptic eschatology predominate in Rom. 1:1–5:11, while those of cosmic apocalyptic eschatology prevail in Romans 6–8. Romans 5:12–21 is a key transitional passage in which the two patterns interpenetrate.[60] More will be said about this when de Boer's argument is taken up again in chapter 6. For now, suffice it to say that Paul is adapting both patterns of Jewish apocalyptic eschatology in light of his Christology and that Barth's own forensic apocalyptic eschatology is fully consonant with Paul's adaptations of both patterns.

Two things need to be said about the "forensic apocalypticism" as it is used to describe Barth's theology of justification. The first is that insofar as apocalyptic eschatology, of which forensic apocalyptic is but one version, is focused on bringing out the differences between this age and the age to come, Barth's theological corpus as a whole could be characterized as apocalyptic eschatology. After all, Barth is famous for stating that if "Christianity be not altogether thoroughgoing eschatology, there remains in it no relationship whatever with Christ."[61] Ingolf Dalferth suggests that from the first edition of the

58. Ibid.
59. Ibid., 362.
60. Ibid., 365.
61. Karl Barth, *Der Römerbrief* (Zürich: Evangelischer Verlag, 1967), 298. Eng. trans., Karl Barth, *The Epistle to the Romans*, trans. from 6th ed., ed. Edwyn C. Hoskyns (London: Oxford University Press, 1968), 314.

Romans commentary to the end of his life, Barth did not deviate from stressing that "the reality to which theology refers is the eschatological reality of the risen Christ and the new life into which we are drawn by the Spirit."[62]

The second thing to point out is that while this study proposes to use de Boer's phrase "forensic apocalyptic eschatology" to describe Barth's mature doctrine of justification, the actual content needed to fill out the specifics of this phrasing, as it describes Barth's work, must be provided by Barth, not de Boer. Indeed, Barth's version of forensic apocalyptic eschatology looks considerably different from the description de Boer provides of the version found in Jewish intertestamental literature. First of all, Barth follows Paul in understanding the eschatological event by which God deals with sin and the sinner to have already happened in the death and resurrection of Jesus Christ. Second, rather than stressing the importance of one's relationship to the law in determining one's final destiny, Barth follows Paul in noting that the important relationship is between an individual and Christ, established by God.

Moreover, on a formal level, Barth's forensic apocalypticism is not set over against cosmic apocalypticism. Rather, Barth adapts the forensic approach to the doctrine of justification set by the Reformers, making it more christocentrically focused by way of his historicized theological ontology. It is in this way that Barth's forensicism gains its apocalyptic thrust. The doctrine of justification in the later Barth is an integration of a revised version of Reformational forensicism and Pauline apocalyptic eschatology. Again, this means that his version of forensic apocalypticism is not characterized by the same dimensions described by de Boer. Indeed, even as the second edition of Barth's Romans commentary is apocalyptic in tone and thrust, in a manner consonant with Pauline apocalyptic eshatology, it is Barth's engagement with the Reformation reading of Paul that introduces the forensic framework into his theology and, coupled with the revision

62. Ingolf U. Dalferth, "Karl Barth's Eschatological Realism," in *Karl Barth: Centenary Essays*, ed. S. W. Sykes (Cambridge: Cambridge University Press, 1989), 21.

of his doctrine of election, brings a new facet to his own apocalyptic eschatology.

Barth's attention to Paul's apocalyptic witness to Jesus Christ in *A Shorter Commentary on Romans*, *Christ and Adam*, and *CD* IV allows him to highlight the real connection between a forensic doctrine of justification and Paul's apocalyptic eschatology in Romans. When considering the features to any doctrine of justification, several key questions must be addressed: (1) What is justification? (2) How is it accomplished? (3) Who is the person who is justified? and (4) Where is justification located in the eschatology of salvation? Further, any attempt to construct a doctrine of justification on the basis of an exegesis of Paul's letter to the church in Rome brings together a constellation of doctrinal themes that not only can be mined in seeking to answer the questions above but also arise organically out of Paul's theology in Romans.[63] As Käsemann notes, the "various aspects of Pauline theology are thematically linked and have a mutual bearing. This theology possesses systematic power and completeness, with which we must not interfere . . . unless we are prepared to imperil the whole."[64] Guided by Rom. 1:16–17, Barth understood Paul's reason for writing to the church in Rome to be that he wanted them to know that Jesus Christ himself is the gospel—the good news of God's powerful work of salvation. In Jesus Christ, God has reconciled sinful humanity to Godself by putting sinful humanity to death and creating a new humanity in its place. Thus with Paul, Barth understands Jesus Christ to be the active subject of reconciliation. Such a christological understanding of justification implies several other overlapping and interrelated doctrinal themes, all of which are implied throughout various chapters in Romans and which will be treated in the chapters of this book.

63. This is not to imply that Romans is simply Paul's version of systematic theology. More on target, N. T. Wright has compared Romans to a symphony score, noting that "themes are stated and developed (often in counterpoint with each other), recapitulated in different keys, anticipated in previous movements and echoed in subsequent ones." See Wright, *Romans*, New Interpreter's Bible 10l (Nashville: Abingdon, 2002), 396.

64. Ernst Käsemann, "On Paul's Anthropology," in *Perspectives on Paul*, trans. Margaret Kohl (Philadelphia: Fortress Press, 1971), 29.

The first doctrinal theme, implied in Romans 1 and consistent with Paul's proclamation of Jesus Christ himself as the content of the gospel, is that of revelation or apocalypse. Revelation is an event that happens outside us. The truth of God's action to make right what has gone wrong must be told to us. Atonement is the second, interrelated doctrinal theme answering the question of how justification is enacted, and Paul considers it in Romans 3. Sinful humanity is abolished insofar as Jesus Christ suffers the wrath of God for us and in our place. Justification, the twin doctrine of atonement, whose contours are explored most fully in Romans 5, is accomplished as the event of atonement not only justifies us but also God. God's glory is maintained, and our sinful nature is brought to an end as a new humanity is ushered in. The question of who is the justified person implies the doctrine of humanity, and Barth finds Paul's discussion in Romans 7 instructive. Our true humanity is subjectively realized as we turn away from our sinfulness and turn toward our true humanity, which is found objectively only in Jesus Christ. Finally, just as revelation is an event that happens outside us, so the reality that Jesus Christ is the subject of reconciliation implies that it is the perfect tense of salvation that is most decisive in Barth's eschatology. Romans 8 is Barth's guide here—Jesus Christ is God's efficacious promise of eternal life, and thus it is in him alone that we hope.

Given that these five doctrinal themes, which belong to any christologically focused doctrine of justification, find a certain expression in Romans 1; 3; 5; 7; and 8, respectively, the task of the second chapter of this study is to undertake a comparison of Barth's own theological exegesis of these themes in the second edition of his Romans commentary with the theological exegesis of a handful of the scholars of Paul's cosmic-apocalypticism: namely, Ernst Käsemann, J. Christiaan Beker, J. Louis Martyn, Beverly Gaventa, Paul Meyer, Martinus de Boer, Charles Cousar, and Leander Keck. The goal of this dialogue is twofold. The first is to identify stronger links between Barth's work and current Pauline apocalyptic scholarship so that Barth's work might be seen as a legitimate resource and dialogue partner in debates over Pauline theology. The second is to highlight the way Barth's own exegesis and theological reflection in his second Romans commentary anticipate and complement cosmic-apocalyptic readings of Romans.

However, as this study proposes that Barth's mature theology of justification is best described as forensic-apocalyptic, it will be important to establish, in chapter 3, the precise nature of Barth's theological development after writing the second edition of the Romans commentary so that it is clear how he went from basic agreement with the cosmic-apocalyptic reading of Romans to his own version of forensic apocalypticism, which in turn shaped his mature doctrine of justification. In chapters 4–8, this study will analyze and evaluate the mature Barth's exegetical and dogmatic moves in his treatment of the doctrinal themes that arise out of a forensic-apocalyptic doctrine of justification—based on Romans 1; 3; 5; 7; and 8—in *A Shorter Commentary on Romans*, *Christ and Adam*, and *CD* IV/1 and 3.1. Throughout this investigation into Barth's forensic-apocalyptic doctrine of justification, I will argue that Barth's attention to Paul's apocalyptic witness to Jesus Christ allows him to highlight the real connection between a Reformationally grounded doctrine of justification and Paul's apocalyptic eschatology in Romans. I will also argue that Barth's commitment to and radical restating of the Reformation doctrine is a result of his intensifying of forensicism, which comes as he establishes his historicized theological ontology, works out a mature Christology from that, and then returns once again to listen to Paul's apocalyptic witness to the subject matter of the biblical text—Jesus Christ. Where the cosmic-apocalyptic readings seem to want, at times, to put distance between the Reformation doctrine of justification and Pauline apocalyptic eschatology, Barth's forensic-apocalyptic reading of Romans allows him to formulate a doctrine of justification that creates stronger ties between the Reformation doctrine and Pauline apocalyptic eschatology. The study concludes in chapter 9, where I summarize the gains made by Barth's forensic apocalyptic doctrine of justification and argue that the discussion about the relationship between Pauline apocalyptic eschatology and the Reformation doctrine of justification must take a different approach.

A Different Approach

The concept of a new approach to the relationship between Paul and Reformation theology comes from the example set by Barth in his own treatment of Paul and the Reformers. In the preface to the second edition of the commentary on Romans, we find Barth extolling Luther and Calvin for their "genuine understanding and interpretation . . . that creative energy which Luther exercised with intuitive certainty in his exegesis; which underlies the systematic interpretation of Calvin."[65] Barth finds in the Reformers a willingness to listen carefully to what Paul has to say. He praises Calvin for the way in which he, "having first established what stands in the text, sets himself to re-think the whole material and to wrestle with it, till the walls which separate the sixteenth century from the first become transparent! Paul speaks, and the man of the sixteenth century hears."[66] It is clear to Barth that the Reformers are not at odds with Paul, but rather eager pupils. However, he never advocates listening only or unquestioningly to the Reformers. "'Back to the Reformers,' cannot promise us the help that we need to-day. 'Back to . . .' is never a good slogan."[67] The danger lies in the fact that "it is sometimes precisely some insight that once opened up with fresh vitality the force of Paul's gospel that now, taken as self-evident in another situation and frozen into convention, impedes the interpreter's ability to cross the differences of historical space and time in order to approach again that elusive intent of the author."[68] Barth wants us to go to Scripture to hear Paul for ourselves. So, while he upholds the Reformers for listening closely to Paul, he is not above criticizing their interpretation or theology. When Barth is found

65. Barth, *Epistle to the Romans*, 7 [xi].
66. Ibid.
67. *CD* IV/1, 372 [411].
68. Meyer, "Worm at the Core of the Apple," 65.

critiquing the theology and biblical interpretation of the Reformers it always stems from one main issue: namely,

> the lack of attention which was . . . paid to Christology . . . no independent attention was paid to this central theme. . . . It was, of course, said that Holy Scripture is the Word of God to the extent that it presents Christ. But the programme of Reformation theology did not allow for any radical consideration of the meaning, importance and function of Christology in relation to all Christian knowledge.[69]

This book will demonstrate the ways in which Barth, by listening to Paul for himself, not only had ears tuned in to Paul's proclamation of the apocalyptic horizons of the death and resurrection of Jesus Christ, but that, as a result, also heard Paul in the interpretation and theology of the Reformers. Therefore, if anything, Barth's forensic apocalyptic doctrine of justification and reading of Romans constitute not a departure from Protestant theology but a radical recentering of it on the subject matter to which it must be beholden. His approach to Paul's apocalyptic eschatology and the Reformation doctrine of justification opens up new possibilities for the current relationship between Pauline apocalyptic studies and Protestant theology by establishing that Barth is, indeed, a guide worth following.

69. *CD* IV/1, 366 [404].

2

Pauline Apocalyptic Eschatology and Barth's *Römerbrief*

> By the Gospel the whole concrete world is dissolved and established.
>
> —Karl Barth, *The Epistle to the Romans*

> The whole of God's eschatological saving activity in Jesus Christ, from beginning to end, is apocalyptic.
>
> —Martinus C. de Boer, "Paul, Theologian of God's Apocalypse"

This study contends that Barth, in his steadfast focus on the problem of revelation, was keyed in to many of the strands of Paul's adaptation of cosmic apocalyptic eschatology, as indicated by Douglas Harink's incisive observation of the "powerful *apocalyptic* tone and message" in the second edition of Barth's *Römerbrief*. Indeed, it is this feature within the second edition of Barth's Romans commentary that leads Harink to suggest that Barth has actually anticipated some of the "discoveries" of recent Pauline scholarship. In this chapter I will undertake an analysis of the cosmic apocalyptic features of Barth's own theological exegesis in the second edition of the Romans commentary. To this end, we will put Barth's work in conversation with the work of a handful of scholars who each seek to highlight various dimensions of Pauline apocalyptic eschatology.

The goal of such an exchange is twofold. The first is to identify stronger links between Barth's work and current Pauline scholarship so that Barth's work might be seen as a legitimate resource and dialogue partner in debates over Paul's theology of justification. The second is to highlight, through sustained analysis, the way Barth's own exegesis and theological reflection in the second edition of the Romans commentary contain important cosmic-apocalyptic strands that he will later integrate into his revision of forensic justification. Within Barth studies, the second edition of Barth's commentary on Romans is commonly relegated to brief passing comments, rarely studied or quoted in depth. This chapter intends to change that by carefully attending to Barth's exegetical reading of Romans in the second edition of his commentary. This approach has the advantage of achieving one of the main objectives of this study, namely, laying the groundwork necessary for determining exactly how Barth's later development of his own forensic apocalyptic doctrine of justification takes up some of the major concerns and emphases of Pauline cosmic-apocalyptic eschatology and incorporates them into his forensic approach to justification.

This chapter will proceed as a series of five investigative conversations between Barth's work in the second edition of the Romans commentary and a handful of noted scholars of Pauline apocalyptic eschatology. Each conversational section focuses on: (1) a text in Romans (proceeding with Romans 1; 3; 5; 7; and 8); (2) the cosmic-apocalyptic themes brought out by our selected Pauline scholars; and (3) Barth's own treatment of these cosmic-apocalyptic themes. The aim of each section is to provide a close reading of Barth's commentary in order to compare his reading of Paul with cosmic-apocalyptic readings of Paul. While the scholars of Pauline apocalyptic eschatology will set the stage for each conversation, the goal is always to hear Barth as he understands Paul. In the conclusion to this chapter, we will advance two points in order to further the larger argument of this study. First, we will offer a summary of what Barth's reading offers to the picture of each of the doctrines (namely, revelation, atonement, justification, theological anthropology, and eschatology) that are interrelated to a full account of the doctrine of justification. Second, we will briefly sketch some of the missing ingredient elements in Barth's account of justification in the second edition of his Romans commentary—elements that will find their way into Barth's subsequent readings of Romans and his explication of justification in the mature doctrine of reconciliation set forth in *CD* IV. Chapter 3, appropriately, will thus follow up with a survey of how Barth's genetic development, following the writing of the second edition of the Romans commentary, contributed to the mature reading of Romans and subsequently revised forensic doctrine of justification that we find in *A Shorter Reading of Romans* and *CD* IV.

Conversation 1: Käsemann, de Boer, and Barth on Revelation, Apocalypse, and God in Romans 1:16–17

For Ernst Käsemann, Paul's message in Romans can be summed up under the phrase "the self-revealing righteousness of God."[1] Indeed, as he sees it, "the central problem of Pauline theology is concentrated in this theme."[2] He acknowledges the voices of the Reformation in interpreting Paul's genitive construction (δικαιοσύνη θεοῦ) as sometimes an objective genitive. However, he notices that a double eschatology is at work in Paul's talk of not only the righteousness bestowed on us but also God's own righteousness. Käsemann describes this as a Pauline dialectic. At times, God's righteousness is a gift received by us that is already present. At other times, it is only possessed "by hope[,] and its ultimate realization [is] lying still in the future."[3] Käsemann discerns an insistence on God's righteousness as power as crucial to Paul's approach. "The key to this whole Pauline

1. Ernst Käsemann, "'The Righteousness of God' in Paul," in *New Testament Questions of Today*, translated by W. J. Montague (London: SCM Press, 1969), 168.
2. Ibid.
3. Ibid., 170.

viewpoint is that power is always seeking to realize itself in action and must indeed do so."[4] He further articulates, "God's power becomes God's gift when it takes possession of us."[5] However, God always retains God's lordship in this giving, and the gift is never separated from God, its giver. Thus Paul never makes power and gift to be irreconcilable opposites. This plays out in Rom. 1:16–17 as "Paul designates the gospel which is revealed and given to a Christian simultaneously as the power of God."[6]

Käsemann's goal is to locate the center from which Paul unites both his present and future eschatology. While "the gospel is the power of God because in it the divine righteousness breaks into the world as eschatological revelation,"[7] he urges that it is only in Christ that Paul is able to maintain the dialectic of this double eschatology. "Δικαιοσύνη θεοῦ is for Paul God's sovereignty over the world revealing itself eschatologically in Jesus."[8] Käsemann argues that Paul articulates his Christology such that it is none other than Christ himself who is both our Lord and the gift of God given for us. For Paul, the righteousness of God is nothing less than the power of God invading our fallen world in the person of Jesus Christ. Furthermore, the salvation of the world depends on the power of God recapturing it and making it right. "Because of his Christological connection and basis Paul must identify the righteousness of God with the righteousness of faith and let the stress fall on the conferred gift of salvation. On this account, however, standing in salvation is both here and everywhere standing in obedience, that is, in the presence and under the power of Christ."[9] Indeed, Käsemann insists: "we may summarize the whole message of the epistle in the brief and paradoxical statement that the Son of God is as our Kyrios the one eschatological gift of God to us and that herein is

4. Ibid., 175.
5. Ibid., 173.
6. Ernst Käsemann, *Commentary on Romans*, ed. and trans. Geoffrey W. Bromiley (Grand Rapids: Eerdmans, 1980), 28.
7. Ibid., 30.
8. Käsemann, "'Righteousness of God' in Paul," 180.
9. Käsemann, *Commentary on Romans*, 29.

revealed simultaneously both God's legitimate claim on us and also our salvation."[10]

Turning to Barth's commentary on Rom. 1:16–17, we hear a similar emphasis on the "not yet" aspect of Pauline eschatology. With vivid apocalyptic imagery, Barth writes that we are "imprisoned"[11] in this world and that even the "Resurrection, which is the place of exit, also bars us in, for it is both barrier and exit."[12] The reality of sin and death, the current state of the world, presses in on us and remains the truth of our present existence. Nevertheless, the resurrection is a place of exit—"[t]he barrier marks the frontier of a new country. . . . We have therefore, in the power of God, a look-out, a door, a hope. . . . The prisoner becomes a watchman. Bound to his post as firmly as a prisoner in his cell, he watches for the dawning of the day."[13] We see here an example of one of Barth's many articulations, in the second edition of the Romans commentary, of the infinite qualitative difference between God and humanity, which is what Barth, at the time, believed to be the *Sache* pointed to in the biblical text. Yet as determined as Barth is, at this point in his theology, to guard the self-revelation of God from being co-opted in the event of its being given, he still acknowledges the other side of the Pauline dialectic brought out by Käsemann. In the resurrection of Christ from the dead, there is a door, a hope; the prisoner watches for the dawning of a new day. Like Käsemann, Barth names Christ as the center from which to understand Paul's double eschatology. Indeed, it is because the "now" and the "not yet" cohere only in Christ that Barth sounds the note of future eschatology so insistently. However, we must keep in mind that what is important about Christ for Barth, at this stage, is what he reveals about the true God, "a God whose very being means the negation and reconstitution of all things."[14]

10. Ibid.
11. Barth, *The Epistle to the Romans*, translated by Edwyn C. Hoskyns (London: Oxford University Press, 1933), 37 [12]. Interestingly, Paul himself uses the language of imprisonment in Rom. 11:32: "For God has imprisoned [the verb συγκλείω] all in disobedience so that he may be merciful to all."
12. Ibid., 38 [13].
13. Ibid.
14. Bruce L. McCormack, "Can We Still Speak of 'Justification by Faith'?: An In-House Debate with Apocalyptic Readings of Paul," in *Galatians and Christian Theology: Justification, the Gospel, and Ethics*

Barth, too, considers the Pauline understanding of the righteousness of God, calling it "the consistency of God with Himself"[15] in Christ. The righteousness of God means that God affirms himself "by denying us as we are and the world as it is" and then gives himself to be known "as the Redeemer of the prisoners. . . . He guarantees our salvation by willing to be God and to be known as God—in Christ; He justifies us by justifying Himself."[16] In a corresponding manner, Käsemann remarks that "justification is the specifically Pauline understanding of Christology just as the latter is the basis of the former."[17] For both, the righteousness of God is descriptive of the sovereign, high God. Contained within this phrase is a total and radical distinction between God and humanity. And yet, at the same time, it is this sovereign, high God whom Paul proclaims has not left us to our own devices. In Christ, God is faithful in righteousness first to himself, and because to himself, so also to us. The gospel that Paul is at pains to communicate to the church in Rome proclaims the power of God not to abandon us, but to save us in righteousness. Such is the faithfulness of God, which Barth says is revealed to faith. "To those who have abandoned direct communication, the communication is made. . . . Those who take upon them the divine 'No' shall themselves be borne by the greater divine 'Yes.'"[18] Barth understands faith to be our acceptance of the judgment of God on us, by which God righteously maintains consistency with himself, as revealed in the resurrection. We are righteous only insofar as we live by God's faithfulness to God's righteousness. "The righteous man is the prisoner become watchman. . . . There is no other righteousness save that of the man who sets himself under judgment, of the man who is terrified and hopes. He shall live."[19] We are saved by the wholly Otherness of God, who shows forth the power of his righteousness in Jesus Christ and thus saves us by remaining true to

in Paul's Letter, ed. Mark W. Elliott, Scott J. Hafemann, N. T. Wright, and John Frederick (Grand Rapids: Baker Academic, 2014), 179. For example, see Barth, *Epistle to the Romans*, 97 [72].

15. Barth, *Epistle to the Romans*, 40 [15].
16. Ibid., 40–41 [16].
17. Käsemann, *Commentary on Romans*, 24.
18. Barth, *Epistle to the Romans*, 41 [16].
19. Ibid., 41 [17].

himself. Therefore, for Barth, as for Käsemann, the righteousness of God revealed in Christ and by which we live is the theme of Romans.

De Boer and Barth

Martinus De Boer takes up the question, "how does Paul himself use the language of revelation, what we may call his 'apocalyptic language,' the noun *apokalypsis* and the verb *apokalyptō*?"[20] Against Christopher Rowland, he maintains that Paul's use of the language of revelation is neither focused on human experience of the divine world nor simply on the revelation of information that a prophet must pass on to others; rather, Paul's particular form of apocalyptic is centered on "God's own revelatory action of rectifying a world gone awry."[21] De Boer goes on to clarify that because apocalyptic eschatology contains a cosmic formulation of two world ages, the notion of revelation within apocalyptic eschatology consists of both ages. "It is only through the disclosure of the coming age that the present can be perceived as 'this (evil) age,' destined to be brought to an end by God."[22] De Boer argues that, for Paul, apocalyptic properly concerns the action of God, which brings the present world age to an end and replaces it with a new one.

Paul uses apocalyptic language in relationship to the gospel for which he has been called to proclaim. While the gospel for which Paul is set apart had already been promised in the Scriptures, it is Christ's resurrection from the dead that proclaims the good news that he is the Son of God. Thus God's revelatory action in the death and resurrection of Jesus Christ is the foundation on which Paul preaches the gospel. De Boer points out that while Paul makes use of the term "apocalypse" in connection with the parousia in Rom. 2:5 and 8:18–19, in Rom. 1:16–17 he uses the term to describe the gospel he preaches about the death and resurrection of Christ. He directly relates God's power to the verb ἀποκαλύπτω. "The gospel evidently involves an apocalyptic-eschatological event in the present."[23] The gospel powerfully reveals

20. Martinus C. de Boer, "Paul, Theologian of God's Apocalypse," *Interpretation* 56 (2002): 24.
21. Ibid.
22. Ibid., 22.
23. Ibid., 26.

God's righteousness and creates faith. Through faith the believer can perceive this powerful apocalyptic action of God in the world. "Faith (*pistis, pisteuō*) is, for Paul, a form of sharing in God's eschatological revelation, that is, in God's eschatological activity and movement. . . . The movement and presence of God are to be seen in the crucified and risen Christ."[24] Thus de Boer aptly surmises that the definitive invasion of God's apocalyptic action in the world to deliver humanity from the present evil age is seen in Christ's death and resurrection. For this reason, Pauline apocalyptic eschatology is not concerned with a decision human beings must make, but instead with the decisive action God has already enacted on their behalf. "According to Paul, God has done this in the apocalyptic-eschatological event of Jesus Christ, who (so Paul claims) died for human beings and was raised by God. Paul presents himself primarily as a theologian of this revelation, this apocalypse of God."[25]

If de Boer's focus is to illuminate Paul's apocalyptic understanding of the gospel, centered on God's powerful rectification revealed in the death and resurrection of Christ and creating faith in its hearers, then Barth's commentary on Romans 1 could not be more complementary. As Barth finds it, Jesus Christ is both the gospel and the meaning of history.[26]

> In this name two worlds meet and go apart, two planes intersect, the one known and the other unknown. . . . The relation between us and God, between this world and His world, presses for recognition, but the line of intersection at which the relation becomes observable and observed is Jesus. . . . The name Jesus defines an historical occurrence and marks the point where the unknown world cuts the known world.[27]

Barth's description of Jesus Christ as the place of the event of the revelation of God resonates not only with the idea of the cosmic two world ages contained in apocalyptic eschatology but also, more specifically, with what de Boer brings out in Paul's apocalyptic

24. Ibid.
25. Ibid., 33.
26. Barth, *Epistle to the Romans*, 29 [5].
27. Ibid.

eschatology regarding God's rectifying action to make right a world gone wrong. "By the Gospel the whole concrete world is dissolved and established."[28] Furthermore, Barth hears Paul describing God's revelation as an event that breaks forth into our world while also remaining utterly unique, never becoming part of our world. This event of revelation occurs in Jesus Christ, but "because it is the revelation of the righteousness of God, [it] must be the most complete veiling of His incomprehensibility. In Jesus, God becomes veritably a secret: He is made known as the Unknown, speaking in eternal silence."[29] In other words, God reveals Godself to us in Jesus Christ only ever indirectly. This means that for Barth, too, the notion of apocalyptic is not simply a disclosure of information to an individual, who is to pass it on to others. The singular focus on God's rectifying action, which de Boer finds characteristic of Pauline apocalyptic eschatology, could not sound a stronger note than it does in Barth. God is the sole actor. God does not become a possession of humanity. Revelation is not a predicate of history. Rather, in complete freedom, God reveals himself as the unknown God. "The Epistle moves round the theme (1:16, 17) that in Christ Jesus the *Deus absconditus* is as such the *Deus revelatus*. . . . The Moment when God, not man, speaks and acts, is the Moment of Miracle."[30]

Barth uses paradoxical and dialectical language to emphasize that God is only known indirectly. This is characteristic of the one-sided focus, in the second edition of Barth's Romans commentary, on the wholly other God who self-reveals becoming a human possession. Barth's reading is made possible on the apocalyptic grounds of Romans 1. Apocalyptic revelation speaks to God's action alone, not our own. It is action that brings the present age to an end and replaces it with a new one. For Barth, this event of revelation is concretized in the cross and resurrection. He argues that the resurrection occurs in history without being an event of history, while the cross makes revelation concrete in history. "The Resurrection is the revelation: the disclosing of Jesus as

28. Ibid., 35 [11].
29. Ibid., 98 [73].
30. Ibid., 422 [408].

the Christ, the appearing of God and the apprehending of God in Jesus. . . . In the Resurrection the new world of the Holy Spirit touches the old world of the flesh, but it touches it as a tangent touches a circle, that is, without touching it."[31] Insofar as the resurrection is the apocalyptic action of God's self-revelation, Barth says it is the power of God to save imprisoned humanity. The gospel of the resurrection reveals God as humanity's creator and redeemer. "It is pregnant with our complete conversion; for it announces the transformation of our creatureliness into freedom."[32]

Just as de Boer emphasizes that faith for Paul is created by the gospel, so Barth also stresses that the powerful work of the gospel converts and transforms our creaturely existence. De Boer describes faith as the form of a believer's participation in the eschatological revelation seen in the death and resurrection of Christ. Similarly, Barth defines faith as "the affirmation of the resurrection as the turning-point of the world; and therefore it is the affirmation of the divine 'No' in Christ, of the shattering halt in the presence of God."[33] Both hear Paul making God's powerful apocalyptic action in the death and resurrection of Christ to be the highest priority. What follows after is a believer's participation, by faith, in God's rectifying action. "Faith, therefore, is never identical with 'piety', however pure and delicate. . . . Faith lives of its own, because it lives of God."[34]

Faith is a gift given by God. By faith we know the truth of God's apocalyptic action in the world. Here in the second edition of the Romans commentary, Barth writes of faith as "negation" in order to guard against the idea of it being something we contribute to our salvation. Faith is a void in which God reveals God's own faithfulness. In this way, like revelation, faith is understood apocalyptically. It, too, is never a possession we can control. It is always something that is given to us in the event of God's revealing.

31. Ibid., 30 [6].
32. Ibid., 37–38 [13].
33. Ibid., 39 [14].
34. Ibid., 40 [15].

Conversation 2: Cousar, de Boer, Beker, and Barth on Rectification, Faith, and Atonement in Romans 3:21–26

If Rom. 1:18–3:20 is touted as Paul's epic rhetorical alignment of all of humanity under the same inescapable plight of accountability before God, Rom. 3:21–26 is rendered as the solution. Yet Paul's complicated syntax about Jesus' death forbids any scholarly consensus. Scholars of Pauline apocalyptic eschatology are keen to make sure that these six verses are not isolated from the earlier parts of chapter 3, nor do they want Paul's cosmic horizons pushed aside in the attempt to understand the relationship of Paul's use of terms such as ἱλαστήριον, πίστεως, and δικαιοσύνη and its cognates. Charles Cousar notes that as early as 3:5, the theme of verses 21–26—δικαιοσύνη θεοῦ—is announced.[35] He describes the expression as Paul's way of designating not only God's faithfulness to God's promises but also God's moral integrity.[36] Furthermore, the expressions in verses 3 and 7, respectively "the faithfulness of God" and "the truthfulness of God," are functional synonyms for the theme of 3:21–26—"the righteousness of God."[37] This is the very character of God that seems to be in question in the early part of Romans 3, yet verses 21–26 demonstrate that God is indeed righteous in that "God graciously sets right (or rectifies) humans as a free gift"[38] in the Christ event. God's moral integrity is safeguarded because Christ's death "vindicates God's dealing with previously committed sins"[39] by placing the ungodly into right relationship with God. Similarly, God is shown to be faithful to God's promises in that "God's righteousness is made known apart from the law—in the faithfulness of Jesus Christ."[40] Following Richard Hays,[41] Cousar suggests that the reference to Ps. 143:2 in 3:20 anticipates Paul's

35. Charles B. Cousar, *A Theology of the Cross: The Death of Jesus in the Pauline Letters* (Minneapolis: Fortress Press, 1990), 39.
36. Ibid. For a more thorough explanation of the phrase, see Leander E. Keck, *Paul and His Letters*, 2nd ed., Proclamation Commentaries (Minneapolis: Fortress Press, 1988), 119–21.
37. Cousar, *Theology of the Cross*, 37n21.
38. Ibid., 40.
39. Ibid.
40. Ibid., 41.
41. Richard B. Hays, "Psalm 143 and the Logic of Romans 3," *Journal of Biblical Literature* 99 (1980): 107–15.

argument in 3:21–26, since the psalmist prays in 143:1: "'Lord, heed my prayer; give an ear to my supplication by your faithfulness; answer me by your righteousness' (from the LXX)."[42] Thus the faithfulness prayed for by the psalmist is answered by Jesus' faithful activity, which upholds the righteousness of God.

Such an interpretation, however, runs contrary to most English translations, which render the prepositional phrase "through faith" (διὰ πίστεως) as a human response to God's action rather than Christ's own faithful obedience unto death. Cousar suggests a more logical rendering would be to make "through faith" (3:25) parallel to "in his blood," such that "Jesus is precisely faithful at the cost of his blood."[43] The theological take-home of this translation is that it better communicates how God effects change in the human situation. God's righteousness is a power reaching "'out for the world, and the world's salvation lies in its being recaptured for the sovereignty of God.'"[44] This is a cosmic-apocalyptic reading of the verb "to justify" (δικαιούμενοι in 3:24) and its object—"all" (πάντες in 3:23), which is too often construed along exclusivist and individualistic lines. Cousar remarks that the verb "to justify" (δικαιοῦντα) in 3:26

> carries a less apocalyptic and more forensic cast because of its object. Now the recipient of God's action is designated not as "all" who have sinned, but "the one who shares the faith of Jesus." . . . God acquits the believer. . . . It appears as if "faith" has been made some sort of stipulation for justification. . . . Should 3:23–24, in the light of 3:26, be understood to imply that "all who have sinned but have now come to faith" are being justified as a gift?[45]

In answering this question, Cousar follows Arlend Hultgren,[46] who argues that apocalyptic and forensic statements on justification, such as those found in Rom. 3:24 and 3:26, respectively, "need to be thought of as separate but obviously related topics, and that methodologically

42. Cousar, *Theology of the Cross*, 38–39.
43. Ibid., 58.
44. Ibid., 59.
45. Ibid., 60.
46. Arland J. Hultgren, *Paul's Gospel and Mission: The Outlook from His Letters to the Romans* (Philadelphia: Fortress Press, 1985), 82–98.

the universal statements demand prior consideration."[47] Cousar concludes that at the heart of Paul's gospel stands the death of Jesus, which has "an apocalyptic, world-transforming character because it effects a complete change in the situation between sinful humanity and God."[48] The atoning death of Jesus is the "eschatological event by which God deals with human sin . . . once-for-all."[49]

In a similar vein, de Boer argues that "Paul does not preach apocalyptic eschatology, not even Christian apocalyptic eschatology; he preaches the crucified Christ whom God raised from the dead, nothing else (cf. 1 Cor. 1:23; 2:2)."[50] Applying this understanding of how Paul works to Romans 3, de Boer concludes:

> [t]hus, while Paul speaks of faith (or of rectification by faith) primarily when he is combating the claim (among both Jews and Christians of his time) that "works (observance) of the law" provide the righteousness that will lead to eschatological justification (acquittal) and thus to life in the new age, the meaning of faith is actually determined by the cosmological-apocalyptic disclosure of God's righteousness and of sin in the crucifixion of Christ. Christ's death cannot be understood in exclusively forensic terms, since it marks God's triumphant invasion of the world "under sin" (Rom. 3:9) to liberate human beings (the ungodly) from sin's deadly power.[51]

De Boer insistence on Paul's cosmological apocalyptic thrust to his interpretation of Christ's death, makes sense only if one reads Romans 3 in light of Romans 6–8. However, Beker also insists that Paul has an apocalyptic interpretation of Christ's death.[52] He delineates four dimensions to the apocalyptic nature of Christ's death. First, the apocalyptic powers are defeated in the death of Christ, making the event itself apocalyptic. Second, Christ's death is a judgment on the old age. Third, Christ's death is inextricably linked to his resurrection

47. Cousar, *Theology of the Cross*, 61.
48. Ibid.
49. Ibid., 66.
50. Martinus C. de Boer, "Paul and Apocalyptic Eschatology," in *The Origins of Apocalypticism in Judaism and Christianity*, vol. 1 of *The Encyclopedia of Apocalypticism*, edited by John J. Collins (New York: Continuum, 1998), 367–68.
51. Ibid., 366.
52. J. Christiaan Beker, "Paul's Apocalyptic Theology: Apocalyptic and the Resurrection of Christ," in *Paul the Apostle: The Triumph of God in Life and Thought* (Philadelphia: Fortress Press, 1980), 189.

"[b]ecause the resurrection is the apocalyptic-cosmic event that inaugurates the cosmic triumph of God, it draws the death of Christ into its apocalyptic orbit."[53] Fourth, Paul understands the salvific elements of Christ's death and resurrection not only apocalyptically but also dialectically. Beker finds Paul, in Rom. 3:24–26, to be reinterpreting traditional understandings of "the righteousness of God as covenant renewal, of Christ as expiation ... in terms of his understanding of the death of Christ as the judgment of the powers of this age."[54] However, he does not think Paul does the work of reinterpretation in Rom. 3:24–26, but rather, like de Boer, his new take comes in Rom. 5:12–21; 6:1–10; and 8:3. The cosmic-apocalyptic features of Romans 3 are located in verses 9 and 23—"[b]ecause all have sinned, all must die. The death of Christ signifies the apocalyptic judgment on all humankind, and his resurrection signifies the *sola gratia* of new life in Christ for all."[55] At the end of the day, a cosmic-apocalyptic understanding of Christ's death "is the consequence of its inseparable connection with the resurrection of Christ."[56] As Beker understands Paul,

> the events of cross and resurrection cohere in a single meaning. Paul correlates God's act of love in Christ (Rom. 3:25) and the obedience of Christ (Rom. 5:19; Phil. 2:6). Thus, the death of Christ is both God's "own" love for the world (Rom. 5:6–8) and God's judgment over human sin (1 Cor. 1:18–23); it is both Christ's obedience, self-surrender, and sacrificial love for us (Rom. 5:19; Gal. 1:4; Phil 2:6; 2 Cor. 8:9) and God's surrender of "his own Son" (Rom. 8:32).[57]

Turning to Barth's interpretation of Rom. 3:21–26, we see this theme of δικαιοσύνη θεοῦ taken up in Barth's focus on the freedom of God. The righteousness of God is God's "nevertheless [that] contradicts every human logical 'consequently,' and is itself incomprehensible and without cause or occasion, because it is the 'nevertheless!' of God."[58] It

53. Ibid.
54. Ibid., 191.
55. Ibid., 193.
56. Ibid., 194.
57. Ibid., 209–10.
58. Barth, *Epistle to the Romans*, 93 [68].

comes to us freely, from the outside, as God's sovereign power, without becoming our possession, and judges all humanity only according to the standard of God's own righteousness. Insofar as this happens "a radical alteration of the relation between God and man [takes place] which explains why, though human unrighteousness and ungodliness have brought the world to its present condition . . . He nevertheless continues to name us His people in order that we may be His people."[59] In other words, because God pronounces God's enemies to be God's friends, God's righteousness is an action that effects a complete change between sinful humanity and God. This is the "but now" of the passage in which the mercy of God triumphs. And it is a "but now" that effects all humanity and all creation. "God can be known only when men of all ranks are grouped together upon one single step."[60] Furthermore, Barth writes that the righteousness of God, now manifested, "is the meaning of history, . . . [and] the redemption of all creation."[61] Clearly attentive to the cosmic-apocalyptic emphasis of Paul's understanding of the gospel, Barth maintains that God's work of justification is nothing short of the "renewal of heaven and of earth," a declaration that is "*creatio ex nihilo*."[62]

Translating διὰ πίστεως in a rather novel way, Barth renders the phrase "through his faithfulness in Jesus Christ," remarking that the "faithfulness of God is established when we meet the Christ in Jesus."[63] For Barth, the stress is consistently on the righteousness of God. Jesus Christ is the place where God's faithfulness is manifested. Barth speaks metaphorically of the day of Jesus Christ as the "Day of all days," by which it is revealed that it is not humans who wait, but God, in God's faithfulness.[64] Thus the role of Jesus Christ is revelatory, and his death functions as such. "In His light we see light."[65] Jesus is "the place of propitiation above which God dwells and from which He speaks."[66]

59. Ibid.
60. Ibid., 100 [74].
61. Ibid., 95 [70].
62. Ibid., 102 [76].
63. Ibid., 96 [70].
64. Ibid., 95 [71].
65. Ibid., 97 [71].
66. Ibid., 105 [79].

Through the blood of Jesus we are reminded that "God gives life only through death."[67] This is the meaning of atonement for Barth. Atonement occurs "only through the faithfulness of God," by which the "impossible possibility of our redemption" is declared.[68] As such, Jesus Christ is "the righteousness of God Himself."[69] Barth states that Jesus lived a life of perfect obedience to the will of the faithful God and placed himself under the judgment of God, not making himself a hero but ridding humanity of all of its futile possibilities in his death. "The Messiah is the end of mankind, and here also God is found faithful."[70] In other words, Jesus acted in obedience to the will of God and then, on the cross, acknowledged God's righteous judgment on sinful humanity as just. Therefore, in Christ's death, God demonstrates God's righteousness through judgment on all humankind, which Barth calls the "impossible possibility . . . acquittal in condemnation."[71] But also, in the resurrection, Jesus Christ is the righteousness of God through the demonstration of God's faithfulness. "On the day when mankind is dissolved the new era of the righteousness of God will be inaugurated."[72] In his death and resurrection, Jesus reveals God's righteousness to be a paradox—one only indirectly accessible by faith.

Having prioritized Paul's focus on faithfulness and righteousness of God, when Barth does address Paul's notion of faith he stresses that "[o]ur hearing can then be nothing more than faith in God, faith that He is because He is."[73] Christ's death confronts us with a paradox that can only truly be comprehended with the eyes of faith. "Believing in Jesus, we believe in the universal reality of the faithfulness of God. Believing in Jesus, to us the righteousness and justification of God are manifested and displayed."[74] Yet, while Barth speaks here of human belief in Jesus, he does so without assuming that faith is something we come to possess on our own. On the contrary, because "faith is

67. Ibid., 105 [80].
68. Ibid.
69. Ibid., 96 [70].
70. Ibid., 97 [72].
71. Ibid., 92 [67].
72. Ibid., 97 [72].
73. Ibid., 101 [76].
74. Ibid., 107 [81].

the faithfulness of God," it means conversion for an individual, "the radically new disposition of the man who stands naked before God."[75] Faith, for Barth, like revelation, is actualistic in nature. It is a giving that takes place in a moment that has neither a before nor an after—"There are no human avenues of approach."[76] For humanity, faith is impossible. But, in the moment when God grants faith, it becomes the impossible possibility in which God is made intuitable as the unintuitable. Thus Barth concludes that faith in Jesus, too, "like its theme, the righteousness of God, is the radical 'Nevertheless.'"[77]

Conversation 3: De Boer and Barth on Sin, Death, and Christ in Romans 5

In his published dissertation study of 1 Corinthians 15 and Romans 5, de Boer seeks to answer two interlocking questions: "How does Paul's christologically determined apocalyptic eschatology inform his understanding of death on the one side and how does his understanding of death serve to define his apocalyptic eschatology on the other?"[78] Taking as his starting point the connection that both Käsemann and Beker make between Paul's apocalyptic eschatology and his treatment of "death," de Boer argues that death for Paul is a cosmic power that has already been defeated in Christ's death and resurrection. In Romans 5 death as a cosmic power means that no help can be gained from the law or law observance. Only Christ can defeat death. De Boer's focus is on the second subunit within Romans 5, that of verses 12–21, which contains the Adam-Christ typology. He classifies Romans 5:1–11 as a reformulation of Paul's main theme, already articulated in 1:16–17 and 3:21–26, concerning "the gracious and reconciling work of God in the death of Christ."[79] As this theme is carried over into 5:12–21, Käsemann notices that God's grace is set over

75. Ibid., 98 [72].
76. Ibid., 99 [74].
77. Ibid., 99 [73].
78. Martinus C. de Boer, *The Defeat of Death: Apocalyptic Eschatology in 1 Corinthians 15 and Romans 5* (Sheffield: JSOT, 1988), 19.
79. Ibid., 145.

against the law. Such a comparison, however, is made not within a forensic framework, but a cosmic one, with the introduction of Adam as the signal that Paul is now placing the justifying work of Christ into a cosmic context. Christ's death brings the cosmic effect of eternal life. Working between the polarity of death and eternal life, de Boer maintains that Paul recasts both cosmic themes christologically, thereby disrupting the presumed forensic connection between works of the law and justification or eternal life. For this reason de Boer proposes that the forensic apocalyptic themes that Paul works with in chapters 1–4, and even 5:1–11, are ultimately circumscribed and overtaken by cosmic ones,[80] even as texts such as 8:1 and 8:33–34 "indicate that forensic categories have hardly been given up or left behind."[81]

De Boer offers a careful rendering of the structure and framework of Rom. 5:12–21, with the goal of illuminating Paul's insistence that Christ's death "marks God's triumphant invasion of the world under the power of sin to liberate human beings (the ungodly of Rom. 4:5; 5:6) from its destructive and death-dealing power."[82] In the first part of verse 12, sin and death are characterized as "cosmological intruders into the human cosmos."[83] Verse 21, as the conclusion of the section, shows grace also to be a cosmological ruler, and one that is ultimately triumphant in the conflict with sin and death. De Boer further discerns a pattern at work within verses 15–17 and 18–19. In each set of verses, Paul begins with a statement with a forensic framework that he then interprets cosmologically by the end. In other words, the fact that death exercises dominion through one man's trespass and the gift of righteousness exercises dominion in life through Jesus (v. 17) explains

80. De Boer makes an important clarification about the points of contact with Jewish cosmological apocalyptic eschatology in Romans, however, when he states that "Paul is certainly not interested in pursuing the type of angelological speculation frequently found there." De Boer goes on to agree with Käsemann's acknowledgment of Bultmann's point that "with respect to evil powers opposed to God, 'Paul did in a decisive sense develop this cosmology as anthropology.'" See de Boer, *Defeat of Death*, 179.

81. Ibid., 153. Insofar as forensic Jewish apocalyptic eschatology emphasizes that "death signifies the separation of Adamic human beings from God," de Boer purports that Paul is greatly indebted to it. Ibid., 180.

82. Ibid., 156.

83. Ibid., 161.

why the free gift is not like the trespass (v. 15). Likewise, because one man's disobedience made sinners of many, and by one man's obedience many will be made righteous (v. 19), so we understand that the one trespass led to condemnation for all, while one man's act of righteousness leads to justification and life for all. In both cases, the pattern communicates that "God's abundance, powerfully effective in the justifying work of Christ, is His gracious response to a multitude of trespasses, a situation much worse than the single trespass that issued in condemnation."[84]

Looking to Paul's understanding of the law in verses 13–14 and 20, de Boer surmises that the law is not part of the solution but the problem. Why this is so does not become clear until Romans 7, but given the introduction of sin and death as cosmological powers in chapter 5, Paul begins a reappraisal of the law in this light. While in forensic apocalyptic eschatology the law "is the God-given solution to the sentence of death that was meted out to Adam (and/or Eve) and all their descendants for repudiating God,"[85] Paul's retrospective reinterpretation from the viewpoint of the grace that has "more than abounded" in the death of Jesus shows that "sin is so strong that it turns those who rely on the Law into the unwitting (and perhaps not so unwitting) instruments of its murderous control . . . [such that] the human predicament is much worse than its appears before or apart from"[86] Christ's crucifixion. Yet de Boer urges that Paul's message about sin and death is not meant to terrorize but rather to lift up the miracle of grace that is seen both in the gift of justification in 5:1–11 and in the moral righteousness powerfully created by God's rectifying power. "If the consequence and mark of sin's reign is the reign of death (where one reigns the other does also), the consequence and mark of God's rectifying power is of course 'eternal life' (where the former is the latter must be also)."[87]

Returning to the question of whether the defeat of death is a present

84. Ibid., 164.
85. Ibid., 167.
86. Ibid., 169.
87. Ibid.

or future reality, de Boer goes a step further than Beker's conclusion that Christ conquered all the powers for us except death and hones in on Paul's dialectical rendering between the old reality of the reign of sin and death and the new age of justification, righteousness, and life. He argues that this new life

> is present now *only and always as a gift of God's own rectifying, life-giving power*, i.e., of His grace (5:21). This gift never becomes a "possession" of believers. Yet precisely because it is *God's* gift, i.e., God's liberating power, Christians can affirm the present reality of eternal life *in the midst of* and *in the face of* the seemingly continuing reign of death and its partner and cause, sin.[88]

He reasons that Paul's use of the future tense (5:9, 10, 17, 19; 6:5, 8, 14; 8:11) serves the purpose of driving home the point that salvation or eternal life is "always dependent upon the invasive divine power present in the gift. . . . [T]he premise of salvation posits the promise of salvation."[89] Eternal life is paradoxically a present reality because Christ has redeemed humanity from the powers of sin and death. Therefore, if sin and death appear still to reign, "believers yet know that these tyrants do *not* reign, that they have been deprived of their power to determine human destiny, that they are the human 'past' not the human 'future.'"[90]

Barth treats Romans 5 under the heading of "the approaching day" (*der nahende Tag*), with verses 1–11 sectioned off as *der neue Mensch* and verses 12–21 as *die neue Welt*. Already within his treatment of verses 1–11, he remarks that the triumphant miracle of grace means that "[d]eath is deprived of its power."[91] He immediately highlights the paradox present in Paul's dialectic between the old and new age in verse 1. It is only by "faith [that] we are what we are not."[92] The truth of our newness, the meaning of the resurrection, is only visible to us in the cross. "By hope we are His. Thus the new subject emerges in

88. Ibid., 175–76.
89. Ibid., 177.
90. Ibid., 178.
91. Barth, *Epistle to the Romans*, 157 [133].
92. Ibid., 149 [125].

the negation of the old, known, human subject."[93] Like de Boer, Barth connects the peace that comes with our justification to the earlier themes Paul has already presented in chapters 1 and 3. "Peace is declared when imprisoned truth (1:18) is set at liberty and when the righteousness of God is made manifest (3:21)."[94] But again, the paradox of this peace remains. It never implies union with God or the dissolution of death.[95] "The bitter conflict between flesh and spirit remains as intense as before; man remains man, and God is still God."[96]

Careful to define faith not as "a steady growth in experience, but through the action of God upon him," Barth urges that the faith of which Paul speaks is one that glories in the hope of the final consummation and "never appeal[s] to it as an experience or possible possibility of our own."[97] Faith is not a human capacity. It is the "creative and redemptive power"[98] of the Holy Spirit. The eyes of faith enable us to see what cannot be seen in day-to-day life—the truth that we stand in grace and have peace with God. Bringing life out of death is work that is God's alone and we see it only by faith.

> We, as believers, stand in the negation of the negation of the suffering of Christ (5:6). . . . What at first seems nothing but mere human suffering becomes the action of God, the Creator and Redeemer. . . . [F]or we recognize that we stand under judgment, and we love the Judge, because He lets it be known that He is not to be identified with the god of this world. As Judge, He manifests Himself as utterly different from us and from our life.[99]

Barth has here picked up on the forensic images of 5:1–11. Yet he hears Paul's cosmic apocalyptic eschatology interwoven throughout and so uses military and warfare imagery as well: "We possess a divine artillery [i.e., knowledge that suffering and death are God's way of

93. Ibid., 150 [127].
94. Ibid.
95. "Paul has nothing to say concerning the peace of God, nothing even concerning his own existence, which is not spoken in a paradox." See ibid., 152 [129].
96. Ibid., 150 [127–28].
97. Ibid., 153 [130].
98. Ibid., 157 [134].
99. Ibid., 156 [133].

saving us] which silences the enemy and inflicts upon him the damage he would inflict upon us."[100]

Barth understands Paul in 5:6–11 to be stressing that the death of Jesus is that which turns us away from every human positive and negative possibility except that of death. Only in death can we become new. That Christ died for us means that

> by His death we recognize the law (*Erkenntnisprinzip*) of our own dying; in so far as in His death the unintuitable God becomes *for us* intuitable;[101] in so far as His death is the place where atonement with God takes place . . . ; and in so far as in His death the paradox of the righteousness and the identity of His holy wrath . . . becomes *for us*—the Truth.[102]

Without a doubt, the atonement is *satisfactio vicaria* because Christ died for us who are weak and godless. Christ's death is juxtaposed with all that we are, have, and do. Connecting Paul's talk of the glory of God in verse 2 with the death of Christ, Barth says it is "not merely a new object; it requires a new subject."[103] In this move, we find that Barth actualizes justification. The new subject is identical with our old self only by faith, which means that the death of Christ requires the new person "who with unquenchable certainty knows himself in Christ to be beloved of God."[104] He speaks of the justification that is ours by the blood of Christ as the answer to the question of all questions: "Whence are we?"[105] Yet this is who we are only as we believe that by Christ's own death we, too, have died. "The new man has no existence except non-existence."[106] Barth is trying here, in every way possible, to describe our justification through Christ's death in dialectical terminology so as to emphasize that it is never something that is in our

100. Ibid., 156–57 [133].
101. Hoskyn's translation of *unanschauliche* and *anschaulich* as "invisible" and "visible" is better rendered as "unintuitable" and "intuitable" in order to make more plain not only Barth's commitment to Kantian epistemology's rejection of metaphysics but also his commitment to overcome Kant by means of Kant (where the knowledge of God is concerned). See Bruce L. McCormack, *Karl Barth's Critically Realistic Dialectical Theology: Its Genesis and Development 1909-1936* (Oxford: Clarendon Press, 2004), 216–35.
102. Barth, *Epistle to the Romans*, [137], *rev.*
103. Ibid., [139].
104. Ibid., 162 [139].
105. Ibid., 163 [140].
106. Ibid.

possession. Our newness comes into being only by faith, which itself is the faithfulness of God.

When he turns to the second half of chapter 5, Barth notes the connection between Paul's talk of the new human and the new world. Neither can exist side by side with the old, "nor do the old and the new man compose two men. For the possibility of the one involves the impossibility of the other; and the impossibility of the one involves the possibility of the other. . . . But only in the light of the critical 'Moment' . . . does the distinction between the two become apparent."[107] In Adam we experience judgment leading to death. In Christ we experience judgment leading to life. Sensing Paul's unequal weighting of the two, Barth notes that neither is there a balance to be struck between them, nor are they equal in importance. There is no repeating cycle of sin and righteousness, death and life, between Adam and Christ. Instead, there is a "unity of movement" between the two, but only as the second is triumphant over the first. It is the critical moment, which we understand as faith or resurrection, that ultimately disturbs the balance between the two. "The new world is therefore more than a variation of the old. . . . There is a death which is the death of death: and this is the theme of the Gospel (1:16). The Gospel is the power of God, the power of the Resurrection, . . . it is faith, as the primal and creative factor."[108]

Examining Paul's language about sin, death, and the law, Barth summarizes death as that which defines our world and sin as the sovereign power in our world "like God."[109] Death is "the supreme law of our life," before which we are powerless, while sin manifests concretely in death and "occurs before it has taken concrete form consciously or unconsciously . . . and it is powerful before it takes control of his [a man's] will or disposition."[110] The world in which sin entered is a world imprisoned by principalities and powers. Death came into this world of sin and now has "universal sovereignty" and

107. Ibid., 165 [142].
108. Ibid., 166 [143].
109. Ibid., 177 [155–56].
110. Ibid., 173 [151].

"points backwards to the unintuitable sovereignty of sin."[111] The law, sin's contrast, "is an intuitable factor in history (2:14–16) constantly reawaking in men the recollection of that relationship with God which they have—lost."[112] Moreover, through the law sin itself "becomes intuitable."[113]

It is in Adam's shadow, however, that the light of Christ is seen. "Both figures stand close upon the barrier between sin and righteousness, death and life; but the one looks backwards, the other forwards."[114] This distinction between Adam and Christ is, according to Barth, the concern of the whole passage. The old and the new, represented by Adam and Christ, "is a dualism of one movement . . . . This unity of direction is necessitated by an identity of origin and of purpose. Both have their origin and their purpose in God, and to Him they point. They move forward of necessity from guilt and destiny to reconciliation and redemption."[115] The law is also in Adam's shadow, which makes sin intuitable. "The law, as an intuitable and concrete historical fact, is, rather, the point at which men become consciously aware of the two worlds."[116] The law, glossed by Barth as "religion," is an entirely human possibility, even as it has its "unintuitable foundation and meaning from God,"[117] and so it still stands in the shadow of sin and death. Religion, as the highest human possibility, strives in vain to reach God, but only results in sin abounding. Yet precisely there, "men encounter God; and there breaks forth the krisis of God, the sickness unto death."[118] The light of the resurrection reveals to us that it is Christ, as both the revealer and recipient of the divine justification and election, who is "the secret of divine predestination, by which all history is constituted anew and given a pre-eminent and victorious meaning."[119] Notably, "the death of all death"[120] occurs as

111. Ibid., 175 [153].
112. Ibid., 173 [151], *rev.*
113. Ibid.
114. Ibid., 176 [154].
115. Ibid., 177 [155].
116. Ibid., 183 [161], *rev.*
117. Ibid., 184 [163], *rev.*
118. Ibid., 186 [165].
119. Ibid., 181–82 [160].

the righteousness of Christ brings justification to all. Barth talks here of revolution and "overthrowing the dynasty."[121] In that God has acted on behalf of humanity, freedom from sin and death have been won for them. "Grace is grace, where the possibility of religion in the full bloom of its power is earnestly accepted—and then offered up as a sacrifice."[122] God alone can save, and God does so by grace, yet this does not spare us from judgment. "Life is not life, if it be not life from death. And God is not God, if he be not the End of men."[123]

Conversation 4: Meyer, Martyn, and Barth on Justification and Pauline Anthropology in Romans 7

Paul Meyer's focus in his reading of Romans 7 is to draw attention away from the "I" of the passage and toward the characters of sin and death instead. Rather than reading Rom. 7:7–25 as being about a kind of psychological split in the "I," he finds it to be about the law and the way that the law has been victimized by sin. Yet the passage is about more than that. It is also about a vindication of the law, which is carried out not "by directly defending the goodness of the law but by giving an account of how it has been used by sin."[124]

A key factor in Meyer's interpretation is his decision to link 7:1–6 with what has come before it in chapter 6 rather than to connect it to what follows it in 7:7–25. He starts with Paul's legal definition of justification in 6:1–7:6. Christ's death rescues us from the power of the law by putting sin to death (6:1–14) and ushering us into "a new righteousness and integrity that alter life's previous patterns"[125] thereby making us obedient slaves to God (6:15–23 and 7:1–6). Meyer points out that the grammatical antecedent of the relative clause of 7:6—"that which held us captive"—is the law. He submits, therefore,

120. Ibid., 182 [160].
121. Ibid., 175 [153–54].
122. Ibid., 186 [165].
123. Ibid., 187 [166].
124. Paul W. Meyer, "The Worm at the Core of the Apple: Exegetical Reflections on Romans 7," in *The Conversation Continues: Studies in Paul and John in Honor of J. Louis Martyn*, edited by Robert T. Fortna and Beverly Roberts Gaventa (Nashville: Abingdon, 1990), 69.
125. Ibid., 68.

that Paul writes 7:7–12 in order to prevent an antinomian interpretation. In other words, Paul's angle in emphasizing the goodness of the law is to focus on the other side of the mistaken confusion—sin. Thus sin, not the law, is the personified power and adversary of the "I" in not only 7:7–12 but all of 7:7–25.

Furthermore, Meyer understands 7:7–25 to be a retrospective. It looks back on the sin that had previously bound us in order thus to prepare us for the discussion in chapter 8 of what God has done to restore human life by means of the Spirit. The law figures into this section only as it is shown in verses 7–12 to be completely unable to prevent what it prohibits as well as to actually produce in us the very thing it is supposed to prevent. Meyer locates the center of this section at verses 10b–11, arguing that "the effect of *sin* on the genuinely religious person who looks to God's Torah for life has been to produce exactly its opposite, death."[126] Rather than locating the core of the dire situation, as it is explicated in Romans 7, in the divided self, he locates it in "the self's enslavement to the power of Sin, precisely as Sin has wrested the Law out of the hands of God."[127] In other words, Paul sets up two laws (7:22–23, 25; 8:2), rather than two parts of the self. The first law is the Mosaic law working as the law of God, and the second is the Mosaic law as it has fallen into the hands of sin.

> "By hijacking the law . . . by using something essentially good—and God-given—to bring death to the human race, sin revealed the magnitude . . . of its own evil." . . . This Law taken in hand by Sin, and employed by Sin to deceive and kill, is nothing other than the holy and spiritual Law of God (Rom. 7:12). It is God's own Law corrupted by Sin, indeed conscripted by Sin into a lethal alliance with Sin.[128]

This view of sin's power over the law—effectively splitting the law into two—is supported particularly in verses 21–25, where the law resurfaces as a major theme. The first law is "the law of God," in verses

126. Ibid., 71.

127. J. Louis Martyn, "A Formula for Communal Discord!" in *Theological Issues in the Letters of Paul* (Nashville: Abingdon, 1997), 272.

128. J. Louis Martyn, "Nomos Plus Genitive in Paul: The History of God's Law," in *Early Christianity and Classical Culture: Comparative Studies in Honor of Abraham J. Malherbe*, ed. J. F. Fitzgerald et al. (Leiden: Brill, 2003), 581.

22 and 25b, and "the law of my mind" in verse 23. The second law is "the law of sin" that is in "my members" in verses 23 and 25b. "Verse 22 confesses allegiance and delight in the first. Verse 23 reports the discovery of the second. The contrast could scarcely be sharper."[129] Martyn clarifies, "The terrifying *fundamentum* to the whole of Paul's argument is the fact that the Mosaic Law is not only God's Law, but also Sin's Law, a tool of Sin."[130] It is but a short step from 7:7–13 to the expression ὁ νόμος τῆς ἁμαρτίας, by which Paul refers to the law of God as it has fallen into the hands of sin. "Using the term *nomos* to refer specifically to the Torah, Paul presupposes an *event* in what would appear to be a history of the Law. Are there, then, junctures in Paul's letters at which he clearly speaks of the Law's history? There are, indeed, two."[131] The law of God has a history. In this history are two decisive events—"its falling under the power of Sin, so that it leads to death, and its being taken in hand by the Spirit in Christ, so that it leads to life."[132]

For Meyer, the cleavage painted by Paul in Romans 7 is not within the self but with the law, when it is co-opted by sin. This is not to say that the law is no longer God's. On the contrary, 7:13 indicates that "the law has remained God's and has continued to serve the divine purpose of disclosing and intensifying sin."[133] The law is indeed good, and what it offers is good; thus 7:10 indicates that the law promises life. Paul's own Jewish allegiance to the Torah is neither illegitimate nor misplaced. The real problem comes when one is sold under sin and discovers that "just what one hoped to avoid in one's reliance on the law (v. 15)"[134] is actually what is produced in reliance on the law.[135]

129. Meyer, "Worm at the Core of the Apple," 75.
130. Martyn, "Nomos Plus Genitive in Paul," 273.
131. Ibid., 282.
132. Ibid., 283.
133. Meyer, "Worm at the Core of the Apple," 72.
134. Ibid., 73.
135. Martyn makes this point, too. "Paul was well acquainted with the riches of this tradition, having enjoyed a blameless life as he followed the precepts of the God-given Law (Phil. 3:6). Indeed he refers explicitly to this tradition when he says that the commandment had life as its goal (Rom. 7:10). As he now looks back, however, Paul sees a radically different picture, the one in which Sin plays its awesome role as the cosmic power that has turned the Law into its junior ally. For, noting Sin's role as a spoiler, Paul quickly adds that sin employed the commandment to deceive and kill him (Rom. 7:11)." Martyn, "Nomos Plus Genitive in Paul," 586.

Meyer cites Rom. 3:9; 1:31; and 2:2 as evidence that this idea fits with what Paul has already said about the inability of religious people, under the power of sin, to have a relationship with God. In short, he finds the summary of the whole of 7:7–25 to be that "It is the *law* that has been used by *sin* to produce *death*."[136]

In sum, Martyn and Meyer's interpretations steer clear of any talk of a split "I" and instead give a concentrated look at the role played by sin in the passage. They conclude that sin in chapter 7 acts as an anti-God power to such an extent that not only are individuals sold under the power of sin, but God's law is wrested from God by sin and used as sin's tool to produce death in the human. Thus the passage is moved to a level of cosmic drama in which there are three actors on stage—God, the individual/humanity, and sin.

Barth understands Romans 7 to be about the contrast between eternity and time. His interpretation involves the same three actors just mentioned, but religion is also prominently featured in the dynamic created between sin and humanity. In fact, religion is sin for Barth. Far from lessening the drama, Barth's discussion of religion heightens and highlights Paul's cosmic apocalyptic eschatology. Defining religion strictly as a human enterprise allows us to see how it represents "the polar opposite of God's apocalyptic act in Christ."[137] In the same way that Meyer and Martyn understand Romans 7 as telling the history of the law as it is co-opted by sin, Barth understands Romans 7 as telling the story of the meaning and reality of religion, defined as the last human possibility standing in opposition to the grace of God's freedom. Romans 7:1–6 is thus entitled "the Frontier of Religion," which explains religion's positive meaning; 7:7–13 is entitled "the Meaning of Religion," which explains its negative meaning; and 7:14–25 is entitled "the Reality of Religion," which discloses the truth that the problem of life cannot be solved by any human effort. Religion,

136. Meyer, "Worm at the Core of the Apple," 76.

137. J. Louis Martyn, "Galatians, An Anti-Judaic Document?" in *Theological Issues in the Letters of Paul*, 79. Martyn clarifies that Paul is not out to denigrate Judaism, but rather "he is consistently concerned to say that the advent of Christ is the end of religion." See Martyn, *Galatians: A New Translation with Introduction and Commentary*, AB 33A (New York: Doubleday, 1997), 164.

at the end of the day, is limited, and thereby "its ineffectiveness, establishes and authenticates the freedom of God to confer grace upon men."[138] Religion is the highest human possibility within humanity's search for freedom independent of God. In contrast, God's freedom is God's decision to confer grace on humanity to restore them to the relation of union with God. Furthermore, God's grace comes to humanity outside and above the human possibility of religion. We are new people only in Christ, "justified and redeemed . . . endowed with attributes which are not [ours], have not been [ours], and never will be [ours]."[139]

For Barth, 7:1 indicates the parameters of our existence in this world. Being human and living in the world necessarily mean that "we cannot hope to escape the possibility of religion."[140] Religion has a positive and negative function, and precisely in this ambiguity is its danger. In the positive function of a religious person (i.e., in that she bears witness to the relation that exists between God and humans) and in her negative function (i.e., in her, human nature is confronted by God's reality), Barth finds a dualism controlling the whole realm of religion. The consequence of this dualism is that sin abounds (5:20).

The frontier of the dualism inherent in religion comes for Barth in 7:4. Christ's death is the means by which we are freed from the limits of human religion and freed for God's possibility. In Christ, we are under grace. "All human possibilities, including the possibility of religion, have been offered and surrendered to God on Golgotha. . . . Golgotha is the end of the law and the frontier of religion."[141] God's justification of us reveals that our situation under the law will not change in this life. Only as our self-striving is put to death in the death of Christ can we find true freedom. It is a freedom given to us out of God's gracious freedom and made known to us in the death and resurrection of Christ.

Commenting on 7:5–6, Barth notes that religion "stands within the bracket which is defined by the all-embracing word *sin*."[142] Here is a

138. Barth, *Epistle to the Romans*, 230 [212].
139. Ibid., 229 [211].
140. Ibid., 230 [212].
141. Ibid., 233 [215].

connection to what is to come in 7:7–13, when humans become sinners under the scrutiny of the law. Religion is trapped within sin's dominion and so hastens the "inevitable passing to death of the world of the flesh."[143] Not only must we die, but religion, too, must die, as it is our human striving for independence from God. Thus we can only find our true selves "outside the domain of the law" in the place where God is gracious to us. "If we mean that something intuitable has taken place in us and in others, we have returned again to law and to religion."[144] Being under grace is not an experience. If it were, it would fall back under the domain of religion, which is bounded by the power of sin and can only lead to death. Only in the light of the resurrection, "the brilliance of this *But now*," can we "look back upon *the law* and its dialectic as upon that which is *done away*."[145] The resurrection discloses the truth that we are freed from the law and freed for obedience unto God in the death of Christ. Therefore, it is a truth that must be made new by God moment by moment for us as we are joined to the death of Christ. The newness of Spirit talked about in 7:6 has its beginning only in God. It is a newness "beyond the frontier of the old and of every new possibility of religion."[146]

The positive side to religion is that it is the turning point. It is the place where the first unintuitable thing (grace) confronts the last intuitable thing (law). Religion is where the freedom of God seizes us. This is Barth's explanation of 7:7a. Not surprisingly, Barth's description of our radical seizure by God's grace is neither concrete nor this-worldly. The seizure is "nothing but vacuum and void and blankness."[147] Insofar as the divine in Jesus touches our world of space and time, it ceases to be historical, temporal, and directly intuitable. Confronted with the nonworldliness of grace, we discover "[r]eligion, as the final human possibility, commands us to halt."[148] Yet the

142. Ibid., 235–36 [218].
143. Ibid., 235 [218].
144. Ibid., 237–38 [220], *rev.*
145. Ibid., 237 [219].
146. Ibid., 239–40 [222].
147. Ibid., 240 [222].
148. Ibid., 242 [224].

dialectic continues back the other way in 7:7b, and Barth's language fairly bristles with apocalyptic imagery. Religion is merely the loftiest summit in the "land of sin";[149] it is the place where "sin becomes an observable fact of experience."[150] Religion overwhelms us, Barth says, "like an armed man,"[151] for it forces us to be confronted, as worldly people, by the problem of the existence of God. "When human finite existence is confronted by the eternity of God, it becomes sin."[152]

Barth concludes his reading of 7:7–13 by reiterating that religion is "the working capital of sin; its fulcrum; the means by which men are removed from direct union with God and thrust into disunion, that is, into the recognition of their—creatureliness."[153] The meaning of religion is not only that sin is shown to be the power that reigns in the "closed circle of humanity,"[154] but also that "its power is bounded by the freedom of God."[155] Religion's meaning is that "it sharpens our intelligence that we may perceive (7:6) the sheer impossibility of our attaining that freedom from the law."[156]

In the final section of Romans 7, Barth suggests that the theoretical meaning of sin is only truly understood as sin's dominion over humanity is really observed. Yet even as we see sin abounding in the religious person, so we understand better the meaning of grace abounding even more, "the necessity that the divine mercy should act in spite of sin."[157] For Barth, Romans 7 is about the freedom of the grace of God to save us in spite of ourselves. Romans 7:14–25 demonstrates religion as a "yoke which cannot be removed."[158] Religion only brings about dissension—within the religious person herself and between the person and God. Romans 7:14–20 shows that our lives dwell within the four walls of sin. "Religious experience, then, simply bears witness

149. Ibid.
150. Ibid.
151. Ibid., 245 [227].
152. Ibid., 245–46 [228].
153. Ibid., 248 [231].
154. Ibid., 257 [239].
155. Ibid.
156. Ibid.
157. Ibid., 257 [240].
158. Ibid., 258 [241].

to the fact that sin is all-embracing."[159] In 7:21–25 this plays out as we see the disruption that religion brings to our lives. Religion, the working fulcrum for sin, breaks us into two halves. Inwardly, our spirit delights in God's law. Outwardly, our corporeality follows a different law. Who are we? The inward? The outward? Both? We cannot be spirit without nature or nature without spirit; yet, neither can "the desired union . . . be maneuvered merely by ranging the two alongside one another or by amalgamating them, or by conglomerating them."[160] Here is the dilemma, with which the chapter began, of the religious person. We must die, but we can neither live nor die. The ambiguity of religion suspends us between heaven and earth and confronts us with the limitation of our humanity. True religion, Barth concludes, is characterized by Paul's remark of disgust with himself—"O wretched man that I am!" From this, the great "But!" can be stated—"Jesus Christ is the new man, standing beyond all piety, beyond all human possibility. . . . He is—what I am not—my existential I—I—the I which in God, in the freedom of God—I am!"[161]

On this note—the note that it is in God's freedom alone that we are who we are not—Barth urges that Paul is not merely describing his pre-conversion experience: "[w]e must not deprive this *am* of its heavy significance."[162] Barth recalls that this is a point the Reformers understood well. Paul is describing his past, present, and future existence. "Paul is thrust into a dualism which contradicts itself,"[163] but into which the grace of God and God's freedom breaks through.

Conversation 5: Keck, Meyer, Gaventa, and Barth on the Spirit and Eschatological Hope in Romans 8

As Leander Keck rightly points out, Romans 8 is not only the climax to the discussion that first began in 5:12; it is a panorama of Paul's cosmic horizon—the awaited redemption of all creation.[164] The first

159. Ibid., 266 [249].
160. Ibid., 269 [251–52].
161. Ibid., 269 [252].
162. Ibid., 270 [253].
163. Ibid.

seventeen verses mention the Spirit fifteen times, while verses 18–30 make repeated use of "wait" and "hope," with "glorified" serving as bookends in verses 18 and 30. The movement of the passage is between the time of the Spirit—the "now"—and the hope of universal salvation[165]—the "not yet" of redemption. In a similar vein, Gaventa stresses that Romans 8 demonstrates that the conflict with sin and death continues in the present. They have been defeated but are not yet destroyed. Redemption has begun but is yet to be completed.[166]

Meyer fleshes out Paul's focus on the Spirit in 8:1–17. He notes the key contrast is between the ineffectiveness of the law—under the power of sin—to renew life, and the power of God's Spirit to do just that. Human beings are either in the flesh or in the Spirit. It is only God's raising of Jesus that brings an individual to new life in the power of the Spirit. Paul's phrases in verses 9–11 are all interchangeable and together point to the truth that "God is the one who gives life to the dead (4:17); he has raised Jesus from the dead. The Spirit is not the possession of some elite group within the church."[167] Keck points out that references to "flesh" in Paul are signals of his theological anthropology and that his perspective is consistently negative. The thirteen formulations about the "flesh" between 7:5 and 8:15 "express Paul's view of the human plight as a *condition* that must be replaced, and that *is* replaced by solidarity with God's own Son, through whose death God condemned sin in the flesh, and by the residence of God's Spirit, whose work will be completed by the resurrection of the body."[168] Although the awaited "freedom," which is the true opposite of the enslavement to sin and death spelled out 7:7–25, is an anticipated

164. Leander E. Keck, *Romans*, Abingdon New Testament Commentary (Nashville: Abingdon, 2005), 194.

165. Susan Eastman has convincingly argued that the movement in Paul's argument "from the present to the future 'apocalypse of the sons of God' is not from a 'hidden' to a 'revealed status,' but from partial to full redemption, to the salvation of 'all who believe' as promised in 1:16. The eschatological climax of this movement is in Paul's vision of Jew and Gentile glorifying together the God from whom, to whom, and through whom are all things (11:36)." See Susan Eastman, "Whose Apocalypse? The Identity of the Sons of God in Romans 8:19," *Journal of Biblical Literature* 121, no. 2 (2002): 277.

166. Beverly Roberts Gaventa, "Neither Height nor Depth: Discerning the Cosmology of Romans," *Scottish Journal of Theology* 64, no. 3 (2011): 265–78.

167. Paul W. Meyer, "Romans: A Commentary," in *The Word in This World: Essays in New Testament Exegesis and Theology*, edited by John T. Carroll (Louisville: Westminster John Knox, 2004), 190.

168. Keck, *Romans*, 209.

gift of the future salvation (8:21), it also has a certain connection to the present. Paul's image of "heir" in 8:17 affirms new life in the Spirit, albeit in provisional and unseen ways. Because of the Christ event, the power of sin has been undone; its condemnation is not just pronounced, it is carried out (8:3).

As he has already done elsewhere (5:10, 17; 6:5, 8; 8:11), Paul continues his insistence on the futurity of salvation in 8:18–30. Martyn suggests that this apocalyptic perspective finds the world not yet fully subjected to God even as this eschatological subjection has indeed begun, giving glimpses into the awaited end.[169] Meyer, too, observes Paul's contrast between the sufferings of the present time and the awaited future redemption. The correlation between Christ's life and those who are in Christ represents a "hard realism" that allows the trials of the present time to actually verify "the truth of the gospel instead of refuting it."[170] Consequently, the gift of the Spirit "confirms the gap between present and future, but at the same time sustains the expectation and turns it into a certain hope."[171] As Keck puts it, "for Paul the presence of the Spirit combines 'the already' and 'the not yet.'"[172] Furthermore, creation's groaning as with the pangs of childbirth, cosmic imagery drawn from apocalyptic literature, not only signals God's judgment and the advent of the new age, but it also demonstrates that Paul treats nature neither romantically nor with contempt. As part of the created order, creation itself is yet another witness to the hope of God's new future. Gaventa argues that Paul's references to humanity and creation together make up his cosmology, which, on the whole, is neutral. "The *κόσμος* is not inherently bad; it is God's creation and in need of God's salvation."[173] However, this cosmos "(i.e. the human population and indeed the entirety of creation, *κτίσις*) has been taken captive by anti-God powers. . . . and humanity (i.e. the

169. J. Louis Martyn, "Apocalyptic Antinomies," in *Theological Issues in the Letters of Paul*, 113.
170. Meyer, "Romans: A Commentary," 191.
171. Ibid., 192.
172. Keck, *Romans*, 212.
173. Gaventa, "Neither Height nor Depth," 269–70.

human cosmos) is at present the object of a conflict between God and anti-God powers."[174]

In the conclusion to the chapter, Paul returns again to the love of God. God's handing over of his Son proves that God is not against us but irrevocably for us. Meyer insists that this is the message at the heart of Paul's teaching on justification.[175] Gaventa asserts that the question "who is 'against us' (καθ' ἡμῶν)?" likewise powerfully conveys the core gospel message.[176] Meyer further notes that in between Paul's two lists, which unfold the assurance of God for us in verse 35 and verses 38–39, respectively, is an appeal to Ps. 44:22, a lament to God over the abuses of Israel's enemies that Paul universalizes "as an apocalyptic truism that God's faithful are always exposed to violent death."[177] Yet even as there is the apocalyptic insistence that current tribulation is a mark of belonging to God, it is closely followed by an emphatic statement of the cosmic victory that God's love in Christ will achieve over the powers, realities, and beings that would like to separate us from God. Keck concludes that here Paul must have wanted to set his argument to music for "[t]he astounding confidence expressed . . . is grounded solely in the power of God's love, expressed as God's giving"[178] of Jesus Christ. Gaventa, on the other hand, finds verses 31–39 demonstrating that Paul "regards the human cosmos . . . as a place which remains disputed territory. God is in conflict with other powers for rule over the human cosmos."[179] She continues, "what Paul writes here makes no sense if there is not, in his judgment, some intent to separate humans from their rightful lord."[180] Yet Gaventa, too, hears Paul's confidence that "the powers that attempt this separation will be defeated."[181]

When Barth listens to Paul's talk of the Spirit in Romans 8, he hears both the Spirit's negation and the Spirit's affirmation. "The Spirit is the 'Yes' from which proceeds the negative knowledge which men have

174. Ibid., 270.
175. Meyer, "Romans: A Commentary," 193.
176. Gaventa, "Neither Height nor Depth," 273.
177. Meyer, "Romans: A Commentary," 193.
178. Keck, *Romans*, 223.
179. Gaventa, "Neither Height nor Depth," 273.
180. Ibid., 274.
181. Ibid., 275.

of themselves. As negation, the Spirit is the frontier . . . of human life: as affirmation, the Spirit is the new, transfigured reality which lies beyond this frontier."[182] The knowledge brought by the Spirit points to the limits of every human possibility, while also illuminating the new reality and new humanity. "This is the meaning of the words—*in Christ Jesus*."[183] The once-for-all event in which sin and death are finally negated is, for Barth, the possibility of the Spirit. "The Spirit is that new, existential, once-for-all, universal life, which has been revealed in Christ."[184] As Barth has insisted all along the way, the new reality of the Spirit is not a possession that is made ours. The possibility of the Spirit is given only in Jesus Christ. Furthermore, Paul's emphasis on the sending of Jesus by God is the divine answer given to the imprisonment of humanity under the power of sin. "The divine answer is the righteousness of God, of God alone, which as such pre-eminently and victoriously confronts the last possible definition of men, namely, their essential sinfulness."[185] "God sends His Son in the midst of sin-controlled flesh, in order that there—if not there, where—sin and rebellion against God with all its consequences may be condemned and struck down; in order that . . . the curse of death may be done away."[186] God's righteousness is revealed, therefore, in the condemnation of sin in Christ.

Barth understands well Paul's reservation of the language of freedom for the future salvation of verse 21. As long as we remain people of this world, our freedom in God will only be slavery. Only in the miraculous event of our new humanity in Christ is our freedom real. We must "live in the darkness, but not now without the reflection of light uncreated; God's prisoner but as such His freedman; His slave, but as such His [s]on; mourning and yet blessed."[187] For Barth, the "not yet" always sounds the stronger note as even the "now" is an event with neither before nor after. This corresponds well with Gaventa's

182. Barth, *Epistle to the Romans*, 272 [255].
183. Ibid.
184. Ibid., 273 [256].
185. Ibid., 278 [261].
186. Ibid., 281 [264].
187. Ibid., 297 [281].

emphasis on the conflict to which the cosmos is presently subjected. "Living in the flesh, we await and hope for resurrection, we await our body with its new predicates. Of this hope our present life is the reflection, impress, and witness. Pledged to hope, our life finds there its goal. Quite apart from any conceivable change in us, we are constituted by eternity and qualified by what is to us unintuitable."[188] The final day of Jesus Christ "has not as yet dawned but is inscrutably *at hand*" in the "'Now' of 3:21," the moment of "Jesus Christ crucified and risen."[189] It is only in this "Now" that we apprehend eternity in time. Barth, without a doubt, does not see God's triumph in the world around him; it is at hand, but remains unintuitable.

On a more positive note, suffering is unable to bar us from the "Now" of Jesus Christ. In fact, it is in suffering "that He justifies Himself in our presence and teaches us through His Spirit to cry, *Abba, Father*."[190] Suffering is the place, in the present time, where we see Christ. Here, too, we await the revelation of God's glory, which is our only hope. "The *Futurum resurrectionis* reminds us that we have been speaking of God and not of some human possibility."[191] Paul's words in 8:18–25 are a reminder of just how complex our life on this side of the resurrection is. There is no room for romanticism.

> We must rid ourselves of reverence for pseudo-life, if we are to apprehend; for it is not by such reverence that we are led to the apprehension of the divine secret of the cosmos. . . . In God breaks forth the contrasts which mark the vanity of the creature. The suffering, by which the whole created world of men and of things is controlled, is His, His action, His question, and His answer. For this reason the creature is placed under hope.[192]

The Spirit is our confirmation that we stand in an ambiguous place. The Spirit witnesses to the reality that we are children of God in the midst of our temporal and corporal existence, where we are still not yet the new people. We are adopted, yet we remain on this side of the

188. Ibid., 300 [284], *rev.*
189. Ibid., 304 [287, 288].
190. Ibid., 304 [288].
191. Ibid., 306 [289].
192. Ibid., 308, 309 [292, 293].

resurrection "under the Cross, unable to do more than bear witness to the 'Now' of eternity which is ours, to the Day of Jesus Christ, which is no day, but the Day of Days, before and behind and above the days of our life."[193] In line with Gaventa, redemption still awaits us; sin and death still need to be destroyed.

Like Meyer and Keck, Barth hears Paul's strong proclamation of "God for us" in 8:31–39. He takes this to mean "that the realm of contrasts lies behind us, and that the duality in which we stand, which conditions everything we see, and which renders the world darkness to God and God darkness to the world, has been overcome."[194] This realm of contrasts has been parsed out by Martyn to be "apocalyptic antinomies."[195] Where the old world is defined by pairs of opposites, new creation finds a new unity in Christ, as well as a new set of antinomies. "Swept away are the basic guidelines which—in one form or another—all people had formerly considered permanently dependable."[196] In that Christ was delivered up, we know God to be for us because there "the transformation of all things occurs where the riddle of human life reaches its culminating point."[197] Therefore, we have the greatest assurance that Christ—"the new man that I am not"[198]—has triumphed for us. Even as the contrasts set up by Paul are indeed "[m]onstrous to us," yet in God, they are "as negations which have been negated, as positions which have been dissolved, they are at peace, reconciled, redeemed, and resolved; in Him they are one."[199]

***

As stated in the introduction to this chapter, the goal of the conclusion to this chapter is to advance two points that will further the larger

193. Ibid., 313 [297].
194. Ibid., 326 [310].
195. Martyn states that his use of "antinomy" is rather idiosyncratic. His intention is to signify the ancient expressions for various pairs of opposites that were understood as the building blocks of the cosmos. See Martyn, "Apocalyptic Antinomies," 115n13.
196. Ibid., 119.
197. Barth, *Epistle to the Romans*, 327 [311].
198. Ibid., 329 [313].
199. Ibid.

argument of this study. Recall that the larger argument of this study suggests that once Barth becomes acquainted with Reformed theology and subsequently radicalizes such theology through his historicized theological ontology, his subsequent reading of Romans, as well as his exegetically derived doctrine of justification, become at once more Reformed and more thoroughly apocalyptic. Therefore, first we will give a summary of what Barth's readings, in his second commentary, offer to each of the doctrines interrelated to a full account of justification (namely, revelation, atonement, justification, anthropology, and eschatology). Second, we will briefly highlight some of the missing elements in Barth's account of justification in the second commentary—elements that will find their way into Barth's subsequent readings of Romans and explication of justification within his mature doctrine of reconciliation.

First, Barth's comments on Rom. 1:16–17 suggest an understanding of revelation as occurring at "the place" of the resurrection of Jesus from the dead. Revelation is not a predicate of history. While it happens in history, revelation is not a product of history. It is never something given to us directly. We cannot possess or control it, nor is it ever a completed fact lying somewhere behind us. It remains always before us in a present giving. The resurrection of Jesus from the dead is the point of intersection between the unknown world of God and our own known world. Here revelation takes place in hiddenness. What we have not yet seen in Barth's treatment of revelation at this stage, which we will see later, is a strong development of revelation as the history of the person of Jesus Christ. Closely related to this, Barth has not yet developed the positive affirmation that the event of revelation is an event of divine-human union, which perfectly corresponds to the negative affirmation that revelation takes places in hiddenness. What we will see change in Barth's mature theology is the idea that reconciliation is revelation, full stop. "Revelation in fact does not differ from the person of Jesus Christ nor from the reconciliation accomplished in Him. To say revelation is to say, 'The Word became flesh.'"[200]

Second, we have seen that Barth's approach to Rom. 3:21–26 and the theme of atonement has been first of all focused on God's righteousness as revealed through God's faithfulness in Jesus Christ. Jesus is the righteousness of God, meaning that he faithfully goes the way of the cross, destroying all human possibilities. The death of Jesus is an act of the human Jesus done in obedience to the will of God. God's faithfulness to Jesus is thus finally fully disclosed (here again is the priority of revelation over reconciliation) in the resurrection. God was in Christ and his death only to the extent that God was also above Christ and remained distinct from Christ. Jesus' death is the place of God's speaking, and the resurrection becomes knowable only in light of Jesus' death on the cross. Yet the meaning of the cross is only made known in the resurrection. Resurrection light must shine through the cross. Barth is singularly focused on the modern problem of knowledge of God throughout the second edition of the Romans commentary. Thus where revelation occurs, there reconciliation is a consequence. Reconciliation is always understood only in the light of revelation. At this point, Barth has "no way to explain the relation of divine action to human action, and therefore no way to explain how one man's death could be the act of God that triumphs over sin, death, and the devil."[201] Eventually Barth will come to the conclusion that the reconciling activity of God is, as a consequence of the divine election, constitutive of the being of God. There we will see a more robust treatment of the atonement, realized through the lens of the priestly office of Christ as well as a more thorough relating of the death and resurrection of Christ. To sum up, what will change in Barth's reading of Paul: rather than revelation being reconciliation, reconciliation is revelation. This is no mere rhetorical fancywork. It is a change characterized by revamping the understanding of Christ's office in light of the ontological implications of the second Person of the Trinity assuming the human history of Jesus of Nazareth.

Third, Barth's understanding of justification, as it comes to

200. *CD* I/1, 119 [122].
201. McCormack, "Can We Still Speak of 'Justification by Faith'?," 179.

expression in his treatment of Romans 5, brings a strong focus on justification as an eschatological doctrine. For Barth, justification is a forward-looking sovereign declaration that makes us to be in a moment's time that which we are not yet but which we will be. Hence justification is also understood forensically for Barth. The eschatological actualization of justification is fleshed out in Barth's unique understanding of the role that faith plays in justification. Namely, justification is the consequence of the direct act of God on an individual insofar as God creates faith in us, which is then repeated moment by moment, never becoming a kind of precondition on our side. By faith we are made to know that our death takes place in the death of Christ. The unintuitable God is revealed in the death of Christ. The blood of Christ serves a didactic purpose, reminding us of God's faithfulness. In putting to death all human possibilities God not only justifies Christ, and through Christ us, but God also justifies himself. God is faithful to God's self and to humanity in raising Jesus from the dead.

At this point in Barth's development, Jesus is understood as a distinct subject from God, hence Barth is focused on justification as God's faithfulness more than on human justification through the alien righteousness of Christ. Jesus primarily serves an indispensable function in Barth's theological epistemology. As the Christ, Jesus surrenders all human possibilities open to him in order to die. Jesus is thus "the place" where God reveals God's righteousness. In this respect, what will change in Barth's mature doctrine of justification is that justification will become grounded in Christology. The eschatological and forensic casts will remain, but they will acquire more christological precision. Rather than focusing solely, in justification, on God's faithfulness to God's self and to us, to the neglect of the role played by Christ's alien righteousness, Barth will integrate his study of the Reformers, which happens after the publication of the second edition of the Romans commentary, with his reading of Paul, in order to understand the lived obedience of the human Jesus, including his death in God-abandonment, as an event that takes place in the very being of God. The first outcome of this reorientation is that the faithfulness of God simply is the faithfulness of Christ. The second outcome is that our justification is not something that takes place in us as a consequence of the direct act of God on us, creating faith moment by moment. Rather, just as we are elect in Christ, so our justification is objectively accomplished fully and completely in Christ. It is Christ's dying the death of God-abandonment for us and in our place, and his perfectly lived obedience and faith, that justify us. Only because and insofar as justification takes place in Christ is it effective for us. What remains is for the Holy Spirit to awaken us to the truth that in Jesus Christ we are justified sinners, so that we may then live in a way that corresponds to who we already are in him.

Fourth, when we consider Barth's reading of Romans 7, there are several ways he integrates the cosmic and universal horizons of Romans with theological anthropology. In that Barth takes the law to symbolize all religion, the horizon of who is included in his argument includes both Jew and Gentile alike. Religion, either directly or indirectly, encompasses the universal condition of all humanity. Additionally, Barth's emphasis on the "secret of God" and the "frontier of religion" is his unique read on Paul's cosmic outlook, and, importantly, it is not bracketed off from Pauline anthropology. The two are intimately connected for him because both are functions of his more central focus on God as wholly Other. This focus on the otherness of God simply begs the question—wholly Other than whom? The answer is that God is wholly Other than the creation and humanity. Thus not only is humanity implicated in this view of God, but humanity's problem and solution come into focus in it. "That the event of the cross can become *the* parable of the Kingdom means that in and through it is revealed the fact that the Kingdom of God is realized only through the negation of all human, historical, and temporal possibilities."[202] The cross is the place where the reality that religion has split us into two selves, when we were meant to be whole, is revealed to us and death is an instrument of God for restoring us to the

202. McCormack, *Karl Barth's Critically Realistic Dialectical Theology*, 255–56.

relation of direct immediacy we once had with God. Restoration is only available to us through dying to sin and coming under the divine grace revealed in the death and resurrection of Jesus Christ. "In the slain Christ-according-to-the-law, the last and noblest human possibility, the possibility of human piety and belief and enthusiasm and prayer, *is fulfilled by being evacuated*. . . . From death comes life; and what death is, is made known to us in the death of Christ."[203] What comes into focus in Barth's reading of Romans 7 is Paul's insistence on our human inability to restore our relationship with God. "In the inexorable 'No' of death, the 'Yes' of God and of life is presented to us . . . . There is no escape from this vision or from this undoing."[204] Barth wants us to embrace the full paradox of our situation. This is what religion helps us to do. It "sharpens our intelligence that we may perceive the sheer impossibility of our attaining that freedom from the law"[205] in order that we can be exposed not only to our own helplessness but also to the grace of God, which alone can set us free from our sinful existence. No other possibility is open to us except the possibility of being a person of the earth.

What is not yet clear in Barth's explication of Romans 7 is how this Pauline take on theological anthropology is an apt description for the beginning of justification. Romans 7, Barth will later say, portrays the circumstances in which we find ourselves in transition from past sinfulness and rejection into future righteousness and election. This later reading of Romans 7 will be fully unpacked in chapter 7 of this study. For now, suffice it to say that two things shape the contours of this later reading: first, justification is explained within a revised forensic rubric of God's unconditional acquittal (*Freispruch*) of an individual; second, Barth's appropriation of the doctrine of election. The seeds of emphasis that are already in place in the Romans commentary concerning Jesus Christ as "the man who passed from death to life," and "through Jesus Christ our Lord I am not the wretched man that I am,"[206] are more deeply worked out under Barth's

203. Barth, *Epistle to the Romans*, 233–34 [215–16] (emphasis mine).
204. Ibid., 251 [233].
205. Ibid., 257 [239].

historicized theological ontology. With Barth's theological ontology set in place, the transition from Rom. 7:24 to 7:25a gets described as a history—a continual event of the invading work of God.

Finally, Barth's understanding of the Spirit and eschatological hope in Romans 8 is at once both highly actualized and void of any hint of realized eschatology. We have already seen Barth's emphasis on justification as a thoroughly eschatological doctrine lacking any preconditions on our side. It should come as no surprise, therefore, that his take on the Spirit and eschatology in Romans 8 continues that same line of thought. It is only the "eschatological I," the new person, who knows not only what sin is but also that it has been destroyed and taken out of the way in Jesus Christ. The Spirit reveals that the resurrection of Jesus from the dead is the place where eternity confronts time and the turning point where the transition from the old to the new takes place. This "new" humanity that Jesus' resurrection brings into existence is complete only in Christ. That means that where humanity is concerned, any such newness is our future, not our present. In working this out, Barth comes quite close to actually equating the Spirit with this new humanity. Certainly, though, the Spirit is the power of new humanity by bringing it into being. While we are not yet in ourselves what we are in Christ, God has already brought us into relation with Christ. In the same way, while we do not have the Spirit as our possession, that we have the Spirit can only be said where the "we" is "not we"—in other words, where the "we" refers not to ourselves as we are but to ourselves as we will be. We do not have the Spirit, but we can be encountered by the Spirit and brought by the Spirit into relationship with our future selves. This event, in which the Spirit causes us to "be" what we are not, is an event with neither before nor after.

Clearly, Barth is stretching the relation that joins us to God, the relation established by the Spirit in the here and now of our lives, to the breaking point. There is nothing left, really, but the "in Christ" because he has so completely actualized the Spirit's work in our lives.

206. Ibid., 269 [252].

There is, of course, more realized eschatology in Romans 8 than what Barth allows for in his second commentary. What we will see change, therefore, in Barth's later understanding of eschatology is not his understanding that the Spirit is not ours to possess, but rather a commitment to thoroughly working out *how* Jesus Christ, as God's effective promise of eternal life, is our only hope, and furthermore how hope is a form of our here-and-now participation in the risen Jesus Christ. Under the umbrella of Barth's historicized theological ontology, Jesus Christ is what he does; hence, Jesus Christ is himself the event of reconciliation. Jesus Christ is God's promise of our future. This is not to say that the promise is already fulfilled in us. Barth will never go there. But he can now go farther with Paul to embrace that by the power of the Spirit, our frail human responses to God's work can be offered to God, thereby making that which is objectively true of humanity in Christ to correspond subjectively to who we are, by the Spirit, daily becoming. The Spirit is no longer practically equated with new humanity. Rather, the Spirit is now the active power of God in our lives, confirming and fulfilling what is already true of us in Christ. The Spirit makes us, more and more, to correspond to who we really are. Our obedient actions—our faith, our hope, our love—these are all the realizations of our true humanity. Pauline ethics can thus be taken with utmost seriousness.

Having a full picture of Barth's initial take on Pauline apocalyptic eschatology in his second Romans commentary now before us, what we must undertake in the next chapter is a survey of the salient features of Barth's theological development that followed after the second edition of his Romans commentary. First, we will see that Barth acquired a more formal knowledge of the forensic framework the Reformers gave to the doctrines of justification and the atonement and subsequently began to consider himself a Reformed theologian. Second, we will see that as Barth came into his own as a Reformed theologian, he did so in a way distinct to himself. His was a Reformed theology with a historicized theological ontology. The features of this will be laid out by way of a brief look at his doctrine of election in *CD* II/2. Third, through an examination of Barth's treatment of Rom. 1:18–32 in *CD* II/2, we will see how Barth moved beyond his earlier perspective in the second edition of his commentary to both a revised forensicism and a historicized theological ontology, which together nicely complement Pauline apocalyptic eschatology, if in slightly different ways. The aim of this third chapter is to line up the formative pieces of Barth's genetic development. This will allow us to approach chapters 4–8 of this study with the background necessary for understanding the forensic apocalyptic features of Barth's mature doctrine of justification.

3

Barth's Theological Development after *Der Römerbrief*

> I should like to describe it as a Christological concentration—I have been led to a critical (in an exalted sense of the word) discussion of church tradition, the Reformation, and especially Calvin.
>
> I soon saw that it was also necessary to continue it, to arrange the relationship between law and gospel, nature and grace, election and Christology and even between philosophy and theology more exactly and thus differently from the patterns which I found in the sixteenth century.
>
> —Karl Barth, *How I Changed My Mind*

As we made evident throughout the previous chapter, the sharply contoured antitheses of the second edition of Barth's Romans commentary were "concerned quite simply with *God* in his independent sovereignty over against man, and especially the religious man."[1] We further saw how this theme connects well to the cosmic-apocalyptic thrust of Romans. As this chapter moves us beyond the second edition of the Romans commentary, it will survey some key

1. Karl Barth, "Dank und Reverenz," *Evangelische Theologie* 23, no. 7 (1963): 339.

theological developments that come to shape Barth's revised forensic apocalyptic reading of Paul in his shorter commentary on Romans and his mature doctrine of justification in *CD* IV/1.

When Barth reflected retrospectively on the second edition of his Romans commentary, he pointed out three things that helpfully place the commentary within his genetic-historic development. First, he acknowledged that he had to speak the way he did at that particular time. Second, he insisted that he did not put something on Paul that was not inherently there in the letter to the church in Rome, but he did credit himself with being the first to draw out such threads.[2] Finally, Barth remarked that he had to move away from the *diastasis* of the Romans commentary in order to bring Jesus Christ to the center of his thoughts.

> The sentences I then uttered were not hazardous (in the sense of precarious) on account of their content. They were hazardous because to be legitimate exposition of the Bible they needed others no less sharp and direct to compensate and therefore genuinely to substantiate their total claim. But these were lacking. . . . The result was that we could not speak about the post-temporality of God in such a way as to make it clear that we actually meant to speak of God and not of a general idea of limit and crisis.[3]

Hence, even as Barth was faithfully listening to Paul's radical message of the priority of God's in-breaking, revelatory action in the world, he was on the verge of making Paul's witness to the living God into a generalized concept, which would only serve to diminish the disruptive impact of Romans.

It is the thesis of this third chapter that the later Barth moved beyond the perspective of the second edition of his Romans commentary by revising Reformational forensicism in such a way that Paul's apocalyptic eschatology could be highlighted in new ways and from different angles. The overall aim of this third chapter is to line up the formative pieces of Barth's genetic development so that we can

2. Eberhard Busch, *Karl Barth: His Life from Letters and Autobiographical Texts. Translated by John Bowden* (repr., Eugene, OR: Wipf & Stock, 2005), 120.
3. *CD* II/1, 635 [715–16].

approach chapters 4–8 of this study with the background necessary for determining the way Barth's exegetically derived doctrine of justification, within *A Shorter Commentary on Romans* and *CD* IV, is both forensic and apocalyptic.

Barth's Education and Educating in Reformed Theology

Following the publication of the second edition of the Romans commentary, Barth began the journey of acquiring a more formal knowledge of the forensic framework the Reformers gave to the doctrines of justification and the atonement, and as he did so, he began to self-identify as a Reformed theologian. The occasion that most contributed to Barth's education in Reformed theology was the invitation he received, at the beginning of 1921, to a chair in Reformed theology at Göttingen. Barth remarked that it was the first edition of his Romans commentary that led to such an invitation, yet not because of any particular Calvinist content, but rather because "the form of the book . . . suggested that I was passionately concerned with holy scripture."[4] Barth's first semester at Göttingen found him lecturing on the Heidelberg Catechism, and with this course he began in earnest to dive into Reformed theology. He truly began as a novice, not even owning a copy of the Reformed confessions, much less having ever read them. But at Göttingen he discovered the mysteries of Reformed theology, commenting that he frequently burned "the midnight oil" in his struggle over the next four semesters to understand the Reformed tradition.[5] In this way Barth gradually became a committed Reformed theologian, living into his honorary professorship in Reformed theology, "slowly but surely [becoming] intent on pure *Reformed* doctrine."[6]

By the summer of 1922, Barth was giving a series of lectures on Calvin, whom he found to be "a waterfall, a primitive forest, a demonic

4. Karl Barth, preface to German reprint of *Der Römerbrief*, 1st ed. (Zürich: Evangelischer Verlag, 1963), ix, quoted in Busch, *Karl Barth*, 123.
5. Ibid., quoted in Busch, *Karl Barth*, 129.
6. Karl Barth to Eduard Thurneysen, December 19, 1922, in *Karl Barth-Eduard Thurneysen Briefwechsel, 1921-1930* (Zürich: Theologischer Verlag, 1974), 127.

power, something straight down from the Himalayas, absolutely Chinese, strange, mythological; I just don't have the organs, the suction cups, even to assimilate this phenomenon, let alone to describe it properly."[7] The following winter semester, of 1922–23, Barth lectured on Ulrich Zwingli. By the summer of 1923 he took on the task of lecturing on the Reformed confessional writings, and as an offspring of that, he spoke in the fall on "The Nature and Purpose of Reformed Doctrine." While he admitted previously to studying Calvin and Luther to some extent, in Safenwil he had yet to really unpack the theology of the Reformers and admitted to not having access to them in the right way at the time. He attributed this to his formal, academic way of studying texts, left over from his student days. In Göttingen, however, this all changed. "Only now were my eyes properly open to the Reformers and their message of the justification and the sanctification of the sinner, of faith, of repentance and works, of the nature and the limits of the church, and so on. I had a great many new things to learn from them."[8] Yet, for as much as Barth was learning from the Reformers, it must be borne in mind that he never attempted a simple replication of their theology. He always approached their theological texts with imagination and critical judgment, remarking that he continually found them always to be both helpful and unhelpful, and that after having considered their historical context and meaning would decide for himself which classification to give to them.

It also bears mentioning that during this time of personal growth and teaching Barth never lost sight of the importance of theological exegesis. In addition to his various lectures in Reformed theology, he offered lectures on Ephesians, James, 1 Corinthians 15, 1 John, Philippians, Colossians, and the Sermon on the Mount.

McCormack has argued that while there were small shifts in Barth's thinking during his first two years at Göttingen, such as his more positive views on doctrine and the church and his affirmation of the

7. Karl Barth and Eduard Thurneysen, *Revolutionary Theology in the Making: Barth-Thurneysen Correspondence, 1914–1925*, trans. James D. Smart (Richmond, VA: John Knox, 1964), 101.

8. Karl Barth, *Selbstdarstellung* (1964), quoted in Busch, *Karl Barth*, 143.

Reformation Scripture principle, "none of these modifications amounted to a shift away from the eschatological perspective which governed *Romans* II."[9] Instead, the key shift that took place in Barth's thinking while at Göttingen came in May 1924, when he first read two textbooks on Lutheran and Reformed dogmatics by post-Reformation theologians Heinrich Schmid and Heinrich Heppe. Specifically, he learned of the early church's anhypostatic and enhypostatic christological doctrines, which together affirm that the human nature of Jesus Christ has no independent existence alongside the *Logos* but rather acquired its existence from God's own existence in the being of the eternal Son. The outcome of such a discovery meant that Barth could move away from the time-eternity dialectic, which prevailed throughout the second edition of the Romans commentary, as it allowed him to maintain the "Godness" of God in the event of God's self-revelation. Barth had found a way to preserve the critical distance between God and humanity using christological means. Along with this christological grounding came a real space for the incarnation. Revelation was no longer limited to the single event of the cross but could now incorporate the whole of the incarnate life of Jesus Christ. Such christological grounding first comes to expression in *The Göttingen Dogmatics*.[10] Barth affirms that God not only exists above the contradiction of our lives, but also, as the Lord, God freely enters into our contradiction and overcomes it from within. God's hiddenness really takes place in history because "the Subject in whom the humanity of Jesus is made real and exists is a Subject in history."[11] All this being said, the radicalism of Barth's earlier eschatological reservation did not disappear, only this radicalism now found its ground in Christology rather than eschatology.

In sum, Barth's theological development from 1921–24 was concentrated in his attainment of a real depth of knowledge of

9. Bruce L. McCormack, *Karl Barth's Critically Realistic Dialectical Theology: Its Genesis and Development 1909–1936* (Oxford: Clarendon Press, 2004), 318–19.
10. Karl Barth, *"Unterricht in der christlichen Religion" 1924, I*, ed. Hannelotte Reiffen (Zürich: Theologischer Verlag, 1985); Eng. trans., *The Göttingen Dogmatics: Instruction in the Christian Religion I*, trans. Geoffrey Bromiley (Grand Rapids: Eerdmans, 1991).
11. McCormack, *Karl Barth's Critically Realistic Dialectical Theology*, 363.

Reformed theology, which resulted in his self-identification as a Reformed theologian. Yet, importantly, his commitment to Reformed theology was never wholesale agreement, but rather dynamic and creative appropriation of that theology. What we see continuing during this period is a strong commitment to theological exegesis of Scripture. The starkest change in Barth's theology during this time was his switch from an eschatological ground for preserving the distinction between God and humanity to a christological ground. The adoption of the anhypostatic-enhypostatic Christology was thus a major development, allowing Barth to grapple with the effect of God's real, indirect presence in history without the danger of historicizing revelation. This change in his doctrine of revelation also allowed for a more careful distinguishing between the historical event of reconciliation and the eschatological event of redemption. "Reconciliation was no longer absorbed into a future redemption which never arrives."[12]

We are now a step closer to being able to examine the form and content of Barth's forensic apocalyptic doctrine of justification in his exegesis of *A Shorter Commentary on Romans* and the mature Christology of *CD* IV. Our next task is to understand the important role Barth's doctrine of election played as it came to expression in *CD* II/2.

Barth's Historicized Theological Ontology

In the summer of 1936, at a conference in Geneva on Calvin's doctrine of predestination, Barth heard a lecture by Pierre Maury titled "Election and Faith." This lecture had a profound influence in moving Barth toward the christological concentration that would come to characterize his mature theology from *CD* II/2 onward. Maury urged that election must be grounded in Christology rather than being treated in abstraction from the person and work of Jesus Christ. Thus the true subject of election is God's eternal Son, who freely chooses to be for us by taking our sin onto himself.

12. Ibid., 367.

By that September, in a series of lectures given by Barth in Debrecen, Hungary, titled "God's Gracious Election," Barth began working with Maury's argument, suggesting that it is the "*eternal* God and thus also the eternal Son of God [who] is the *electing* God."[13] Matthis Gockel has shown how subsequently, in the Basel lectures between the fall of 1939 and summer of 1941, Barth arrived at a unique, new conclusion that Jesus Christ is both the object and the subject of election. Hence, prior to this, Barth and Maury held that while the eternal Son of God is the subject of election, the object of election is Christ's human nature. It was Barth's groundbreaking conclusion that Jesus Christ is *both* the subject and object of election that transformed the whole of his subsequent theology. Assumed under such a conclusion is a heretofore new, historicized theological ontology.

For Barth to hold that Jesus Christ, the God-human in his divine-human unity, is not only the elect human but also the electing God showed that he had done away with the classical theological distinction between the eternal Word and the incarnate Word. The antimetaphysical tendencies and actualism we saw present in the second edition of the Romans commentary had just increased exponentially. Now "God *is* in himself, in eternity, the mode of his Self-revelation in time—God as Jesus Christ in eternity and God as Jesus Christ in time—thus guaranteeing that the immanent Trinity and the economic Trinity will be identical in content."[14] In other words, the primal decision of election is that event in God in which God differentiates God's self into three modes of being. Election is both the event of God constituting God's self as triune and the event in which God chooses to be God for us. The classical theological gap between the eternal Son and Jesus Christ is now gone, and the distinction between the two is removed. "The eternal Son of God is Jesus Christ as he lived, died, and rose again in time *and he alone*."[15] The being of God is already

13. Matthias Gockel, *Barth and Schleiermacher on the Doctrine of Election: A Systematic-Theological Comparison* (Oxford: Oxford University Press, 2006), 161n8.
14. Bruce L. McCormack, "Karl Barth's Historicized Christology: Just How 'Chalcedonian' Is It?," in *Orthodox and Modern: Studies in the Theology of Karl Barth* (Grand Rapids: Baker Academic, 2008), 218.
15. Ibid., 222.

determined in eternity by what God reveals God's self to be in Jesus Christ—a God of grace who is radically for all humanity.

One outcome of Barth's radicalized understanding of election was that when Barth turned to set forth his Christology within his doctrine of reconciliation in *CD* IV, he replaced the classical ontological category of "nature" with the modern category of "history," thereby "integrating 'history' into his concept of 'person.'"[16] What results is a theological ontology that expresses both the reality that God has elected to take humanity into the event of God's being and the reality that the human Jesus participates in the being and existence of God. God takes humanity into God's life in the incarnation. Thus all that occurs in the human life of Jesus of Nazareth is taken into God's life and made to be God's own. God does not cease to be God in doing this, because God has elected to be God in this way. In the history of Jesus of Nazareth, God truly gives God's self over to judgment, wrath, suffering, and death—the means "in and through which [God's] true being is realized."[17] In the decision for the history of Jesus Christ, the being of God the Son is constituted. In this way, Barth's new doctrine of election assumes a historicized theological ontology.

Furthermore, in an asymmetrical manner, the human Jesus has his being and existence in God by sharing in God's history through actively obeying the will of his Father. The human Jesus participates in God's being and existence indirectly "by freely willing to live in correspondence to the history of God inaugurated in the covenant of grace."[18] Again, the unifying factor in these two histories, which together constitute the unified person, Jesus Christ, is election. God, from all eternity, freely chose to give both to God's self and to humanity essential being in relation to the same person, Jesus of Nazareth. "It is in and through the *one* history of the man Jesus that what is essential to both God and humanity is concretely realized."[19]

The significance of Barth's development of a historicized theological

16. Ibid.
17. Ibid., 225.
18. Ibid., 228.
19. Ibid.

ontology for this study is that this element changes how Barth's mature doctrine of justification is apocalyptic. That both God's own being and humanity's are established through God's self-determination to be God for us in Jesus Christ means that God's justification of sinful humanity has a historical ontological ground. Barth comes to explain justification as an event between God and humanity. Even more, justification is a history that involves a movement from unrighteousness to righteousness. The history of Jesus Christ is the unfolding history of the movement and event of the justification between God and humanity. And because this justification of God and humanity in Jesus Christ is the result of the eternal decision of God, in which God elected that both our being and God's own being would be constituted in the history of the life, death, and resurrection of the God-man Jesus, the main thrust of Pauline apocalyptic eschatology—God's in-breaking action to put the world aright—is upheld. Yet, with this historicized theological ontology in place, the classical Reformation emphasis on the forensic nature of justification takes on new meaning. Not only does it lend itself to a faithful treatment of Paul's apocalyptic eschatology, but it also contributes to the way that forensicism frames all of the doctrines interrelated to justification. Of course the specifics of the form and content of this argument still remain to be worked out in chapters 4–8, but we now have in place the key developmental pieces that ground forensic apocalyptic eschatology within Barth's mature doctrine of justification.

Bringing the Developmental Pieces Together: Barth's Treatment of Romans 1:18—32 in *CD* II/2

In this final section of our survey of Barth's theological development we will examine his treatment of Rom. 1:18–32 in *CD* II/2. This will show us three things. First, we will see how Barth's privileging of Scripture enables Paul's apocalyptic eschatology to shape his formulation of doctrine. Second, we will note that it is exegesis that propels Barth's commitment to Reformed theology as well as his creative contribution to and adaptation of the doctrine of election. Finally, we will begin to discover how Barth's historicized theological ontology, arising as it does from his doctrine of election, shapes his forensic treatment of apocalyptic escahtology in Romans.

Beverly Gaventa has drawn attention to the fact that recent scholarship on Rom. 1:18–32 has neglected to reflect on the significance of the thrice-repeated "handing over" of humanity by God, an element that places this Pauline text firmly within the realm of cosmic-apocalyptic discourse.[20] She demonstrates that when the verb *παραδοῦναι* is used in the LXX, it is overwhelmingly in the context of the handing over of an individual(s) to the "power of another agent."[21] The signal being given by Paul in Romans 1, then, is that "God's handing over of humanity is not simply a response to human action but an event in God's conflict with the anti-God powers."[22] That God, for a time, handed humanity over to the power of sin must be seen in the context of Paul's larger theme of the righteousness of God. This was announced first in 1:16–17 and then repeated in 3:24, with the additional note of God's grace "through the redemption that is in Christ Jesus," which "signals that God has now brought back from slavery the humanity once 'handed over' to the anti-God powers."[23] Finally, in Rom. 8:32, the language of "handing over" is used once more by Paul—this time to describe God's action of handing over God's own Son on our behalf. On the cross, then, the conflict with the anti-God powers reaches its apex. God's victory over sin and death is made real on the cross, and humanity is set free from enslavement to the powers to which God had handed them over.

Barth's treatment of Rom. 1:18–32 in *CD* II/2 also includes significant reflection on the New Testament usage of *παραδοῦναι*. Specifically, his investigation of the term and of the passage in Romans occurs in §35, which treats the election of the individual, in a long, small-print

20. Beverly Roberts Gaventa, "God Handed Them Over," in *Our Mother Saint Paul* (Louisville: Westminster John Knox, 2007), 113–23.
21. Ibid., 115.
22. Ibid., 118.
23. Ibid., 122.

section at the end of §35.4 titled "The Determination of the Rejected." The problem of rejection is concentrated, as Barth sees it, in the New Testament's portrayal of Judas Iscariot, who himself "handed over" Jesus to the authorities. In Judas's shadow, however, is the apostle Paul, who, in contrast to Judas, witnesses to divine election in his "handing over" of the gospel message (1 Cor. 11:23). Paul's witness to divine election, however, comes only after his conversion. Previously he was Saul, the persecutor of the followers of Jesus, and as Saul, a revised version of Judas, the betrayer of Jesus. On this interesting connection between Paul and Judas, Barth observes: "the work of the elect can only be the amazing reversal of the work of the rejected."[24]

In the case of παραδοῦναι, we find that while Judas "handed over" Jesus, Paul received from the Lord that which he also "handed over" to the Gentiles. "The two 'deliveries' are obviously mutually determinative, so that Paul is set in the shadow of Judas, as Judas is set in the light of Paul. There is no apostolic παραδοῦναι which does not have behind it the judgment of Judas' παραδοῦναι."[25] In between Judas and Paul is Jesus Christ, who not only bore the rejection of Judas but whose election also stands first before Paul's. Jesus Christ is the prototype of both Judas and Paul, making "the situation between the elect and the rejected . . . the open situation of proclamation."[26] Thus the παραδοῦναι of Judas, in his betrayal of Jesus, and that of Paul, in his apostolic witness, can each only be understood rightly in the light of the prototype to both: the divine παραδοῦναι.

> There is the mysterious and terrible divine "delivery" according to which God in His burning wrath (cf. Rom. 1:18f.) does to men what Judas did to Jesus. He takes their freedom from them. He makes them so powerless that He gives them over to the authority of a power which is too great for them—the power, in fact, of their enemy—that he may rule them.[27]

Like Gaventa, Barth hears the apocalyptic note of conflict in the use of παρέδωκεν, and so he considers the question: Who is the enemy to

24. *CD* II/2, 480 [532].
25. Ibid., 483 [536].
26. Ibid., 480 [532–33].
27. Ibid., 484 [538].

whom humanity is handed over? To answer this question, he turns to Acts 7:42 and Rom. 1:24, 26, and 28. His conclusion from these passages is that "the mighty enemy to whose power God delivered men is their own work. . . . God abandons them to themselves and therefore to their destruction."[28] Reflecting on the use of παρέδωκεν in verses 24, 26, and 28 in light of 1 Cor. 5:1f. and 1 Tim. 1:19f., Barth concludes that "there is certainly connected, as its earthly counterpart, the technically obscure event which is twice described in the Pauline letters as the handing-over of certain men to Satan."[29] Indeed, Barth argues that while humanity is, in the first instance, left to themselves, this is characterized even "more sharply" by Paul as their delivery to Satan. "They are left alone, under the authority of the one whom they have tried to serve and have actually served with their actions. . . . Abandonment is abandonment, abandonment to Satan, as Paul does not hesitate to describe it."[30] Barth finds God's action of handing over humanity, however, to be perfectly just—giving humanity the existence we have merited.

Yet the handing over of humanity to the destruction we have merited is not an end in itself. There is a limit to the punishment of being handed over. "A final possibility—or, rather, an entirely new possibility beyond the completed judgment, beyond the payment of the last farthing—is not absolutely cut off by these passages from those handed over by God."[31] Furthermore, "the power of Satan, against which man has no power, is certainly limited by the might of the Lord."[32] In light of Rom. 1:17–3:20, Barth argues that God's wrath, for all of its severity, is "but the reverse side of His righteousness," in which Jews and Gentiles are alike judged, "utterly abandoned," and burned "right down to faith . . . that there it [God's righteousness] may promise and give them as believers both freedom and justification."[33] Here we see that Barth finds God's παρέδωκεν of humanity to be less

28. Ibid., 485 [538].
29. Ibid.
30. Ibid., 485 [539].
31. Ibid., 486 [540].
32. Ibid., 487 [540].
33. Ibid.

for punishment than for mercy. "It would not be the love of God which dealt with them in any other way, or spared them in this way. From this end He wills to make a fresh beginning with them. He will awaken them from this death which they must die."[34] From Rom. 3:21 onward, Paul is concerned to communicate that in the divine handing over of all—Jews and Gentiles alike—God actually intends good for them insofar as God's action aims at the "eschatological possibility of faith."[35] Furthermore, it is only as we keep this clearly before us that we can even attempt to understand Paul's use of παρέδωκεν in Romans 1.

With Paul as his guide, Barth reaches even further in his insistence to discern the connection between the human and divine παραδοῦναι. He next considers that God is the one who hands over Jesus in Rom. 4:25 and 8:32 and that Jesus, too, is said to have handed himself over in Gal. 2:20 and Eph. 5:2, 25. Whereas the connection in Romans 1 was to God handing humanity over in the same way that Judas handed over Jesus, now the connection is to God handing over Jesus and Jesus handing over himself in the same way Judas handed him over. "At this point we obviously have to do with the handing-over which takes precedence over all others in value, importance and meaning."[36] Barth concludes that "[a]ll other delivery looks either to or from this. It has its reality in what happened here."[37] In other words, Barth lets Rom. 4:25 and 8:32 interpret Rom. 1:24, 26, and 28. That Jesus is handed over to death by God in 4:25 effectively "removes the obstacle which prevents God from acquitting us as a just Judge,"[38] because in the death of Jesus our sin is destroyed. Romans 8:32 also confirms this. Paul urges that God is not against us but radically for us. The παρέδωκεν of Romans 1 reappears, but this time God delivers Jesus up for our sake. "And in the delivery . . . there is accomplished by the One who alone can be their Judge that which purifies them from every accusation and makes any future accusation irrelevant from the very outset."[39]

34. Ibid., 488 [541].
35. Ibid.
36. Ibid., 489 [543].
37. Ibid.
38. Ibid.
39. Ibid.

The consequence of God delivering up Christ "in powerlessness to [a] strange and hostile overwhelming power"[40] is that Christ is deprived of his freedom, his power is destroyed, and "he has no option but to submit to that which is inflicted on him, for the rest looking only to the higher power of God."[41] Barth also considers John 1:14 as setting forth the original and decisive handing over of Jesus in the incarnation. Regarding this connection between handing over in the incarnation and that of the atonement, Barth remarks that "[t]he first took place for the sake of the second, and the second was the outcome and revelation of the first. We cannot understand the positive divine παραδοῦναι, which is the basis of all others . . . unless we hold to the original and authentic παραδοῦναι."[42]

> The positive divine παραδοῦναι is included in the decree of God's eternal love. Concretely, the sending by the Father and the obedience of the Son are simply this divine παραδοῦναι. It is not for nothing, therefore, that Rom. 8:35, Gal. 2:20, and Eph. 5:25 relate it so emphatically to the divine ἀγαπᾶν. . . . Delivery, handing-over, abandonment by God are themselves included in and necessarily result from the fact that God wills to make man participant in eternal life by giving Himself to be his Covenant-partner.[43]

In this move, we can see that what has most impressed Barth in his study of παραδοῦναι is that Rom. 8:32 flows from the eternal decision of God to constitute God's own being by freely turning toward humanity in the lived history of Jesus of Nazareth.

The situation of Rom. 1:24, 26, and 28 is that in which God makes God's own in giving up Jesus and that for which Jesus offers "His freedom to His love"[44] in giving himself up for us (Eph. 5:2). This is God's great love for humanity, which overcomes our opposition and enslavement and makes us children of God. "So great is His love that He regarded it as worthy of this offering."[45] In this handing over, this

40. Ibid., 490 [544].
41. Ibid.
42. Ibid., 491 [545].
43. Ibid.
44. Ibid., 491 [546].
45. Ibid.

offering, God "does not merely execute judgment upon sin. He takes it upon Himself and suffers so that there can be no further question of suffering it ourselves . . . This is what makes absolutely necessary Paul's defiance in Rom. 8."[46] Therefore, the fate of the Jews and Gentiles handed over to "evil powers"[47] by God's wrath in Romans 1 is no worse "than that which God visited upon Himself in the handing-over of His Son. . . . There is, therefore, all the difference of heaven and earth when, on the one hand, the Son of God is left to Himself, indeed to the power of Satan, and on the other, the same thing happens to Jews and Gentiles."[48] Barth reasons that the handing over in Romans 1, and the punishment it entails, does not have any "independent significance alongside that of Jesus."[49] Jesus did not suffer anything other than what humanity had earned. However, Jesus suffered what he himself had not earned, for us, and in our place. "Jesus Christ is *the* Rejected of God,"[50] and thus "we cannot regard as an independent reality the status and fate of those who are handed over by the wrath of God. . . . We can thus ascribe to it only a reality which is necessarily limited by faith in Jesus Christ."[51]

The embryonic point in Barth's apocalyptic reading of Rom. 1:18–32 and 8:32 is the prior grounding in the event of the incarnation. The divine handing over of the incarnation is the event that grounds the triune being of God in love. Therefore, in the same way, it is because of God's love for us that God hands Jesus over to the powers to suffer for us and in our place that which we alone deserve. Romans 1:18–32 demonstrates God's wrath to be but the underside of God's love. Humanity's handing over can thus be put in perspective. In Christ's death on the cross, God has ultimately defeated, once and for all, that to which humanity was handed over. There is a higher purpose for humanity beyond the handing over—our restoration as God's covenant partners.

46. Ibid., 494 [549].
47. Ibid.
48. Ibid., 494 [549].
49. Ibid., 495 [550].
50. Ibid., 496 [551].
51. Ibid.

We have seen how both Barth and Gaventa have made much of the import of Paul's threefold use of παρέδωκεν. While Gaventa's aim is to place Rom. 1:18–32 within the realm of cosmic-apocalyptic discourse, she ultimately highlights that God's purpose in handing over humanity to anti-God powers is less for punishment than for mercy. With Barth, she recognizes that Rom. 8:32, with its use of the παρέδωκεν clause, shows that God hands over Jesus in order to defeat the powers and thus be merciful to us. Barth's purpose in examining Rom. 1:18–32 is to uncover both the positive and negative side of the divine παραδοῦναι so as to understand what purpose "handing over" plays within the doctrine of election, and specifically within the relationship of rejection to election. We see Barth discovering the key insight of his doctrine of election within this investigation of παραδοῦναι: "that the election of Jesus Christ is the beginning of all the ways and works of God."[52] Barth's apocalyptic reading of Paul is here tightly connected to his historicized theological ontology, which is more forensic than cosmic in its insistence that God's being (and humanity's) is a function of decision and act. Because election is at the heart of Barth's investigation of Rom. 1:18–32 and 8:32, he does not hesitate to put stress on the defining nature of the incarnation. In so doing, he also moves out of Paul and into the Johannine gospel and back again in his quest for the ontological presuppositions of God's handing over of humanity in Romans 1. "Barth begins with the historical facticity of what God has done and then asks (in effect): How must the being of God be constituted in eternity if he can do what we have seen him to do in time? What are the conditions in God for the possibility of the incarnation in time . . . ?"[53] In a parallel manner, Cousar points out that for Paul "God is to be known precisely in the message of the cross as a shameful and scandalous event. . . . Paul does not first reckon with the created order and inductively conclude that behind such beauty, precision, and regularity there must be a divine being to be called

52. Ibid., 454 [504].
53. Bruce L. McCormack, "The Ontological Presuppositions of Barth's Doctrine of the Atonement," in *The Glory of the Atonement: Biblical, Historical & Practical Perspectives*, ed. Charles E. Hill and Frank A. James III (Downers Grove, IL: InterVarsity Press, 2004), 358.

'God.'"[54] Certainly, Paul himself is not developing an ontology.[55] Yet, without a doubt, Paul had a concept of God and believed that Jesus was God. Therefore, Barth is not wrong to make the moves he does as he reads Rom. 1:18–32. In fact, Paul's letter invites such inquiry. Barth is attempting to hear in Paul the witness to the subject matter of all biblical texts, the Word of God, Jesus Christ, and from that, he is inquiring, as a systematic theologian, into the question of what God must be if Jesus is God.

We will continue to see this methodological approach at play as we move into the heart of our study of *CD* IV in chapters 4–8. We will also continue to see the way Paul is Barth's constant guide as his forensic doctrine of justification takes shape through a historicized theological ontology that is apocalyptic to its very core. More specifically, chapter 4 will take us into our first investigation of *A Shorter Commentary on Romans* and *CD* IV/1, where Barth highlights the real connection between a forensic doctrine of justification and Paul's apocalyptic understanding of revelation. Revelation is an event that happens outside us. The truth of God's action to make right what has gone wrong must be told to us. Guided by Rom. 1:16–17, Barth understands Paul's reason for writing to the church in Rome to be that they would know that Jesus Christ himself is the good news of God's powerful work of salvation. In Jesus Christ, God has reconciled sinful humanity to Godself by overcoming sinful humanity and creating a new humanity in its place. Thus with Paul, Barth understands Jesus Christ to be the active subject of reconciliation. Such a christological understanding of justification is consistent with Paul's apocalyptic proclamation of Jesus Christ as the true content of the gospel message. In the words of Käsemann, Barth follows Paul in starting with the cross, with the result that "Christology is transferred from metaphysics, with its sterile logical necessity, into history and thus into the kingdom of our own

54. Charles B. Cousar, *A Theology of the Cross: The Death of Jesus in the Pauline Letters* (Minneapolis: Fortress Press, 1990), 42.

55. This is in opposition to Francis Watson's argument in "The Triune Divine Identity: Reflections on Pauline God-Language, in Disagreement with J. D. G. Dunn," *Journal for the Study of the New Testament* 80 (2000): 99–124.

reality. . . . For the cross of Jesus is for us the truly critical power both of the world and of every individual, because it determines existence as a whole."[56]

56. Ernst Käsemann, "The Saving Significance of the Death of Jesus in Paul," in *Perspectives on Paul*, trans. Margaret Kohl (Philadelphia: Fortress Press, 1971), 34–35.

4

The Dimensions of Revelation in Barth's Forensic Apocalyptic Doctrine of Justification

> Jesus Christ, is the content of the Gospel. He is revealed in the Gospel and God's verdict is revealed in him.
>
> —Karl Barth, *A Shorter Commentary on Romans*

> The work of God in Jesus Christ is also the Word of God—the Word in which He makes known His will even as it is done to those who can hear it.
>
> —Karl Barth, *CD* IV/1

How is revelation understood in Barth's reading of Romans 1, and how does that interpretation contribute to a forensic apocalyptic understanding of justification? As already stated, any doctrine of justification is shaped by the answers to these questions: (1) How is justification enacted? (2) What are the contours of justification? (3) Who is the person who is justified? and (4) Where is justification located in the eschatology of salvation? Barth's mature doctrine of revelation proceeds on the assumption that all of these questions about justification can only be asked and answered on the basis of the enacted history of Jesus Christ. Jesus Christ himself is the reconciliation of humanity to God. Thus the history of Jesus Christ, a unity of his person and work, reveals the reconciliation that has happened. This is the shift that Barth's revision of his earlier doctrine of election produced. Where, earlier, he believed that revelation is reconciliation, now the relationship is reversed. Reconciliation is revelation. To put it this way is to suggest that the doctrine of revelation is no longer his principle concern; reconciliation is. The difference this makes is that humans are not saved simply because they have received the revelation that Jesus reveals about God in his death and resurrection. Revelation does not, as such, save. The reconciling work of Christ himself, which Barth now understands as the history of Jesus' obedience unto death and exaltation to God's "right hand," is what saves. Revelation is a function of the very reconciling activity of the triune God. To say, however, that reconciliation is revelation does not require an alteration of the basic structure of revelation. It is still an apocalyptic event. But now that apocalyptic event has been grounded in the divine decision that is basic to Barth's forensic framework for justification. The thesis of this chapter is that Barth understands Romans 1 to provide an apocalyptic account of revelation as an event that happens *extra nos* in the person of Jesus Christ. For Barth, there is no separation of the person of Jesus Christ from the work of Jesus Christ. The work is the person, and the person is the work. Therefore Jesus Christ is himself the content of the reconciling gospel message of salvation, which is forensically construed as God's just verdict. We will first trace how Barth works this out exegetically in *A Shorter Commentary on Romans* before turning to how this shapes his formulation of the forensic apocalyptic dimensions of justification in *CD* IV/1.

Revelation and Romans 1

As we enter into the main body of this study (chapters 4–8), we enter simultaneously into Barth's *A Shorter Commentary on Romans* and the fourth volume of the *Church Dogmatics.* While the date of the lectures contained within *A Shorter Commentary on Romans* corresponds more closely with *CD* II/2, with *CD* IV/1 coming some years later, the two will be treated together in these chapters for the simple reason that together they provide a fuller picture of Barth's use of Romans in constructing his forensic apocalyptic doctrine of justification. The time gap between the two documents will not be an issue, since *A Shorter Commentary on Romans* contains lectures given by Barth in the winter semester of 1940/41, which was when he was in the final stages of drafting *CD* II/2, and thus marks the point from which his christological concentration (Barth's commitment to reading doctrines off the narrated history of Jesus of Nazareth) is in place.[1] Furthermore, the addition of *A Shorter Commentary on Romans* at this point in the study has the benefit of rounding out Barth's exegetical engagement with Paul's letter to the church in Rome. Certainly *CD* IV/1 and IV/2 are replete with references to texts, words, and phrases in Romans.[2] There is even an extended exegetical discussion of Romans 7, which we will consider in chapter 7. However, in *CD* IV, the nature of much of Barth's commentary on passages in Romans is brief, often occurring alongside discussions of other biblical texts or simply as passing comments. This is not to suggest that Barth neglects a real engagement with Romans in *CD* IV, only to acknowledge that his engagement is often more piecemeal than cumulative. Frequently absent is a sustained look at a particular text in Romans or a sense of how the part fits with the whole. This is what is present, however, in *A Shorter Commentary on Romans*, and it will serve us well to begin with the treatment in *A Shorter Commentary on Romans* of the selected chapter of Romans at the start of each remaining chapter, and from there to move into an analysis of the *Church Dogmatics.*

Before moving into our main discussion of revelation, Romans 1, and

1. For more on this, see Bruce L. McCormack, "Christonomie," in *Karl-Barth Handbuch*, ed. Michael Beintker (Tübingen: Mohr Siebeck, forthcoming).
2. James Wharton notes that the *Church Dogmatics* contain "some 15,000 biblical references and more than 2,000 pieces of painstaking exegetical discussion of particular texts." See James Wharton, "Karl Barth as Exegete and His Influence on Biblical Interpretation," *Union Seminary Quarterly Review* 28 (1972): 6.

Barth's forensic apocalyptic doctrine of justification, a few words are needed by way of background information on *A Shorter Commentary on Romans*. By the time Barth's course of extramural lectures on Romans, given in Basel during the winter of 1940–41, was published in 1959, under the English title *A Shorter Commentary on Romans*, the shock waves of the 1918 and 1921 editions of *Der Römerbrief* had already come and gone with such great force, almost entirely negative, that few scholars took notice of this later and, of course, shorter piece of theological exegesis. The few who did held, to varying degrees, a common opinion that Barth's own system of thought (at times more softly expressed as a "Barthian emphasis") was the basis of his reading of Paul.[3] Not ignorant of these criticisms, in his preface to *A Shorter Commentary on Romans* Barth urges his readers to accept his work in both this and the earlier editions of his Romans commentary as legitimate biblical exegesis. "In both cases it was my intention—and it will remain my intention in the future, if I again have to say something about the Epistle to the Romans—to let Paul speak for himself."[4] As we have already seen, so also in *A Shorter Commentary on Romans*, Barth is concerned to hear Paul witness to the subject matter to which the text points—here focused on God's electing activity.[5] Maico Michielin points out that within *A Shorter Commentary on Romans* there are three dimensions to God's electing activity: "(1) the election of humankind in Jesus Christ; (2) the election of Paul as a witness to this election; (3) and derivatively, the election of the Christian to be a witness."[6] Given the context of Barth's own theological development at the time of these lectures, we should not be surprised to find this new angle in God's electing activity as the subject matter to which Paul witnesses.

3. For a listing of the five reviews see Maico Michielin's introductory essay, "Exegesis That Corresponds to God's Activity," in Karl Barth, *A Shorter Commentary on Romans*, ed. Maico Michielin, trans. D. H. van Daleen (Aldershot, UK: Ashgate, 2007), viii n3.
4. *SR*, xxv [6].
5. Micheilin admits that this phrase is nowhere in *SR*. However, it was chosen to represent Barth's understanding that "the subject matter with which Paul is concerned not only deals with God but with God's continuing dealings with humankind. . . . The subject matter is the living God, who, in Jesus Christ through the power of the Spirit, establishes himself as the subject matter of the text and in so doing elects Christians to be his covenant-partners by means of the biblical witness." See ibid., ix–x.
6. Ibid., ix.

Barth divides Romans 1 into two main sections in *A Shorter Commentary on Romans*. The first contains verses 1–17, which he titles "The Apostolic Office and the Gospel." The second section, 1:18–3:20, is titled "The Gospel as God's Condemnation of Man." Right away Barth has already made certain decisions concerning the thrust of the opening chapters of Romans. The theme of the gospel is announced in connection with Paul's apostolic office. Within Paul's introductory remarks, Barth finds that Paul's reason for writing the letter and main theme is nothing short of the gospel itself. By placing the rest of Rom. 1:18–32 together, he highlights Paul's thematic coherency within these chapters. Whereas the second half of Romans 1 is often cordoned off as its own diatribe against sexual immorality or else defended as demonstrating the possibility of natural knowledge of God, Barth sees it as part of a bigger Pauline argument about the gospel's proclamation of the condemnation of humanity—both the Gentiles (1:18–32) and the Jews (2:1–3:20).

I would contend that the fact that Rom. 1:1–17 comprise their own chapter in *A Shorter Commentary on Romans* indicates the important role that they play in Barth's reading of Paul. He points out that within Paul's opening greetings he has already set down a "substantial" statement about "the cause that moves him."[7] The cause is nothing less than the person of Jesus Christ, for whom Paul is a slave. Jesus Christ himself is the content of the gospel, and Paul's Lord, because he has been revealed as the Son of God by his resurrection from the dead. As Käsemann articulates it: "Christ is not the author of the gospel . . . ; he is its decisive content."[8]

The connection between the apostolic office and the gospel toward which Barth gestures in his title for verses 1–17 occurs when the gift of the Spirit, which Paul desires to pass on (v. 11), is focalized within the gospel, which has been entrusted to him (v. 5). Consequently, then, Barth finds verses 16–17 to fill out the definition of the gospel it is Paul's apostolic office to preach in Rome. The power that *is* the gospel

7. *SR*, 7 [16].
8. Ernst Käsemann, *Commentary on Romans*, edited and translated by Geoffrey W. Bromiley (Grand Rapids: Eerdmans, 1980), 10.

is God's almighty power, not some power among any other power, and therefore the reason Paul has already proclaimed that he is not ashamed of the gospel (v. 16). Again, Käsemann corroborates Barth's reading nicely: "The gospel is more than the message actualized in the church. It is God's declaration of salvation to the world, which is outside human control, which is independent even of the church and its ministers, and which constantly becomes a reality itself in proclamation in the power of the Spirit. It can thus be called δύναμις θεοῦ."[9]

Furthermore, because Paul has already set out that the content of the gospel is the person of Jesus Christ (v. 4), Barth helps us understand how the gospel itself *is* God's power. First, the gospel is God's powerful work of salvation. Barth notices that Paul explains salvation as the revelation of God's righteousness, or just verdict, which takes place in the gospel (v. 17). Since Jesus Christ is the very content of the gospel, he reveals in himself God's just verdict. In other words, "God's just verdict is God's work of salvation,"[10] which Jesus is and does. "The doctrine of justification is the specifically Pauline understanding of Christology just as the latter is the basis of the former."[11] While Barth acknowledges that the phrase in 1:17 "by faith unto faith" is not easy to understand, he finds in it a kind of play on words pointing to the verdict pronounced by Jesus, originating in God's faithfulness, and subsequently aiming at the trust, or faith, of those who hear this verdict. Barth suggests, ultimately, that Paul's words about the person who believes are impossible to understand unless Jesus Christ is in the picture. It is the proclamation of the gospel, whose content is Jesus Christ, that contains God's just verdict and calls for a faithful response to this verdict in its hearers. "Paul himself permits us to reconcile the apparent contradiction, for power and gift are not true antitheses in his eyes."[12]

Barth next observes that the second half of chapter 1, which begins

9. Ibid., 22.
10. *SR*, 11 [24].
11. Käsemann, *Commentary on Romans*, 24.
12. Ibid., 28.

with verse 18, has often been assumed to show Paul abandoning his office as a messenger of the gospel in order to speak in another capacity, such as a religious interpreter of history. If this is what Paul is up to, then Barth likens him to a bad preacher who begins with a long discussion unrelated to the sermon he has already announced. He finds no external evidence, however, that Paul has made such a change, nor does he think Paul's words about the Jews in 2:1ff are coherent if spoken generally rather than from the perspective of the gospel. Following this same line of reasoning, Barth concludes that it makes no sense to understand Paul as speaking from some general perspective about the Gentiles either. The specification that this revelation is "from heaven" (v. 18) makes this clear. God's power is "the sum total of all heavenly majesty";[13] there is simply no other source of revelation. This means that the second half of Romans 1 does not put us in some "outer court, but right in the heart of the matter."[14] Put another way, there is a dark side to God's just verdict—God's wrath. Noting Paul's grammatical cues, Barth finds the "for" (*γάρ*) of 1:18 to form a series with 1:16 and 1:17.[15] Thus the gospel as God's work of salvation also pronounces God's condemnation of humanity because of their sin. "The death of Jesus Christ on the cross is the revelation of God's wrath from heaven. That is the starting-point of Paul's argument."[16] Barth concludes that what Paul has said here is the first thing that must be said when the gospel confronts humans. But because the gospel is Jesus Christ himself, Paul does not stop with God's judgment. The first word to humanity is a word of condemnation. But the good center to such news comes already in 1:17 and again in 3:21–4:25, when Paul proclaims that "the Gospel is the divine justification of those who believe."[17] Käsemann, too, stresses that "[a]s justification, the gospel always means deliverance from wrath, the justification of the ungodly, eschatological

13. *SR*, 13 [28].
14. Ibid., 13 [28].
15. Käsemann exegetes the passage this way as well. See Käsemann, *Commentary on Romans*, 35.
16. *SR*, 14 [30].
17. Ibid., 26 [51].

creation ex nihilo, and anticipation of the resurrection of the dead, as 4:17 clearly says."[18]

What we find in Barth's reading of Romans 1 is a sure insistence that Jesus Christ himself is the content of the gospel. Barth gets at this in several ways, first by highlighting the way Paul's own apostolic office flows from his enslavement to the Lord Jesus Christ, and second by parsing the gospel as God's power for salvation, which itself is the revelation of God's just verdict worked out in Jesus Christ. For Barth, Jesus Christ is both the content and revelation of God's faithfulness as well as the object of faith for those who hear the verdict he has pronounced. The death of Jesus on the cross reveals God's just verdict as wrath against sinful humanity. It is because it is Jesus Christ, who is himself the gospel, that the first word to humankind must be one of condemnation. The good news is not about us. It is rather about the salvation God has powerfully wrought for us in Jesus Christ.

Paul's theology, translated into the language of dogmatic theology, affirms that reconciliation is revelation. The apocalyptic and forensic elements of revelation are brought together in the person of Jesus Christ, who is himself God's reconciling activity for humankind. The apocalyptic elements in Paul's portrayal of the gospel are seen first in that God's power to save comes to us from outside ourselves, from heaven, in the person of Jesus Christ, and second that the gospel first speaks a word of condemnation against sinful humanity. The forensic element comes out in that the content of Jesus Christ, himself the gospel, is nothing less than the revelation of God's just verdict. Barth will continue to work out the forensic imagery of the verdict in Romans 3, but because Paul already announces Jesus Christ as the content of God's righteousness in Romans 1, Barth highlights the apocalyptic and forensic imagery in this opening section.

Our first investigation into *A Shorter Commentary on Romans* makes clear that Barth is now reading Romans with an understanding of the Reformation's emphasis on justification and the positive element contained within the event of revelation, insights both missing in the

18. Käsemann, *Commentary on Romans*, 35.

second edition of his Romans commentary. Certainly, the negative affirmation of revelation as a work of God in hiddenness, as that which takes place without human input, is still very much in play, but now there is an equal insistence on the person of Jesus Christ, in his divine-human union, as himself the very content of revelation. Clearly, Barth has moved away from the time-eternity dialectic, which featured so prominently throughout the second edition of the Romans commentary, and is now implicitly preserving the critical distance between God and humanity using christological means instead. Barth now considers with real seriousness what it means that Paul is an apostle of Jesus Christ and how that connects with his insistence on the gospel as the power of God for our salvation.

We also see Barth working, more than in the second edition of the Romans commentary, with the Reformation concept of justification as God's just verdict. The righteousness of God is construed forensically in terms of God's verdict revealed in Jesus Christ. Barth finds this forensicism in Paul's insistence that the cross is God's condemnation of sinful humanity. Yet because Jesus Christ is himself the content of revelation, condemnation is not the last word; justification is. "God's verdict is God's work of salvation. The Judge is the Savior. When Paul acknowledges the Gospel as God's power of salvation, he has the Man [Jesus Christ] in view, through whom God reveals his verdict, and abides by this verdict."[19] One thing Barth knows for sure: the truth of justification, upheld by the Reformers but so often misunderstood, is nothing if not joyful good news in the hands of Paul. Consequently, Barth harnesses Paul's insistence that justification occurs not in us but in Jesus Christ in order to bring together anew Reformed forensicism with Pauline apocalyptic eschatology. The almighty power of God, the power that comes to us from outside as God's work alone, is the revelation of God's righteousness concretized in the act of God's verdict pronounced in Jesus Christ. This is the heart of Barth's forensic ontology, and it arises out of the crucible of Romans 1 just as it upholds Paul's apocalyptic gospel to its very core.

19. *SR*, 11 [24].

Revelation and Forensic Apocalyptic Justification

Already in the opening pages of *CD* IV/1, we can see the role revelation plays in Barth's doctrine of reconciliation. As rehearsed above, for Barth, revelation flows out of the event of reconciliation. God's reconciling activity is revelatory. Barth speaks of "God with us"—"God Himself in this act of His"[20] as an event. This event is nothing less than the salvation of humanity, which is the redemptive grace of God. The event of God's redeeming act showcases both God's glory and humanity's desperate plight. Käsemann puts it this way: "[t]he cross . . . shows us that from the aspect of the question of salvation, true man is always the sinner who is . . . a member of the lost, chaotic, futile world."[21] Furthermore, it is the event of God with us that reveals "an invasion of our history" in which God "does not will to be God without us," wherein God causes divine history and human history "to take place as a common history."[22] "That is the special truth which the Christian message has to proclaim at its very heart."[23] The reconciliation enacted in the lived history of Jesus' death and resurrection is the apocalyptically invasive truth of the gospel.

Barth goes on to clarify that there is but one revelation: the covenant of God with humanity. The heart of this covenant is the good news that God is for us, and it is Jesus Christ himself, in his history, who reveals the basic will of God, the heart of the covenant, to be *Deus pro nobis*. Like in *A Shorter Commentary on Romans*, reconciliation and revelation for Barth are both located in one name, Jesus Christ. "The name of Jesus Christ covers the whole power of the Christian message because it indicates the whole of its content, because at its heart, which is normative for the whole, it is a message about Him, and therefore a message about the event of that 'God with us.'"[24] In Jesus Christ, the work is the Word. Reconciliation is revelation.

20. *CD* IV/1, 6 [4].
21. Ernst Käsemann, "The Saving Significance of the Death of Jesus in Paul," in *Perspectives on Paul*, trans. Margaret Kohl (Philadelphia: Fortress Press, 1971), 40.
22. *CD* IV/1, 7 [6].
23. Ibid.
24. Ibid., 18 [18].

Barth's ordering of reconciliation and revelation finds an exegetical basis in Romans 1. Barth makes reference to Romans 1 in no fewer than four of the seven paragraphs that comprise the two chapters making up the whole of *CD* IV/1. The largest concentration of the references, as well as Barth's most sustained theological-exegetical observations on Romans 1, occurs within two subsections of §60, titled "The Pride and Fall of Man." Additionally, there are two other important discussions of Romans 1: the first in §59.2, "The Judge Judged in Our Place," and the second in §61.2, "The Judgment of God." We will analyze each of these references in turn in order to discern how and to what extent the forensic-apocalyptic elements of Romans 1 give shape to Barth's doctrine of justification. I will argue that, at each turn, Barth's doctrine of justification is not antithetical to its Reformation roots, even as its fresh hearing of Paul's witness to the gospel causes it to be radically restated at certain points.

With only a cursory glance of *CD* IV/1, it is clear that forensic language governs Barth's treatment of reconciliation. Within the second subsection of §59, Barth begins by stating that the incarnation is the event that reveals the deity of Jesus Christ.[25] He then poses Anselm's question: *Cur Deus homo?* Not wanting to answer this question through speculation or by use of abstract principles, Barth looks instead to the history of what God has done in Jesus Christ. He concludes that God, out of his mercy, freely became human in order not only to save the world, but first to magnify God's own glory.[26] "[B]efore anything else, the act of atonement, and therefore the incarnation of the Word, includes within itself the fact that by His presence, action and self-proclamation in the world, as the King of Glory who comes in through its door and gates (Ps. 24:7f.), God vindicates Himself, and is therefore Himself the meaning and basis and end."[27] Barth's statement here echoes his earlier emphasis in the

25. "[T]he way of His incarnation is as such the activation, the demonstration, the revelation of His deity, His divine Sonship." See ibid., 211 [231].
26. "But God reveals and increases His own glory in the world in the incarnation of His Son by taking to Himself the radical neediness of the world, i.e., by undertaking to do Himself what the world cannot do, arresting and reversing its course to the abyss." Ibid., 213 [233].
27. Ibid., 212 [232].

second edition of the Romans commentary on the righteousness of God as God's maintaining consistency with Godself—with God justifying Godself. That which "God does for Himself is also done for us. Our answer can only be a repetition of the answer which God Himself has given in this fact [of the history of Jesus Christ], in which He Himself has pronounced concerning the end and scope and meaning of his activity."[28] Within this emphasis on God's right as a right God gives to Godself, we find not only a distinguishing element to Barth's forensic doctrine of justification but also a complementation of two key Pauline cosmic-apocalyptic emphases: first, on God's act of rectification as "the first move," as God's initiative, rather than God's response;[29] and second, on divine vindication, in which the sovereign, unconditional action of God sets right what has gone wrong in the world.[30] "Mankind's justification is the actuality of God's right to his creation as this reveals itself as saving power, and this remains the basis, force, and truth of justification—a truth which transcends the individual and is directed toward a new world."[31]

After answering Anselm's question by means of the history of God's activity in Jesus Christ, Barth's next question becomes, "How is God for us?" Once more, he looks to the history of the triune God's giving up of Godself in the person of the Son in order to be a human among all humans. He determines that God is for us in Jesus Christ by making our situation God's own, even to the point of taking our place as sinners and enemies before God. This is the positive affirmation of Jesus Christ as the revelation of the divine-human unity. "The Son of God exists with man and as man in this fallen and perishing state. . . . That the Word became 'flesh' means that the Son of God made His own the

28. Ibid., 214 [234–35].

29. Scott M. Lewis, SJ, *What Are They Saying about New Testament Apocalyptic?* (New York: Paulist Press, 2004), 47.

30. According to Martyn, "Paul's letters reflect a keen awareness of the fact that in the human scene something is terribly wrong, and needs therefore to be set right. In Rom 1:18–32, for example, the apostle speaks at length about the ungodliness of those who by their wickedness suppress the truth. When we . . . note that Paul takes as his major theme the announcing of *good* news, we are not surprised to find him repeatedly referring to the setting right of that which has gone wrong." See J. Louis Martyn, "Apocalyptic Rectification," in *Theological Issues in the Letters of Paul* (Nashville: Abingdon, 1997), 87.

31. Käsemann, *Commentary on Romans*, 93.

situation of man in the sense that with him He faced the impossible in all its power. . . . He was not immune from sin."[32]

Barth finally asks: "What is it that takes place when the Son of God becomes flesh of our flesh?"[33] Here he finds Scripture speaking of two things: salvation ("the great positive answer"[34]) and judgment ("the grace of God is not a cheap grace"[35]). He finds these two themes interconnected in Scripture. "If He were not the Judge, He would not be the Savior."[36] It is the second, forensic theme of Christ as judge of all humanity, "and therefore . . . the judicial work of the Gospel concerning Him,"[37] for which he suggests, above all, Rom. 1:18–3:20 as the "*locus classicus*."[38] Barth urges that we keep in mind that it is God's judgment that Christ executes. In light of Christ's work as judge, the true reality of the human situation is revealed. Here, revelation flows from Christ's person and work. It is the knowledge of the righteousness of Christ's role as judge that reveals the reality of the world given up to destruction. But even more than that, looking at what God has actually done in Jesus Christ reveals that the Son of God became human to judge the world in *grace*. God became human in Jesus Christ in order "to pronounce us free in passing sentence, to free us by imprisoning us, to ground our life on our death, to redeem and save us by our destruction."[39] Barth uses both forensic and apocalyptic language to describe the work of justification that takes place in the person of Jesus Christ. Käsemann, too, finds such a marriage of forensic with apocalyptic to arise out of Paul's theology, for he states that "[t]he dying son of God does not give life without killing; he pardons, but as judge; he glorifies us by humbling us to the deepest degree; he illuminates by confronting us inexorably with the truth about ourselves; he heals by placing us among the poor in spirit."[40]

32. *CD* IV/1, 215–16 [236–37].
33. Ibid., 216 [237].
34. Ibid.
35. Ibid.
36. Ibid., 217 [238].
37. Ibid., 219 [240].
38. Ibid.
39. Ibid., 222 [244].
40. Käsemann, "Saving Significance of the Death of Jesus," 46.

The just verdict revealed in Jesus Christ is the good news of the Gospel. There is only one revelation, after all, that of the covenant, of *Deus pro nobis*. Romans 1:18 speaks of God's wrath revealed from heaven against sinful humanity, but this is not the only word, nor is it the end of the story. God gives Godself not only to encounter the sinner for whom God's wrath must be poured out, but also to take this sinner's place. "In Jesus Christ we see who we are by being seen as those we are—being seen as God in Him acknowledges what we are, accepting solidarity with our state and being, making Himself responsible for our Sin."[41] Here again, forensicism and apocalypticism meet in Barth's historicized ontology: our true being and, hence, our justification, is seen and made real only in Jesus Christ. For Barth, God's eternal decision in the covenant of grace establishes both the being of God and, by anticipation, the being of the human in the election of the one God-human in whom both the humiliation of God and the exaltation of the human take place. This is another germane element to Barth's doctrine of justification: namely, that justification is something that takes place in Jesus Christ, in his death and resurrection. Only because and insofar as it takes place in him is it effective for us. Barth's understanding of justification is deeply Pauline, as Käsemann validates. In Paul "[c]ross and resurrection are here most deeply connected—distinguishable but not divisible. They are distinguishable even as 'true man' is distinguishable from 'true God,' but they cannot be divided because true man only exists in the face of the true God, and the true God only exists over true man."[42]

When Barth, in commenting on Rom. 1:18–32, uses the apocalyptic language of the world's imprisonment and speaks of Jesus Christ as the gospel and the meaning of history, he reinforces the cosmic-apocalyptic themes he first brought out in the second edition of the Romans commentary. Yet the emphasis in *CD* II/2 and *A Shorter Commentary on Romans*, that God's punishment and abandonment of humanity is not the end of the story, is also taken up here. Yes,

41. *CD* IV/1, 240 [264].
42. Käsemann, "Saving Significance of the Death of Jesus," 42.

humanity must die, but from this death will come new life and a fresh beginning. The wrath of God against us can only be rightly grasped in light of the history of Jesus Christ. "Just as it is in the cross of Christ that God has inaugurated the new creation, so there is a significant sense in which Christ *is* the new creation."[43] Here we see that the revelation of God's wrath serves the larger purposes of God's love. "God has signaled in the death and resurrection of Jesus Christ that the time of handing over, of confining all to sin, is past. God has condemned . . . Sin . . . in this definitive action to reclaim the world for God's own self."[44] Indeed, the concentration on the history of Jesus Christ as the indicator of why God became human, how God is for us, and what takes place when God becomes human derives its initial foundation from the working out of a historicized ontology as the divine handing over of the Son by the Father, a theme we first noted in our investigation of *CD* II/2 in chapter 3.

Barth next turns his attention to the examination of the human situation in light of the events of the incarnation and crucifixion, finding that God's verdict, which is revealed in the resurrection of Jesus Christ from the dead, is the standpoint from which the human plight must be considered. In Barth's words, we are "going back a step behind the knowledge that we have already won of the salvation"[45] made actual for all humanity in the death of Jesus Christ and revealed in the resurrection to "the negative presupposition of this event."[46] And yet this process of going back behind the event of salvation to its negative presupposition is not something that can be done in separation from the history of Jesus Christ for us—"only when we know Jesus Christ do we really know that man is the man of sin, and what sin is, and what it means for man."[47] Jesus Christ is himself the revelation of sinful humanity.

43. J. Louis Martyn, "Apocalyptic Antinomies," in *Theological Issues in the Letters of Paul*, 122. Martyn references "the one man, Jesus Christ" in Rom. 5:17 in drawing this conclusion.
44. Beverly Roberts Gaventa, "God Handed Them Over," in *Our Mother Saint Paul* (Louisville: Westminster John Knox, 2007), 123.
45. *CD* IV/1, 359 [395].
46. Ibid., 359 [396].
47. Ibid., 389 [430].

Martyn has observed that Barth's emphasis of this point—both in his exegesis and in his theology—is right in line with Paul. "It was from the event of Christ's crucifixion—perceived to be God's redeeming deed—that Paul came to know the true nature of the human plight."[48] Barth learned from Paul to work from solution to plight, and this is one point on which Barth is critical of the Reformers. As Barth observes it, "the programme of Reformation theology did not allow for any radical consideration of the meaning, importance and function of Christology in relation to all Christian knowledge. . . . This was the case in the doctrine of sin."[49] However, Barth still upholds Reformation theology for the very great care it gave to constructing a doctrine of sin "wholly or mainly out of biblical material," thereby ensuring that "the worst danger of this method [devising a doctrine of sin independent of Christology] will not be quite so acute."[50] Nevertheless, the reason Barth insists that we must ground our knowledge of sin only in the knowledge of Jesus Christ is that God has judged both sin and sinner in the death of Jesus Christ, and in the resurrection revealed that our old selves have been done away with once and for all. Our justification takes place first and foremost in Jesus Christ.

> In this verdict we learn what God knows about us, and therefore how it really is with us. For this reason its content is valid. . . . The fact that man is a sinner, and what his sin is, is something that in the last resort we can measure properly and fully only by that which on the New Testament understanding is man's salvation, the redemptive grace which comes from God to man.[51]

Käsemann notes that only in the death of Jesus are the ungodly justified. This is the center of Pauline theology. "It cannot be anything but a theology of the cross, just as, and just because, it cannot be separated from the message of justification, and counters all enthusiasm with a critical and realistic anthropology."[52]

48. J. Louis Martyn, *Galatians: A New Translation with Introduction and Commentary*, AB 33A (New York: Doubleday, 1997), 95n43.
49. *CD* IV/1, 366 [404].
50. Ibid., 365 [404].
51. Ibid., 391 [433].
52. Käsemann, "Saving Significance of the Death of Jesus," 46.

As he did in *A Shorter Commentary on Romans*, Barth classifies Rom. 1:18–3:20 as belonging to the New Testament message of salvation. Rather than being a digression, it is, instead, "the first and basic statement about the Gospel which Paul has made it his business to expound. . . . The Gospel is God's condemnation of man, of all men and every man."[53] Meyer notes that Paul begins not with human activity, but with God's.[54] God's activity, Barth suggests, taking his cues from 1:18, begins with the judgment revealed in the gospel as the judgment of God's wrath. Yet, because of the threefold γάρ in verses 16, 17, and 18, we see why Paul is not ashamed of this being a core part of the message of the gospel. The gospel is the δύναμις θεοῦ, effective for salvation (v. 16); it is the revelation that God's righteousness is God's judicial decision on all humanity (v. 17), and while God's righteous judgment aims at humanity's redemption, it is also revealed as "burning and consuming wrath"[55] (v. 18). This is almost identical to the reading Barth gave these verses in *A Shorter Commentary on Romans.*

Furthermore, Barth suggests that Paul is communicating that human sin is the disobedience that must be overcome by the obedience of faith (1:5).[56] Barth calls this the "law of faith," by which human sin is revealed and known. This is the "truth" suppressed in the unrighteousness of humanity (1:18).[57] Romans 1:19–23 demonstrates the progressive guilt of the world before God. However, according to 1:24–32, it is only the light of the gospel that reveals all human sin as sin against God. In view of the corruption of humanity, God must say "No." In the threefold repetition of "God gave them up," history is concluded in disobedience.[58] Gaventa maintains that this repetition "indicates an important concern in the letter: the absolute priority of God's election over human wisdom or achievement."[59] Yet, we know that the "history of the world which God made in Jesus Christ, and with

53. *CD* IV/1, 392 [434].
54. Paul W. Meyer, "Romans: A Commentary," in *The Word in This World: Essays in New Testament Exegesis and Theology*, ed. John T. Carroll (Louisville: Westminster John Knox, 2004), 161.
55. *CD* IV/1, 393 [435].
56. Ibid., 394 [436].
57. Ibid.
58. Ibid., 506 [564].
59. Gaventa, "God Handed Them Over," 117.

a view to Him, cannot cease to have its centre and goal in Him. But in the light of this goal and centre God cannot say Yes but only No to its corruption."[60]

Barth knows, however, that Paul is speaking of the No from the standpoint of the cross and resurrection, and so he declares: "God says No in order to say Yes. His Word is the Word of the teleologically established unity of the death and resurrection of Christ."[61] In the same way that the purpose of the judges in the Old Testament was to be helpers and saviors for the people of Israel, so too the New Testament's reference to Christ as the Judge "means basically the coming of the Redeemer and Savior."[62] Furthermore, the connection between God's salvation (the "Yes") and God's judgment (the "No") finds its coherence within the concept of the righteousness of God. God's wrath is revealed against the unrighteousness of humanity (1:18), yet the "righteousness of God means God's negating and overcoming and taking away and destroying wrong and man as the doer of it."[63] Barth could not be more in line with Pauline apocalyptic than he is here in his description of the righteousness of God. Käsemann provocatively suggests that "[t]the Epistle to the Romans subsumes the whole of the preaching and theology of Paul under one head—the self-revealing righteousness of God."[64] Barth also sounds a similar note in the second edition of the Romans commentary when he interprets the righteousness of God as the consistency of God with God's self in Christ, which is displayed in God's "maintaining the distance by which we are separated from Him."[65] Our sin is abominable to God, and in light of God's majesty, it simply cannot exist. It must be destroyed. In the event of God's righteousness there takes place the "breaking of a catastrophe,"[66] in which the sinner who provokes God's wrath has to die. This is the

60. *CD* IV/1, 506 [564].
61. Ibid., 347 [383].
62. Ibid., 217 [238].
63. Ibid., 535 [597].
64. Ernst Käsemann, "'The Righteousness of God' in Paul," in *New Testament Questions of Today*, trans. W. J. Montague (London: SCM Press, 1969), 168.
65. Karl Barth, *The Epistle to the Romans*, trans. Edwyn C. Hoskyns (London: Oxford University Press, 1933), 41 [16].
66. *CD* IV/1, 539 [602].

"hidden grace of the righteousness of God" because it "demands this retribution."[67]

Barth's decision to call God's vindicating righteousness, in Romans 1, a hidden grace is best understood in light of the way he reads the negative divine παραδοῦναι of 1:24, 26, and 28 in light of the positive divine παραδοῦναι expressed in 4:25 and 8:32. "The righteousness of God utterly crushes us. In it God asserts and vindicates His own worth over against the creature. Yet in the election of the creature even this righteousness reveals itself as the grace and loving kindness and favour of God directed towards it."[68] In this reading, therefore, Barth connects the apostle's greeting of "grace and peace from God the Father and the Lord Jesus Christ" (1:7) as that which is spelled out in the event of God's righteousness towards the enemies of grace.[69]

Thus far what has been seen at each point in our exploration of Barth's theological exegesis of Romans 1 in *CD* IV/1 is that Barth has not abandoned the forensic framework by which the Reformers, Calvin especially, understood justification.[70] Yet the way in which Barth grapples with the form of God's judgment has been through the lens of Paul's assertion about the gospel in Romans 1. Calvin explains "justification simply as the acceptance with which God receives us into his favor as righteous men. And we say that it consists in the remission of sins and the imputation of Christ's righteousness."[71] Barth's argument mirrors Calvin's explication of justification in the first sentence. The difference is that Barth uses the language of Paul in Romans 1 to speak of how, in God's righteousness, we are justified as God justifies Godself, how God's No serves the purpose of God's Yes. With regard to Calvin's second sentence, Barth does two things

67. Ibid., 540 [602].
68. *CD* II/2, 33 [34].
69. *SR*, 8 [18].
70. For a detailed account of how the Protestant doctrine of justification took shape over time and arrived in its final form, see Bruce L. McCormack, "What's at Stake in Current Debates over Justification? The Crisis of Protestantism in the West," in *Justification: What's at Stake in the Current Debates*, ed. Mark Husbands and Daniel J. Treier (Downers Grove, IL: InterVarsity Press, 2004), 81–117.
71. John Calvin, *Institutes of the Christian Religion*, ed. John T. O'Neill, trans. Ford Lewis Battles, 2 vols., Library of Christian Classics (reissued, Louisville: Westminster John Knox, 2006), 727.

differently. First, as regards the remission of sins, Barth speaks apocalyptically of the destruction of the sinner, the necessity of the in-breaking of a catastrophe in which we are freed by being imprisoned, saved by our destruction. Barth uses this language because he understands Paul's witness to the in-breaking action of God in the death and resurrection to reveal not only the solution but also the nature of the plight of the whole world and all humanity.

Second, as regards the imputation of Christ's righteousness, Barth relocates the concept, making it "basic to the gracious election of God."[72] It is not something that is applied, in the first case, to us, but rather a decision God makes to be God for us in Jesus Christ. Barth's exploration into the divine παραδοῦναι of Rom. 1:24, 26, and 28; 4:25; and 8:32 gives support for the reworking of this traditional Reformational concept. For Barth, as for Paul, justification takes place in the death and resurrection of Jesus Christ. Barth goes a step beyond Paul in inquiring after the ontological presuppositions of the divine παραδοῦναι. He argues that God determined God's being for the incarnation—that this was the original "handing over" from which all others are to be understood. While this goes beyond Paul's own apocalyptic eschatology, it certainly reinforces the apocalyptic focus on the invasive action of God in the world on our behalf. Thus the Reformation's emphasis on the "alien righteousness of Christ" as our justification, which is described by scholars of Pauline apocalyptic eschatology as God's power revealed in Christ, rectifying the world gone awry, is finally preserved in Barth's own forensic apocalypticism and is a key piece in demonstrating his continuity with the Reformation.

Our study of Barth's theological exegesis of Romans 1 in *A Shorter Commentary on Romans* and his understanding in *CD* IV/1 of the role of revelation, as it is expressed in Romans 1, in relationship to justification has highlighted three important dimensions in Barth's forensic apocalyptic construal of justification. First, Barth is keenly

72. Bruce L. McCormack, "*Justitia aliena*: Karl Barth in Conversation with the Evangelical Doctrine of Imputed Righteousness," in *Justification in Perspective: Historical Developments and Contemporary Challenges* (Grand Rapids: Baker Academic, 2006), 192.

attuned to several dimensions of Pauline apocalyptic eschatology. God's righteousness is understood as the powerful work of God to set right the world gone awry by killing in order to bring about new life. Also, the knowledge of that from which we must be redeemed is only understood from the fact of the resurrection of Christ from the dead; Barth follows Paul in working from God's solution back to the human plight. Finally, the good news of human salvation comes not through the exaltation of human knowledge, striving, or accomplishments, but by acknowledging humanity's condemnation and lifting up God's almighty power to save humanity apart from and in spite of ourselves.

The second dimension of Barth's forensic apocalyptic construal of justification is the shape of his judicial framework. Barth's exegetical work in *A Shorter Commentary on Romans* and his exegetical-dogmatic statements in *CD* IV/1 demonstrate that his forensicism, unlike that of the Reformers, is grounded in Christology. God's decision in election is the ontological basis by which we understand God to be for us in the history of Jesus Christ even as we also understand our true humanity to be perceived rightly only in him. That divine and, correspondingly, human beings are a function of decision and act is the forensic basis out of which Barth's revised christological forensicism continually functions. When we consider, therefore, Barth's use of Reformational concepts, such as justification as God's just verdict, we must understand it from this new grounding or we do not understand it at all.

This leads us to the final dimension of Barth's forensic apocalyptic construal of justification, which is that this new grounding of forensicism in Barth's historicized ontology complements the apocalypticism of Paul's letter to the church in Rome. Barth's reading of Romans, within *A Shorter Commentary on Romans* and the first part of his doctrine of reconciliation in *CD* IV, does not mute or in any way suppress the apocalypticism of Paul's message. Instead, it highlights it from its proper christological foundation. That is to say, Barth has got Paul right in his insistence that Jesus Christ himself is the gospel. Nothing could be more apocalyptic, more eschatologically focused. On this point, Käsemann would heartily agree, for he himself argued that "[t]he Pauline doctrine of justification is entirely and solely Christology, a Christology, indeed, won from Jesus' cross and hence an offensive Christology. Its point is the *ecce homo* presented so that we, confronted with the Nazarene, learn how little our illusions about ourselves and the world can stand up to his reality."[73] Rather than ignoring the cosmic dimensions of Paul's apocalyptic eschatology, Barth pays heed to such dimensions through his thoroughly revised forensicism, which is part and parcel of his adherence to Paul's insistence on the primacy of Jesus Christ, himself God's powerful work of salvation revealed for all.

73. Ernst Käsemann, "Justification and Salvation History in the Epistle to the Romans," in *Perspectives on Paul*, trans. Margaret Kohl (Philadelphia: Fortress Press, 1971), 73.

5

The Place of the Atonement in Barth's Forensic Apocalyptic Doctrine of Justification

When we spoke of Jesus Christ as Judge and judged, and of His judgment and justice, we were adopting a definite standpoint and terminology as the framework in which to present our view of the *pro nobis*. In order to speak with dogmatic clarity and distinctness we had to decide on a framework of this kind. And the actual importance of this way of thinking and its particularly good basis in the Bible were a sufficient reason for choosing this one. But exegesis reminds us that in the New Testament there are other standpoints and terminologies which might equally be considered as guiding principles for dogmatics. . . . In all its contexts theology can speak only approximately. It is a matter of finding and keeping to those lines of approximation which are relatively the best, which correspond best to what we want to express. That is what we have tried to do in this matter of the *pro nobis* with the selection and exposition of four concepts taken from the sphere of law. But we have to recognize that in the New Testament there are other similar spheres and therefore that other lines of approximation are possible in principle.

For example, in addition to the forensic imagery which we have chosen there is also, strangely enough, a financial in which the being and activity

> and even the self-offering of Jesus Christ for us and in our place are described as the payment of a ransom (λύτρον, Mk. 10:45), and therefore as a λυτροῦν (1 Pet. 1:18, Tit. 2:14), an ἀπολύτρωσις (Rom. 3:24), an ἐξαγοράζειν (Gal. 3:13, 4:5). In the majority of these passages, although not all, the important concept ἀπολύτρωσις does, of course, speak of an event which will take place only in and with the appearance of Jesus Christ. This strand is relatively slender. Not infrequently (as in Rom. 3:24) it crosses the one of which we have been particularly thinking. And it would be difficult and not very profitable to try to think out the whole event within the framework of this imagery. . . .
>
> There is perhaps also a military view of the work of Jesus Christ behind passages like Mk. 3:27 . . . or Col. 1:13 . . . or even the πανοπλία θεοῦ of Eph. 6:22f. The Eastern Church especially, but also Luther, loved to regard and describe this work as a victorious overcoming of the devil and death which took place on our behalf. But it may again be asked whether it is advisable to try to work out systematically our thinking in this direction. What is clear is that a place should be found for this group of images and the particular truth it presents.
>
> —Karl Barth, *CD* IV/1

In this chapter we are seeking, ultimately, the answers to these questions: how does Barth understand Paul's portrayal of the significance of Christ's death in Romans 3, and what is the outcome of that understanding on his forensic apocalyptic understanding of justification? In theology, justification and atonement are twin doctrines that together provide answers to the questions "What is justification?" and "How is it accomplished?" This chapter will seek to identify Barth's answer to the latter question, while chapter 6 will address the former. In Barth's mature doctrine of reconciliation, the atonement functions to provide the objective realization of humanity's justification in Christ. Barth maintains that in the death of Christ, Jesus Christ caused sin and sinful humanity to be utterly abolished in his own person, thereby saving us from destruction and rescuing us from eternal death. Put another way, Jesus Christ simply is the atonement. Barth treats Christ's death as *the* radical divine action that attacks and destroys, at its very root, sin and sinful humanity, thereby inaugurating a new world and a new humanity.[1] Because Barth

1. *CD* IV/1, 254 [280]. For further discussion on this idea see Bruce L. McCormack, "Divine

understands justification to be an event that takes place in Jesus Christ, we find his construal of how Christ's death atones to be guided by a thoroughly forensic framework, within which he incorporates cosmic-apocalyptic consequences.

This chapter argues that Barth's choice of a forensic framework for his understanding of the atonement does not diminish its apocalyptic dimensions in that the basis of our justification resides in *the abolishment* of sinful humanity in the death of Christ and the raising of the elect as new creation in Christ's resurrection. Insofar as sinful humanity is put to death in the atonement and new creation is established in the resurrection, the justice of God's judgment is upheld.[2] Our investigation will first consider the dimensions of Barth's forensic reading of Romans 3 in *A Shorter Commentary on Romans*, where we will discover that, at that stage in his development, Barth's reading still retained the classic character of penal substitution. For that reason, we will next turn our attention to Barth's mature doctrine of atonement, in *CD* IV/1, where we will see Barth not only reference Romans 3 in his construction of the doctrine but also fully incorporate the doctrine of election into his understanding of the atonement. What

Impassibility or Simply Divine Constancy? Implications of Karl Barth's Later Christology for Debates over Impassibility," in *Divine Impassibility and the Mystery of Human Suffering*, ed. James F. Keating and Thomas Joseph White, OP (Grand Rapids: Eerdmans, 2009), 150–86. McCormack argues that Barth's cautious retrieval of the post-Reformation idea, closely related to the "communication of attributes," of a *genus tapeinoticum* (literally the "genus of humility") provides the building blocks not only for treating Christ's death as divine action but also for enabling it to be a true statement about the experience of suffering and death by God. McCormack maintains that "'the man Jesus' is the performative agent of all that is done and experienced by the God-man" (174). He suggests that Barth's affirmation of the *genus tapeinoticum*, when coupled with his ascription of humility and obedience to God in his mode of being as Son, leads to the conclusion that "[t]he *only* act of the Son of God in relation to his humanity is the act in which he gives it existence in his own being and existence. All subsequent acts of the God-man made possible by *this singular act* are acts performed by the man Jesus. The *genus tapeinoticum* creates the possibility that the man Jesus should be the performative agent of all that is done by the God-human in his divine-human unity. But that possibility is itself grounded in the reality of the eternal *receptivity* of the Son of God vis-à-vis his human nature, a receptivity that is the consequence of that humility and obedience proper to his mode of being" (177). For Barth's discussion of the *genus tapeinoticum* see *CD* IV/2, 85 [93]. For Barth's understanding of the hypostatic union as a history see *CD* IV/2, 105–6 [117–18]. For Barth's ascription of humility and obedience to God in his mode of being as Son see *CD* IV/2, 84–85 [92–93].

2. Although this chapter focuses its attention to the way Christ's death's provides the ground for our justification, Christ's death and resurrection together provide the basis for acquittal. Both Christ's vindication and new creation occur in the resurrection, therefore substantiating the truth of the innocence of humanity elected in Christ. In *CD* IV/1, Barth treats this material in §59.3, under the title "The Verdict of the Father."

will be evident in our exploration is the way that Barth's mature Christology enables the whole of his soteriological framework for justification to be at once forensic and apocalyptic. Finally, rounding out our discussion of *CD* IV/1 is a brief excursus on Barth's take on the role of faith in the doctrine of justification. There we will see how Barth's theological ontology enables the unique Pauline interweaving of δικαιοσύνη and πίστις to bring a new dimension to the Reformation principle of justification by grace through faith without at all diminishing the cosmic scope of God's action on the cross.

Barth's Classical Take on Christ's Atonement according to Romans 3

In Barth's second Romans commentary we saw that the death of Christ was primarily revelatory and didactic. Jesus is the place of propitiation, yet God dwells and speaks from above this place. In other words, Barth understands that God was in Christ and his death, yet only by remaining above and distinct from Christ. Furthermore, Jesus' blood serves as a reminder to us that God grants life only through death. Such a revelation comes only as the resurrection light shines through the cross. Where this revelation occurs, reconciliation comes as a consequence.

Turning to Barth's commentary on Romans 3 in *A Shorter Commentary on Romans*, we see Barth now focusing our attention on Jesus Christ, "the Judge himself,"[3] who contains in himself the content of the just verdict rendered by God as "an act of his righteousness which does not mean our damnation."[4] Commenting on 3:5–6, Barth points out that God remains the Judge of the whole world, and he understands Paul's focus on the righteousness of God as both God's faithfulness to Godself as well as God's grace. Barth's observation is here in line with Charles Cousar's concern that the theme of 3:21–26, God's "rectifying activity vis-à-vis the world," is already at play as early as 3:5.[5] Barth observes Paul's cosmic focus in 3:9, noting that all humanity is under

3. *SR*, 26–27 [52].
4. Ibid., 26 [51].

"the dominion of sin."[6] Beker similarly remarks: "Pre-Christian life is indeed 'under the power of sin' (Rom. 3:9)."[7] Unlike, however, the scholars of Paul's cosmic apocalypticism, who look to Romans 6–8 to fill out their cosmic-apocalyptic reading of Paul's discussion of Christ's death, Barth remains firmly in chapter 3 and thus in its mostly forensic outlook. Barth connects Paul's discussion of Jesus Christ to the forensic image of a Judge who in himself is the very demonstration of God's righteousness coming to us as God's free grace.

Barth's reading of Romans 3 sounds like the classical Reformation understanding of justification as a forensic declaration. Barth clearly knows this and the objections this reading often receives, and so he tackles head-on the issue of how such a declaration of our justification is not merely a legal fiction. Barth's explanation is that God declares sinners to be what they are not—justified—by delivering them *in* Jesus Christ. In other words, only because and insofar as justification takes place in Jesus is it effective for us. In the event of the atonement, Jesus Christ accomplishes not the mere possibility of reconciliation but the reality of it. This focus on the reality of humankind's reconciliation with God, rather than its mere possibility for justification, lines up surprisingly well with Paul's focus on the apocalyptic invasion of God into human history to set the world aright. In God's righteous verdict the sinner is "neither damned, nor merely granted an amnesty, he is acquitted by God, declared innocent and therefore justified."[8] To anticipate what we will see in chapter 6, for Barth, justification is acquittal. Therefore, in order to explain how Christ's work provides the basis for such a divine judgment with this content, he must interpret the atonement as the death of the sinner and the new creation (from the ground up) of the same person as the elect of God.

Commenting on 3:24, Barth remarks that God "has redeemed them from the whole dominion of sin under which they are because of the

5. Charles B. Cousar, *A Theology of the Cross: The Death of Jesus in the Pauline Letters* (Minneapolis: Fortress Press, 1990), 39.
6. *SR*, 23 [47].
7. J. Christiaan Beker, "The Dilemma of Sin and Death: Equivalent or Disparate Powers?," in *Paul the Apostle: The Triumph of God in Life and Thought* (Philadelphia: Fortress Press, 1980), 215.
8. *SR*, 25–26 [50].

Law and from the whole curse which according to the Law should therefore fall upon them: as slaves whose freedom has been paid for and on whom their former master therefore has no more claim."[9] This redemption, which transpires for them in Jesus Christ, is enacted in the giving up of Christ's life. Because Christ is himself the Judge, before whom all sinners are called to account, he is able, following 3:25, to be the "propitiatory sacrifice for the entire people of those who believe in him. He has shouldered the responsibility for the punishment which needs follow their condemnation, and for all the effects of God's wrath. . . . In his death God has made the necessary angry end with the sinners."[10]

Barth's reading here, as evidenced by his use of the term "propitiatory sacrifice"[11] and his language of Christ's punishment by God's wrath and God's angry end with sinners, follows, for the most part, classical Reformed theology, most specifically Calvin's theology of the cross. Calvin held that Christ was made sin for us through the imputation of the guilt that makes the sinner worthy of punishment.[12] As McCormack points out, such an imputation of our guilt to Christ is the "judicial act of God in which the God-man is made liable for our sins and judged in our place."[13] Furthermore, "[t]he righteous demands of God are satisfied through punishment, a punishment consisting in the death of the sinner."[14] Christ's death as the Sinner in our place is not only "the expression of the wrath of God," but it is also "the punishment ordained by God in response to human sin."[15] Only by

9. Ibid., 27 [53].

10. Ibid.

11. The German term used here is *Versöhnungsopfer*, which, out of context, might be translated "reconciliatory sacrifice." However, Hirsch's *Hilfsbuch zum Studium der Dogmatik* defines the term as *sacrificium propitiatorium*. See Emmanuel Hirsch, *Hilfsbuch zum Studium der Dogmatik: Die Dogmatik der Reformatoren und der altevangelischen Lehrer quellmäßig belegt und verdeutscht* (Berlin: de Gruyter, 1951), 338. According to two searches performed using the Digital Karl Barth Library on September 26, 2011, and January 26, 2013, Barth never uses this term in the *KD*, and its only other appearance in his writings is in *The Göttingen Dogmatics III*. See Karl Barth, "*Unterricht in der christlichen Religion*" *Teil 3: Die Lehre von der Versöhnung/Die Lehre von der Erlösung 1925/26 (GA II.38), §29 Christus Jesus: sein Werk*, ed. Hinrich Stoevesandt (Zürich: Theologischer Verlag, 2003), 122.

12. John Calvin, *Institutes of the Christian Religion*, ed. John T. O'Neill, trans. Ford Lewis Battles, 2 vols., Library of Christian Classics (reissued, Louisville: Westminster John Knox, 2006), 507–10.

13. Bruce L. McCormack, "For Us and Our Salvation: Incarnation and Atonement in the Reformed Tradition," *Studies in Reformed Theology and History* 1, no. 2 (1993): 20.

14. Ibid., 25.

Christ's death is God's wrath satisfied and God made gracious toward us.

One of the main weaknesses in Calvin's theology of the cross, and likewise here in Barth's reading of Rom. 3:21–26, is the implication that God's favorable position toward us is only made possible by Christ's death on the cross. Such an understanding does not line up with God's prior gracious sending of the Son to redeem us in the incarnation. More serious still is the tendency in Calvin and likewise Barth, at this point, to abstract God's righteousness—which is satisfied in Christ's atoning death—from God's love. In other words, God's mercy toward us is effectually held captive until God's righteousness is satisfied. Such a position ultimately produces a rift in the being and activity of God. In Calvin, we find little treatment on the being and attributes of God, and so it is not surprising that this problem occurs in his doctrine of atonement.

Barth, however, in *CD* II/1, discusses the atonement under his treatment of the perfections (attributes) of God,[16] and he helpfully orders God's holiness and righteousness under the perfection of divine loving. Barth pairs the holiness of God with God's grace, and God's righteousness is paired with the mercy of God. This means that God's wrath, which is poured out against sin on the cross, serves God's merciful purposes of redeeming humanity. Yet Barth still finds the cross to express God's righteousness in the form of wrath and condemnation. "The meaning of the death of Jesus Christ is that there God's condemning and punishing righteousness broke out, really smiting and piercing human sin, man as sinner. . . . It did so in such a way that in what happened there . . . the righteousness of God which we have offended was really revealed and satisfied."[17] In other words, "[a]t the crucial point, he [Barth] repeated the error of the sixteenth- and seventeenth-century Reformed theologians and made the death of Christ a satisfaction offered to the divine righteousness."[18] In his

15. Ibid., 26.
16. *CD* II/1, 351–406 [394–457].
17. *CD* II/1, 396 [446].
18. McCormack, "For Us and Our Salvation," 30.

commentary on Paul's message in Romans in *A Shorter Commentary on Romans*, Barth does a little better, now expressing the cross as the righteous satisfaction of the gospel. Not only summing up 1:18–3:20 but also connecting it to 3:21–4:25, Barth submits: "For it is the Gospel which reveals to us this wrath of God. . . . [T]he issue is not the rejection of men, but their salvation, their welfare and beatitude. . . . God's just verdict itself has now been revealed as an act of his righteousness which does not mean our damnation."[19] Likewise, Beker notes that where the Reformers and the Reformed tradition tend to make God's mercy conditional on the satisfaction of his justice, Paul correlates God's love and judgment in Christ's death and resurrection.

> In Paul, the death and resurrection of Christ emphasize God's righteousness as the power of love that bears the burden of its moral character within itself and so expresses the costliness of love in the cross of Christ. . . . The unitary meaning of the death and resurrection of Christ points to the fact that the suffering Son of man and the victorious Son of God cannot be polarized.[20]

Barth's work on the perfections of God in *CD* II/1 and his exposition on Romans 3 in *A Shorter Commentary on Romans* are a definite improvement on Calvin's theology of the cross. Yet in his treatment of the atonement in II/1, Barth still speaks of the death of Christ as that which is offered to satisfy God's righteousness. Somewhat inconsistent with what we saw of his summary of Rom. 1:18–3:20 and 3:21–4:25 in *A Shorter Commentary on Romans* is his exposition of 3:21–26.

> By shedding his blood as a man, and giving up his life, the Judge himself . . . has shouldered the responsibility for the punishment which needs follow their condemnation, and for all the effects of God's wrath. . . . For in the death of the Judge Jesus Christ . . . an effective end has been made of . . . themselves as sinners. That they are his people . . . is a gift, that is grace. But that God justifies them, that is a word of purest truth, that is an act of his strictest righteousness.[21]

What this demonstrates is that Barth, despite his improvement over

19. *SR*, 25–26 [49, 51–52].
20. J. Christiaan Beker, "The Scandal of the Cross," in *Paul the Apostle*, 210.
21. *SR*, 27 [53–54].

Calvin, still has not yet found a way to avoid separating the mercy of God from the righteousness of God. For all his insistence on Jesus Christ himself as the content of the gospel, the Judge who in himself is the Savior, where it most counts in Rom. 3:21–26, Barth lacks in sustained christological reflection on the history of Jesus Christ. To be sure, the groundwork is in place. As Maico Michielin points out, Barth's theological exegesis throughout *A Shorter Commentary on Romans* is centered on God's electing activity—most especially, the election of humanity in Jesus Christ. "God condemns Jesus to die on the cross in order to elect him; likewise, God condemns us in the death of Jesus in order to elect us."[22] But to be consistent with his doctrine of election Barth should have provided an explanation of the way that the suffering and death of Jesus Christ are in themselves the very self-giving of God—that Christ's satisfaction of God's wrath against sin is God bearing God's own wrath for us and in our place, that Christ's humble and obedient death is an event in God's own life, that God in Jesus Christ has taken our place. In other words, Christ's death is a satisfaction of God's *love* because God's wrath always only serves God's love and is never independent from it.

Again, the groundwork is in place for this—Barth repeatedly emphasizes that the gospel reveals God's condemnation against us only as part of the good news of our salvation—"[Paul] sees the Gentiles as well as the Jews in the reflected light of that fire of God's wrath which is the fire of his love."[23] But the strands do not all come together in *A Shorter Commentary on Romans*. Barth is not yet fully self-consistent in the way that he will be in *CD* IV/1.[24] Rather, Barth's forensicism is more

22. Maico Micheilin, "Exegesis That Corresponds to God's Activity," in Karl Barth, *A Shorter Commentary on Romans*, ed. Maico Michielin, trans. D. H. van Daleen (Aldershot, UK: Ashgate, 2007), x.

23. *SR*, 15 [31].

24. Barth will subsequently point out that the concept of punishment in relationship to the atonement does not occur in the New Testament. Considering a text like Isaiah 53, he cautiously notes that "If Jesus Christ has followed our way as sinners to the end to which it leads, in outer darkness, then we can say with that passage from the Old Testament that He has suffered this punishment of ours. But we must not make this a main concept as in some of the older presentations of the doctrine of the atonement . . . either in the sense that by His suffering our punishment we are spared from suffering it ourselves, or that in so doing He 'satisfied' or offered satisfaction to the wrath of God. The latter thought is quite foreign to the New Testament. And of the possible idea that we are spared punishment by what Jesus Christ has done for us we have to

classically Reformed in his articulation of how the atonement justifies sinful humanity. The forensic cast of his historicized theological ontology, which comes to expression in his innovative doctrine of election, is here missing in his reading of Romans 3. For this reason, Paul's focus on the crucified cross of Christ as the defining event of the gospel is not appreciated to the fullest measure. In the following section, we will see all of that change as Barth unites the insights of his doctrine of election to his doctrine of the atonement, making the forensic cast to the atonement to be a function of his focus on the history of Jesus Christ, a move that will ultimately allow him even greater adherence to Paul's apocalyptic focus on the death of Christ.

Atonement and Forensic Apocalyptic Justification in *CD* IV/1

As we saw in chapter 4, by the time Barth is working out his doctrine of reconciliation in *CD* IV/1 he has made reconciliation, not revelation, the doctrine with which he is primarily concerned. The life, death, and resurrection of the God-man, which together comprise the lived history of Jesus of Nazareth, rather than the reception of divine revelation, is that which saves humanity.[25] Such reconciling activity does, of course, have a revelatory function. But the apocalyptic event of revelation is now grounded in God's decision in election to be God for us, and this decision is the basis for Barth's revised forensicism.[26] "The most basic content of the doctrine of election is a choice God makes with respect to himself. God chooses to be God only in the covenant of

notice that the main drift of the New Testament statements concerning the passion and death of Jesus Christ is not at all or only indirectly in this direction." See *CD* IV/1, 253 [279].

25. In his 1956 essay "The Humanity of God," Barth clarifies: "Since God in his deity is human," theology now "must occupy itself neither with God in Himself nor with man in himself but with the man-encountering God and the God-encountering man and with their dialogue and history." See Karl Barth, "The Humanity of God," trans. John Newton Thomas, in *The Humanity of God* (Richmond, VA: John Knox, 1960), 55.

26. At its heart, forensicism is deeply ontological. "At the very root of forensic thinking lies the recognition that human being is the function of a decision which gives rise to a willed relation. Human being is the function of a decision God *made* in eternity past in his electing grace. And it is a function of a decision God *makes* in time in justifying the ungodly. The former is the ground of the latter; the latter actualizes the content of the former in time." Bruce L. McCormack, "What's at Stake in Current Debates over Justification? The Crisis of Protestantism in the West," in *Justification: What's at Stake in the Current Debates*, ed. Mark Husbands and Daniel J. Treier (Downers Grove, IL: InterVarsity Press, 2004), 115.

grace."[27] There is nothing more basic to a forensic framework than the concepts of divine decision, declaration, and verdict. In the early post-Reformation period, Protestant theologians even began to understand the divine declaration as constitutive; that which God declares us to be in justification, his declaration itself (as an "effective Word") makes us to be. We might go so far as to say justification is itself regenerative. It is but a short step from this understanding to Barth, who makes the divine decision in eternal election to be constitutive not only of what we are but what God is. To take this step with Barth is to make forensicism basic to theological ontology. We see this play out in Barth's explanation of the justification of God and humanity in Jesus Christ as an event resulting from the eternal divine decision in which God elected that both humanity and God's own being would be constituted in the history of the life, death, and resurrection of the God-man Jesus. With this as Barth's unique forensic-ontological construal of justification, the core of Pauline cosmic apocalypticism—a prioritizing of *God's* in-breaking action to put the world aright—is upheld from a christocentric angle. As Nathan Kerr explains, Barth's Christology in the *Church Dogmatics* follows an apocalyptic logic in that "history is what it is just insofar as *God acts*, and acts *apocalyptically*, precisely as revealed in the concrete, particular history of Jesus of Nazareth."[28]

When we view Barth's unique take on forensic justification from the vantage point of the atonement, what appears most striking is his notion that "we know God and have God only in Jesus Christ . . . [thus] we can know Him and have Him only with the man Jesus of Nazareth and with the people which He represents. Apart from this man . . . God would be a different, an alien God."[29] This means that in the event of the death of Christ the being of God is fully known.[30] God's judgment

27. Bruce L. McCormack, "The Ontological Presuppositions of Barth's Doctrine of the Atonement," in *The Glory of the Atonement: Biblical, Historical and Practical Perspectives*, ed. Charles E. Hill and Frank A. James III (Downers Grove, IL: InterVarsity Press, 2004), 359.

28. Nathan Kerr, *Christ, History and Apocalyptic: The Politics of Christian Mission* (Eugene, OR: Cascade Books, 2009), 77.

29. *CD* II/2, 7 [6].

30. "Paul interprets the event of the cross *theo*logically. His Christology makes it possible to see Jesus' action as God's action." Cousar, *Theology of the Cross*, 27. McCormack points out that in the event

and wrath, revealed against humanity on the cross, must, if God is to be God, result in the destruction of both sin and the sinner. In the death of Christ, sin and death are both taken into the life of the triune God and there extinguished and conquered.[31] Recall that in the second edition of his Romans commentary the emphasis Barth brought out in regards to sin and death in Rom. 3:21–26 was on Christ's death as an act of the human Jesus done in obedience to the will of God, who remained above and distinct from Christ and his death. Now, in *CD* IV/1, Barth insists that the form and content of the atonement must be centered on a Christology in which Jesus Christ accomplishes reconciliation not apart from or distinct from God, but with the Godhead in the unity of his concrete existence as both God and man. "The gracious God is in this history, so is reconciled man, so are both in their unity. And what takes place in this history, and therefore in the being of Jesus Christ as such, is atonement."[32]

Barth provides a helpful clarification for why he uses the concept of history in relationship to the person of Jesus Christ. He notes that we cannot describe the particular, unique unity of the Creator with the creature, such as we see in the God-man, as a state.

> In consideration of the otherness and newness of the Creator in relation to the creature, we can understand it only as history. This creature is what it is as creature in a dynamic movement of the Creator to itself and itself to the Creator. It exists in this movement from another to itself and itself to this other—a movement which, since God the Creator is this Other, it is quite impossible to describe as a movement within itself.[33]

In other words, it is out of consideration for the dynamic and

of the atonement "The subject who delivers Jesus Christ up to death is not the Father alone. For the Trinitarian axiom *opera trinitatis ad extra sunt indivisa* means that . . . [t]he triune God takes this human experience [of the 'penalty of death' that humans have merited through their sinfulness] into his own life; he 'drinks it to the dregs.' And in doing so, he vanquishes its power over us." See McCormack, "Ontological Presuppositions of Barth's Doctrine of Atonement," 364.

31. Such a move is possible only with a Christology that includes a realistic communication of the attributes of Christ's human nature (and the experiences they make possible) to the Person of the union. Such a Christology also requires Barth's doctrine of election, and specifically, the thought that Jesus Christ is the Reprobate human, so that it can also be shown at the same time that God remains God and is unchanged by the experience of the death of the human. See footnote 1 in this chapter.
32. *CD* IV/1, 126 [138].
33. *CD* III/3, 159 [190].

apocalyptic nature of Christ's own being-in-relation that Barth takes up the concept of history.

To deal with sin and the sinner God chooses reprobation for Godself and mercy for us. This act of God's eternal decision is basic to Barth's theological ontology. McCormack explains that "[i]t is an eternal decision in which both the being of God *and the being of the human* are constituted by way of anticipation, by looking forward to the appearance in time of the one God-human in whom both the humiliation of God and the exaltation of the human take place."[34] Because election is an eternal event that is constitutive of God's being, we have received the mercy of God in God's decision to turn toward humanity in the incarnation. Jesus Christ, in perfect unity with the triune God, was elected to take God's own judgment and wrath on himself on the cross, so that all humanity might be elected for new creation and life in communion with God. The unity of the divine and the human in the incarnation means that reconciliation takes place in and through a unitary movement of God toward the human in Jesus Christ.

In his theological exegesis of Romans 3 in *CD* IV/1, Barth names the atonement as the event in time of God's eternal covenant to be *Deus pro nobis*, building such a conclusion from Paul's reference in Rom. 3:3 to πίστις τοῦ θεοῦ, the faithfulness of God, "which cannot be destroyed by any unfaithfulness of man."[35] Barth further suggests that this faithfulness of God is the very foundation of the gospel. It is the very first statement—"that God shows Himself to be just: εἰς τὸ εἶναι αὐτὸν δίκαιον, and only then and for that reason: καὶ δικαιοῦντα τὸν ἐκ πίστεως Ἰησοῦ (Rom. 3:26). In it God Himself is right. He is at one with Himself. He is faithful to Himself. That is its basic ontological content."[36] Again paraphrasing Rom. 3:26, Barth remarks: "In this work of the justification of unrighteous man God also and in the first instance

34. Bruce L. McCormack, "*Justitia aliena*: Karl Barth in Conversation with the Evangelical Doctrine of Imputed Righteousness," in *Justification in Perspective: Historical Developments and Contemporary Challenges* (Grand Rapids: Baker Academic, 2006), 191.
35. *CD* IV/1, 532 [593].
36. Ibid., 532 [593].

justifies Himself."[37] That God is just in himself "is the backbone of the event of justification."[38] Barth's reading here aligns nicely with Cousar's observation that Paul announces the theme of 3:21–26, the righteousness of God, with the expressions in verses 3 and 7, respectively, "the faithfulness of God" and "the truthfulness of God."[39] Keck refers to this as Paul's designation of God's own moral integrity,[40] which is the very point Barth highlights in stating that God is just in Godself. "The right of God will always be wrongly construed where it is based in some conception of natural law or general moral principles."[41] We recall that Barth's interpretation of 3:21–26 in the second edition of his Romans commentary also highlighted that God's freedom is God's righteousness, which is without cause or occasion, totally incomprehensible, and contradicting of all human logic. All humanity is judged by the standard of God's righteousness, which belongs to God alone.[42]

In Rom. 1:18–3:20 Paul works backward from the unfaithfulness of humanity to the righteousness, or faithfulness, of God, which is the only foundation from which to understand the extent of human sinfulness and the salvation achieved for humanity in Jesus Christ. Remarking on Rom. 3:19, Barth notes: "The formulation in which Paul gathered together the results of the first part of the Epistle to Romans is not too stringent to fit here: that every mouth will be stopped, and the whole world guilty before God."[43]

Expounding on Paul's view of the reality of sinful humanity, Gaventa highlights that Paul's determination to "stop every mouth" (3:19)

37. Ibid., 561 [626].
38. Ibid., 531 [592].
39. Cousar, *Theology of the Cross*, 37n21.
40. Leander E. Keck, *Paul and His Letters*, 2nd ed., Proclamation Commentaries (Minneapolis: Fortress Press, 1988), 119–21.
41. McCormack, "*Justitia aliena*," 184.
42. Jüngel states that "Barth's understanding of justification as God's self-justification relates to the interpretation . . . advocated by E. Käsemann . . . that Paul's concept of the righteousness of God . . . be understood out of the apocalyptic tradition [and] primarily denotes God's power and therefore God's gift." See Eberhard Jüngel, *God's Being Is in Becoming: The Trinitarian Being of God in the Theology of Karl Barth*, trans. John Webster (Grand Rapids: T&T Clark, 2001), 93n71.
43. *CD* IV/1, 225 [247].

stems from his earlier condemnation of human speech that refuses to glorify God.

> In Paul's analysis, at the very root of human entrapment in the power of Sin lies the refusal to glorify God, the refusal to give thanks to God. That is, speech that belongs to God in thanks and praise is foundational to the human condition. It should not surprise us, then, to find that Paul pulls this entire section together with the conclusion that the law itself "speaks" in order that "every mouth might be stopped."[44]

In a similar fashion, we can also see Barth's reading of not only Rom. 1:18–3:20, but also more specifically Rom. 3:10–18 in the background of his reflection on the human partner called to answer God's covenant:

> The covenant engages man as the partner of God only . . . to gratitude. . . . The only answer to *χάρις* is *εὐχαριστία*. Here, at any rate, . . . this correspondence cannot fail. Its failure, ingratitude, is sin, transgression. Radically and basically all sin is simply ingratitude—man's refusal of the one but necessary thing which is proper to and is required of him with whom God has graciously entered into covenant.[45]

Barth's understanding of the proper human response to God's grace is the exact opposite of what Paul states to be the tragic reality of all humanity, expressed throughout 1:18–3:20 and especially summed up in 3:9 and 3:23.

Barth knows, then, from Paul, that all of humanity is enslaved to the power of sin. In Rom. 3:9, Paul portrays sin as "a dominion under which humanity exists."[46] As always, Paul, and Barth following after him, works from solution to plight. As Barth follows Paul's mounting case for the cosmic scope[47] of sin's power in 3:6, 19, 23, and 27, he remarks that "in the first part of his letter Paul brings us into the

44. Beverly Roberts Gaventa, "From Toxic Speech to the Redemption of Doxology in Paul's Letter to the Romans," in *The Word Leaps the Gap: Essays on Scripture and Theology in Honor of Richard B. Hays*, ed. J. Ross Wagner, C. Kavin Rowe, and A. Katherine Grieb (Grand Rapids: Eerdmans, 2008), 404.
45. *CD* IV/1, 41–42 [43].
46. Cousar, *Theology of the Cross*, 57.
47. When speaking about the relationship of Jesus' death to sin, Barth, even in one sentence, will use a variety of terms that together provide a picture of sin's cosmic scope as well as Christ's abolishment of every dimension of sin in his death on the cross. Here is an example: "The man of sin, the first Adam, the cosmos alienated from God, the 'present evil world' (Gal. 1:4), was taken and killed and buried in and with Him on the cross." See *CD* IV/1, 254 [279].

darkness in order to bring Jew and Gentile out of the darkness."[48] The knowledge of sin made known by the law in 3:20 is thus misunderstood if it is

> a Law which is different from the Gospel, a Law by which we are confronted and have to be confronted if we are to come to a knowledge of sin and to be led to repentance and to become . . . ready for the Gospel. The Law of which Paul speaks in Romans 2–3 is the Law of God, which, as the Law of His covenant of grace, calls man away from any attainment of his own righteousness to repentance and obedience in the form of trust in God's goodness.[49]

Barth's take on the cosmic-apocalyptic picture Paul paints of this world's captivity to sin, then, is that this is neither the end of the story nor the main point. Rather, the point of highlighting the catastrophe of the world enslaved to sin is to magnify the good news that it is in Christ's justifying death that God's covenant faithfulness to Godself and humanity is fulfilled. "The long and dreary story of humanity's slavery is ended."[50] Yes, all mouths must be stopped in the death of Jesus. "The interruptive event of Jesus' history . . . bring[s] to an end . . . the 'old,' fallen history in its inherent sinfulness. . . . Barth reads the cross as the *judgment* of God upon human history."[51] "What took place on the cross of Golgotha is the last word of an old history and the first word of a new."[52] The cross reveals "not a Yes and No but the plain Yes of God."[53] This is what Barth calls "the second part of the history," narrated in the gospel story, in which "[t]he Judge allows Himself to be judged."[54] In the history of Jesus, we see *Deus pro nobis* in the fact that Jesus took the place of us sinners. He does this as very man but also as very God, thereby exercising the righteousness of God. As Jesus takes our place and makes our sin to be his, "it ceases to be our sin."[55]

48. Ibid., 393 [435].
49. Ibid., 395 [437].
50. Cousar, *Theology of the Cross*, 62.
51. Kerr, *Christ, History and Apocalyptic*, 76.
52. *CD* IV/1, 176 [192]. Barth is here talking about the "previously existing order," which the Old Testament attests to, as consisting of "the grace of God in the form of His judgment on man and man's perishing before Him in suffering and death." See *CD* IV/1, 175 [191–92].
53. Ibid., 532 [593].
54. Ibid., 226 [248].
55. Ibid., 236 [260].

Here is "the mystery of the divine mercy. God acted in this way because He grieved over His people, because He did not will to abandon the world in its unreconciled state and therefore on the way which leads to destruction, because He willed to show to it an unmerited faithfulness as the creator, because in His own inconceivable way He loved it."[56] Paul expresses God's character most clearly, Cousar surmises, "when the contours of grace are most sharply in focus. . . . God is a faithful promise keeper. . . . God's righteousness is made known apart from the law—in the faithfulness of Jesus Christ."[57]

Remarking on the stark Νυνὶ δέ in 3:21, Barth further notes that Jesus' actions as the Judge, the judged, and the judgment are "the justice or righteousness of God in the biblical sense of the term: the omnipotence of God creating order"[58] over and against the present evil age and a new world reconciled with God in Jesus Christ. Beker remarks that "the death of Christ is the proleptic division of this age of judgment and death and the new age of life; it is an abyss that no one escapes and before which all humankind comes to nought."[59] As opposed to the approaches in the second edition of the Romans commentary and *A Shorter Commentary on Romans*, in *CD* IV/1 Barth synthesizes Paul's apocalyptic focus in Rom. 3:21–26 on the righteousness of God and the death of Christ such that the narrated history of Jesus reveals the very will and being of the triune God from all eternity.[60] "Ontologically, . . . the covenant of grace is already included and grounded in Jesus Christ, in the human form and human content which God willed to give His Word from all eternity."[61]

Furthermore, it is only in, by, and with the Word, who is Jesus Christ, that we are able to learn about the covenant—the decision and being

56. Ibid., 237 [260].
57. Cousar, *Theology of the Cross*, 41.
58. *CD* IV/1, 256 [282].
59. Beker, "Scandal of the Cross," 193.
60. Beker rightly cautions that "[w]e must . . . not read later Trinitarian developments into Paul. Paul's 'Trinitarian' construal is apocalyptic-monarchic (1 Cor. 15:28), that is, Christ and the Spirit function as apocalyptic heavenly 'assistants' of God." See ibid., 200. Certainly, though, Paul had the building blocks in place for a more sustained elaboration of the triune God, and so Barth proceeds not by reading a doctrine of the Trinity back onto Paul, but by assuming church teaching on the doctrine in order to make further sense of Paul's theology.
61. *CD* IV/1, 45 [47–48].

of God for us. Jesus of Nazareth is "in this form and with this content the basis and meaning of the covenant."[62] Barth is intent to drive this point home throughout *CD* IV/1, noting such things like: "the first and eternal word of God . . . means in fact Jesus Christ. It is identical with the One who . . . accomplishes the atonement";[63] "Jesus Christ—not an empty *Logos*, but Jesus Christ the incarnate Word, the baby born in Bethlehem . . . the man whose history this is—is . . . alone the content of the eternal will of God which precedes the whole being of man and of the world";[64] and "God is in Jesus Christ *pro nobis. Cur Deus homo?* Because God, who became man in His Son, willed in this His Yes to do this work of His, but His human work, and therefore this work of the reconciliation of the world which is effective for us men."[65]

The significance of Jesus Christ as both the basis and meaning of God's covenant of grace cannot be underestimated for understanding Barth's approach to the atonement. Whereas the traditional Reformed emphasis on penal substitution came out in Barth's reading of Romans 3 in *A Shorter Commentary on Romans,* now, in *CD* IV/1, Barth makes sure that this is no longer the main concept driving his interpretation of Paul's focus on Christ's cross. Instead, he does two things. First, understanding the heart of the atonement as the overcoming of sin, Barth makes the apocalyptic annihilation of both sin and sinner to be the decisive *negative* element of Christ's death on the cross. "The issue is not that wrong should be 'punished'; what is at stake is its removal."[66] "In His person He has delivered up us sinners and sin itself to destruction. He has removed us sinners and sin, negated us, cancelled us out. . . . The man of sin, the first Adam, the cosmos alienated from God, the 'present evil world' . . . was taken and killed and buried in and with Him on the cross."[67]

Second, Barth makes divine love the subject that is satisfied in

62. Ibid., 46 [48].
63. Ibid., 51 [54].
64. Ibid., 53 [56].
65. Ibid., 257 [283].
66. Eberhard Busch, *The Great Passion: An Introduction to Karl Barth's Theology*, trans. Geoffrey W. Bromiley, ed. Darrell L. Guder and Judith J. Guder (Grand Rapids: Eerdmans, 2004), 207.
67. *CD* IV/1, 256 [282].

Christ's death. Along with the radical annihilation of both sin and sinner, which occurs when Christ the Judge is judged, it is God's love for humanity, anchored in the covenant of grace, that creates space for God to do something entirely new for the cosmos and for humanity.

> For the sake of this best, the worst had to happen to sinful man: not out of any desire for vengeance and retribution on the part of God, but because of the radical nature of the divine love, which could "satisfy" itself only in the outworking of its wrath against the man of sin, only by killing him, extinguishing him, removing him. Here is the place for the doubtful concept that in the passion of Jesus Christ, in the giving up of His Son to death, God has done that which is "satisfactory" or sufficient in the victorious fighting of sin to make this victory radical and total.[68]

Here Barth makes the love of God that which is satisfied and thereby achieves salvation.[69] Now he can make clear that the concept of punishment is not the main concept driving the doctrine of atonement.

> The decisive thing is not that He has suffered what we ought to have suffered so that we do not have to suffer it. . . . This is true, of course. But it is true only as it derives from the decisive thing that in the suffering and death of Jesus Christ it has come to pass that in His own person He has made an end of us as sinners and therefore of sin itself by going to death as the One who took our place as sinners.[70]

Having been revised, penal substitution now functions in a subordinate position, as an instrument of God's love, because what is ultimately satisfied in the atonement is not some abstract conception of the wrath of God (Barth notes that this is foreign to the New Testament presentation[71]), but rather God's holy love.[72]

McCormack submits that because God's love is holy God must do what is worthy of Godself in achieving the ends of love.[73] That God did in fact pour out his wrath on sin and sinful humanity tells us that

68. Ibid., 254 [280].

69. Cousar acknowledges that the "action aimed at the sin ('expiation') also has an effect with respect to God. In this sense, the propitiation is a secondary result rather than a primary cause of the atonement." See Cousar, *Theology of the Cross*, 64.

70. *CD* IV/1, 253 [279].

71. Ibid.

72. McCormack, "For Us and Our Salvation," 31.

73. Ibid.

such wrath was necessary to accomplishing God's covenant of grace with humanity. Hence God's wrath still has a place in the discussion of the atonement. However, Barth now grounds God's wrath in God's holy love and makes sure it functions only as the means to God's gracious end. "Yes, the atonement is the filling of this abyss of nothing, of human perdition. And it is by the abyss of the divine mercy that that other abyss is filled. It is this pure divine mercy which fills the abyss."[74] Barth widens his focus beyond Romans 3 to highlight the way passages such as Rom. 5:9; 4:25; 6:10; and 8:3 set up both this positive and negative relationship between Christ's death and sin.[75] Barth's exploration of these passages leads him to conclude that Christ's death releases

> man from a legal relationship fatal to him, from an intolerable commitment which he has accepted, from an imprisonment in which he finds himself. . . . As the subject of sin, sins and transgressions man finds himself in this fatal relationship, under this intolerable commitment, in this imprisonment. He cannot release himself from it. But at one stroke he is wholly and finally released from it when Jesus Christ takes his place

and "judges and destroys [sin] in His death."[76]

Ultimately, Barth's reading of Paul compels a prioritizing of God's own faithfulness to Godself, to his covenant to be God for us, and thus to our justification, peace, sanctification, and liberation as the foundational point from which to understand God's holy love. Furthermore, from this light alone can we rightly contemplate God's setting forth of God's own Son as a sacrifice for the sin of all people, which is the ἱλαστήριον of 3:25. "In this passion there is legally reestablished the covenant between God and man, broken by man but kept by God. On that one day of suffering of that One there took place the comprehensive turning in the history of all creation—with all that this involves."[77] Paul's language in 3:25 indicates that he has embedded a cultic term in explaining the solution to a dilemma that is

74. *CD* IV/1, 89–90 [95].
75. Ibid.
76. Ibid., 256 [282].
77. Ibid., 247 [271–72].

forensically described. Barth, still privileging the forensic framework for the atonement, concludes that the imagery of Jesus as the sacrifice offered is simply another way of stating that God in Jesus was judged for us and in our place. This imagery of "the ἱλαστήριον of the covenant, could only signify for the people of the old covenant: the demonstration, the revelation, the event, the ἔνδειξις τῆς δικαιοσύνης θεοῦ on earth (Rom. 3:25). Because it is this Priest, the Son of God, who makes this offering, which is Himself, therefore in contrast to all others His sacrifice is effective and complete."[78] Paul's use of cultic language makes clear that repeated sacrifices are no longer necessary. "Jesus as an expiation for sin effects the full and final redemption of God's people."[79] Jesus Christ is the one and only real sacrifice for sin because, in his person, he is the fulfillment of the reconciliation of humanity with God. In Jesus Christ, "God Himself has intervened in His own person."[80] Cousar's study of Rom. 3:24–26 agrees with Barth here, even if the point is not made as sharply as it could be. Christ's death "shows that God is not indifferent to human disobedience"[81] because in "the Christ-event, through which God graciously sets right (or rectifies) humans as a free gift, God's own righteousness is manifest."[82] The righteous demands of God and the sacrificial giving which is required in response "are a single related decision in God Himself. For that reason real satisfaction has been done."[83]

> [N]ow it is God Himself who not only demands but makes the offering. . . . In [Jesus Christ] God not only demands but He gives what He demands. In Him He does that which has to take place to set aside sin and remove the conflict. He shows Himself to be pure and holy and sinless by not refusing in Him to become the greatest of all sinners, achieving the penitence and conversion which is demanded of sinners, undertaking the bitter reality of being the accused and condemned and judged and executed man of sin, in order that when He Himself has been this man no other man can or need

78. Ibid., 277 [305].
79. Cousar, *Theology of the Cross*, 66.
80. *CD* IV/1, 280 [308].
81. Cousar, *Theology of the Cross*, 41.
82. Ibid., 39–40.
83. *CD* IV/1, 281 [309].

> be, in order that in place of this man another man who is pleasing to God, the man of obedience, may have space and air and be able to live.[84]

The truth pervading both the positive and negative elements that together comprise the wholly good news of Christ's death on the cross finally comes down to "[t]he will of God towards us [that] is the purpose of this sacrifice, and His good pleasure towards us is its end."[85] Cousar puts it this way: "what dominates . . . is the stunning news that *God* is the protagonist. Behind the drama of the self-giving Christ is the self-giving love of God."[86]

Interestingly, Käsemann misses this point when he states that Jesus' death cannot be called a sacrifice because Paul "accounted [it] as God's action and God cannot very well sacrifice to himself. The cross's consequences for men dominate all Paul's statements to such an extent that the consequences for God simply do not enter his field of vision."[87] For Käsemann, Paul is simply appropriating a cultic tradition about Christ's death on the cross for his doctrine of justification. Barth, on the other hand, takes Paul's use of cultic language seriously, not giving it pride of place but thinking it through in the light of Paul's forensic language of God's righteous verdict, which is the outworking in time of the covenant of grace. Because God's good pleasure and perfect will undergird Christ's sacrifice, Barth points out that "[i]t is no longer a question of a *Quidproquo*, an 'as if,' beyond which we still need something more perfect, a real reconciliation which has still to come."[88] Barth is critical here of the Reformers' language of the imputation of Christ's alien righteousness, as it could be taken to imply that our justification is in some sense improper, which would contradict justification's basis in the perfect love of God.

> [T]he alien righteousness which has been effected not in and by us but in the sacrifice of Jesus Christ does become and is always ours, so that in

84. Ibid., 280–81 [308–9].
85. Ibid., 282 [310].
86. Cousar, *Theology of the Cross*, 26.
87. Ernst Käsemann, "The Saving Significance of the Death of Jesus in Paul," in *Perspectives on Paul*, trans. Margaret Kohl (Philadelphia: Fortress Press, 1971), 43.
88. *CD* IV/1, 283 [311].

> Him we are no longer unrighteous but righteous before God, we are the children of God. . . . What He has done He has done in order that being done by Him it may be done by us; not only acceptable to God, but already accepted; our work which is pleasing to Him; our being as those who are dead to sin and can live to righteousness.[89]

Barth has set aside the Reformation idea of imputation understood "as a *distinct* act of God the Father in the power of the Holy Spirit, an act in which the work of Christ is made to be efficacious for the individual to whom it is 'applied'"[90] and instead employed, in his own way, the notion of a positive imputation of Christ's righteousness in terms of the covenant of grace, which is revealed in time in God's divine verdict pronounced in Christ's death on the cross. The original Pauline concept that our justification comes to us from outside ourselves through Christ's redeeming death is thus safeguarded in Barth's rearticulation of a key Reformation concept.

The Role of Faith in Barth's Forensic Apocalyptic Doctrine of Justification

Barth believes strongly that the Reformation concept of justification by grace through faith (alone) is a rediscovery of Paul's teaching on justification. Indeed, he submits that it is one of the most basic of all Protestant doctrines, though it is has been understood and misunderstood from all sides in a variety of ways.[91] In chapter 2 of this study, we saw that the cosmological-apocalyptic reading of Rom. 3:21–26 wants to distinguish between the forensic focus on the faith of the individual and the cosmic-apocalyptic focus on the death of Christ as the eschatological event that deals with sin once and for all. Thus the cosmic-apocalyptic line is always to uphold God's initiative in the event of salvation. As Cousar states: "the text [Rom. 3:24–26] gives little warrant for a two-staged soteriology: first what God 'objectively' does in Christ and then what happens 'subjectively' to change the situation

89. Ibid.
90. McCormack, "*Justitia aliena*," 192.
91. *CD* IV/1, 615 [687].

of sinful people. The passage conveys a single movement of God in Christ for the salvation of humanity."[92] Likewise, Cousar summarizes the conclusion drawn by Arland Hultgren's study of Paul's justification texts this way: Paul's apocalyptic statements of God's justification of all humanity and his forensic ones, which mention faith and so serve to designate the identity of God's people in the new age, must be kept separate. The universal statements are to be given first consideration, and only in their light can the more specialized statements of justification by faith be understood.[93]

Following Paul, Barth, too, shares this prioritizing,[94] yet he does so in a way that is not disconnected from an individual's response of faith, precisely because he finds the objective and subjective sides of justification to cohere in the person of Jesus Christ, who is himself the event of justification.[95] Barth reiterates that the backbone of Paul's gospel begins always, in the first instance, with an emphasis on δικαιοσύνη θεοῦ, and only then and because of that does Paul speak of δικαιοσύνη πίστεως. Barth notes that the particular combination of the words δικαιοσύνη and πίστις is a hallmark unique to Paul's theology.[96] Barth submits that in the contexts where Paul connects δικαιοσύνη and πίστις, faith means simply this:

> the confidence of sinful man in the demonstration of the undeserved faithfulness of God as given in Jesus Christ. . . . As he [sinful man] gives

92. Cousar, *Theology of the Cross*, 65.
93. Ibid., 60–61.
94. Barth's shared concern here can be noted in the fact that he spends the first six hundred pages of *CD* IV/1 concentrating solely on what he calls the "objective" content of the doctrine of justification, which is the justifying action of God.
95. Barth refers to πίστις Ἰησοῦ Χριστοῦ as "the so-called *genetivus mysticus*," writing that πίστις "denotes the state created by God's revelation in Christ, the being of Christians, their being ἐν Χριστῷ, by which they are put in a position to achieve for their part the knowledge of God or of Christ as the Kyrios, the reality of man in which this achievement is an event. In the πίστις Ἰησοῦ Χριστοῦ we see the divine decision made about man. Only then and on this basis does the word slip down, as it were, into the sphere of human actions." See *CD* I/1, 228 [240]. This fits with Martyn's point that "for Paul, *God's* deed of rectifying us . . . precedes *our* deed of placing our trust in that Christ. . . . [F]or Paul faith does not lie in the realm of human possibility. Even to speak of faith as a 'possibility granted by God' can be misleading. For faith is not an option human beings can choose. Thus, when Paul speaks about placing one's trust in Christ, he is pointing to a deed that reflects not the freedom of the will, but rather God's freeing of the will." See J. Louis Martyn, *Galatians: A New Translation with Introduction and Commentary*, AB 33A (New York: Doubleday, 1997), 276.
96. *CD* IV/1, 614 [686].

> God this confidence, he finds himself justified, but not otherwise. That was what the Reformers maintained. They did not have the unequivocal backing of Paul for all their statements. But they undoubtedly had it for this statement.[97]

Thus for Barth, no dichotomy exists between God's apocalyptic initiative to justify all humanity and the proper human response of faith in God's work of justification. Commenting on Paul's threefold repetition of πίστις Χριστοῦ in Gal. 2:16, Barth writes that this is "the faith in which man knows and apprehends his justification, the justification which can be known and apprehended and realized only in this work" not "because faith as such is better than . . . works"[98] but because justification has been accomplished for us in Christ. "Of the three factors—justification, faith and Christ—the basic and controlling one is obviously the last."[99] Martyn would agree: "The point is that the Christ in whom we faithfully place our trust is the Christ who has already faithfully died in our behalf (cf. Rom 5:8) and whose prevenient death for us is the powerful rectifying event that has elicited our faith."[100]

Barth understands reconciliation between God and humanity as an event that occurs in the person of Jesus Christ.[101]

> God does not ask sinful human beings if they would like to be saved. In Jesus Christ, he just saves them. In Jesus Christ, the salvation of humanity is objective, real, and perfect. . . . Thus, while our salvation is an accomplished reality in Jesus Christ, not merely a possibility, this does not exclude but includes the fact that this reality awaits confirmation and fulfillment in the lives of individuals by the power of the Holy Spirit.[102]

In Jesus Christ, sinful humanity is abolished once and for all. However,

97. Ibid., 626 [699].
98. Ibid., 639 [714].
99. Ibid.
100. J. Louis Martyn, "God's Way of Making Right What Is Wrong," in *Theological Issues in the Letters of Paul* (Nashville: Abingdon, 1997), 151.
101. It is helpful here to remember, as Neder points out, that Barth's actualistic theological ontology is not preconceived in his mind; rather, it is "an attempt to offer a fitting description of the living Lord Jesus Christ himself, as attested by Holy Scripture." See Adam Neder, *Participation in Christ: An Entry into Karl Barth's Church Dogmatics* (Louisville: Westminster John Knox, 2009), 61.
102. Ibid., 46.

this apocalyptic ending is not the end itself but the establishment and anticipation of the end. True humanity is only realized in obedient human action that corresponds to the lived obedience of Jesus Christ. The active participation of human faith is the true response to God's grace in justifying us in Jesus Christ even as human faith contributes nothing to making justification effectual. Following Paul, grace is the divine justifying event in Jesus Christ in which old humanity is replaced with the new prior to and apart from human faith. As "faith in Jesus Christ who is risen from the dead it believes in a sentence which is absolutely effective, so that man is not merely called righteous before God, but is righteous before God."[103] Such faith is both a gift of the Holy Spirit[104] and the actualization within the Christian person of her true being as it is in Jesus.

In a long small-print passage exploring the New Testament sense of the word "faith," Barth makes the following helpful comment:

> We have called it [faith] the factual, objective, ontological standing of man—not all men, but certain men—in a concrete relationship with Jesus Christ and the God who is active and revealed in Him. Those who believe do so in this status—because, as Paul says, they are "in Christ," they belong to Him, they are set at His side. It is in virtue of this that they believe. The act or work of their faith derives from their being, just as a shoot does from a root. . . . Those who believe in the New Testament sense do so, as their own free act, because they have the freedom to do so from the One in whom they believe. . . . They cling to Jesus, to the God active and revealed in Him. And they are sustained by this ontological reality both behind and before. . . . The secret of faith is that as the work of man it has this origin and this goal. . . . That is why Paul can make the important statement in Rom. 3:21f. that a man is not justified in the verdict of God, and therefore in truth, by any work that is demanded by the Law, but διὰ πίστεως, ἐκ πίστεως, πίστει, as πίστεύων. He is justified in truth because in faith he has both his origin and goal in this One who is in truth, in Jesus Christ.[105]

103. *CD* IV/1, 95 [102].

104. A point frequently misunderstood about the traditional Reformation teaching on faith is that for Luther faith is not a human work like observance of the law but is instead a gift of God's grace, effected by the Holy Spirit in a human individual, who is passive in receiving the gift. The human act of receiving the gift of faith has no importance in and of itself. The significance lies entirely in that which is received, such that Luther states that "Faith takes hold of Christ and has Him present, enclosing Him as the ring encloses a gem." See Martin Luther, *Lectures on Galatians 1535, Chapters 1–4*, ed. Jaroslav Pelikan, Luther's Works 26 (St. Louis: Concordia, 1963), 132.

105. *CD* IV/2, 240–41 [266–67].

Barth's explanation of a right understanding of faith seems to be a fitting application of de Boer's conclusion that in Paul "the meaning of faith is actually determined by the cosmological-apocalyptic disclosure of God's righteousness and of sin in the crucifixion of Christ."[106] In Barth's estimation, Paul's various combinations of δικαιοσύνη and πίστις (he lists Rom. 4:11, 13; 9:30; 10:6; and Phil 3:9 as examples) all indicate "the place where and the manner in which man's relationship to the redemptive activity accomplished in the judgment and sentence of God . . . is in fact 'realised' on the part of man."[107] On the human side, faith is both an attitude and action that properly corresponds to the divine attitude and action described by Paul as δικαιοῦν. Faith's relationship to God's justifying action is, however, one that does not anticipate, compete, or cooperate with God's action, nor is it identical to it. Faith is the only human work that properly corresponds to God's divine justification of us. Why? Not because of any intrinsic value or virtue it contains, but simply "because God accepts it as the human work which corresponds to His work. . . . God recognizes, not that by this action man fulfills a condition or attains something which makes him worthy of the divine acquittal, but that in this action of man, and this action alone, his acquittal actually comes fully into its own."[108]

In upholding the important place of human faith in justification, Barth appeals to Rom. 3:3, where he finds πίστις to denote both God's action and the analogous human action. But he is also careful not to understand the role of faith at the expense of the saving action of God in Christ. He submits that even in our faith, we are in need of justification. "There is as little praise of man on the basis of his faith as on that of his works."[109] Barth here follows Calvin's insistence

106. Martinus C. de Boer, "Paul and Apocalyptic Eschatology," in *The Origins of Apocalypticism in Judaism and Christianity*, vol. 1 of *The Encyclopedia of Apocalypticism*, ed. John J. Collins (New York: Continuum, 1998), 366.
107. *CD* IV/1, 614–15 [686].
108. Ibid., 615 [686], *rev.* McCormack suggests that "What happens as we believe is that we begin to live from and toward *the Christ in whom justification is already fully effective*." See Bruce L. McCormack, "Can We Still Speak of 'Justification by Faith'?: An In-House Debate with Apocalyptic Readings of Paul," in *Galatians and Christian Theology: Justification, the Gospel, and Ethics in Paul's Letter*, ed. Mark W. Elliott, Scott J. Hafemann, N. T. Wright, and John Frederick (Grand Rapids: Baker Academic, 2014), 174.
109. *CD* IV/1, 616 [688].

that the Catholic notions of infused grace and virtue are grave misinterpretations of Paul's texts on faith and justification. Faith, for Barth, is best seen in the light of the Christology that has informed his doctrine of reconciliation. Just as Jesus was humbly obedient for our sake and in our place in his life, death, and resurrection, so human faith is "the humility of obedience . . . it is an obeying."[110]

Barth recognizes that he is going beyond the first and second editions of his Romans commentary, where he described faith as a vacuum. He still maintains the truth of such a description, but he clarifies that this negative form of faith cannot "be asserted as a singular magnifying of the glory of God, as though that glory were the greater the less man is before it, and greatest of all when man is absolutely nothing. . . . God is far from finding pleasure in the nothingness of man as such."[111] The reason faith has this negative form of emptying is that the positive form of faith clings to the justification of all humanity in the humble obedience of the Son who was crucified and risen in our place and for us, thereby abolishing sin and death and becoming the new and righteous human for all people. In other words, the shape of the negative form of faith is controlled by the positive content of faith, which is simply that our justification takes place as an event in Jesus Christ, the God-man. "He is our man, we are in Him, our present is His, the history of man is His history, He is the concrete event of the existence and reality of justified man in whom every man can recognize himself and every other man—recognize himself as truly justified."[112] Faith accepts as true the fact that Jesus Christ is humanity's justification. Faith knows that Christ has accomplished the reality of reconciliation, not merely the possibility of it. "For because it is faith in Jesus Christ; it can be true and living faith only as the humility of obedience; it has to be an empty hand, an empty vessel, a vacuum."[113]

110. Ibid., 620 [692].
111. Ibid., 628 [702].
112. Ibid., 630 [703].
113. Ibid., 631 [705].

There need not be any separation between Paul's apocalyptic focus on God's in-breaking action to set the world aright and his declaration that God justifies the one who has faith. As Barth follows Paul, both emphases cohere in the one person of Jesus Christ. There is no need to fear an individualistic preoccupation in Barth's reading. But neither is the individual neglected. Rather, the individual clings to the truth that her true humanity, justification, faith, and humble obedience are all found in the enacted history of the person of Jesus Christ even as the Spirit makes her to correspond in herself to what is already true about her in Christ.

In conclusion, our study of Barth's theological exegesis of Romans 3 in *A Shorter Commentary on Romans* and his later construal, in *CD* IV/1, of the doctrine of atonement, which is undergirded both by his doctrine of election and key themes from Romans 3, has served to underscore five important dimensions to understanding Barth's forensic apocalyptic account of justification. First, just as the main argument of this study proposes that significant development occurred in Barth's portrayal of justification following his second edition of the Romans commentary, so this chapter has shown a movement from Barth's initial alignment with classical Reformation notions of forensic justification and penal substitution in *A Shorter Commentary on Romans* to *CD* IV/1's important corrective to penal substitution and reenvisioning of justification's positive imputation of Christ's alien righteousness in terms of the covenant of grace, revealed in God's divine verdict pronounced in Christ's death on the cross. This does not, however, put Barth at odds with the Reformation. Indeed, where the Reformation is most faithful to Paul, such as on the place of faith in justification, Barth is in complete agreement. But, where the Reformation's construal of Paul's discussion of God's action in the death of Christ results in a faulty understanding of the being of God made known in the history of Jesus of Nazareth, Barth offers a helpful corrective in returning to Paul's steadfast focus on the crucified and resurrected Lord.

Second, as we saw, Barth makes Jesus Christ to be both the basis and meaning of God's covenant of grace. This affects his doctrine of atonement in several key ways. First, the concept of punishment is no longer the main concept driving the doctrine of atonement. Now, in understanding the heart of the atonement as the overcoming of sin in Christ's death, Barth makes the apocalyptic annihilation of both sin and the sinner to be the decisive *negative* element of Christ's death on the cross. Further, Barth makes divine love to be the subject that is satisfied in Christ's death. Along with the radical annihilation of both sin and the sinner, which occurs when Christ the Judge is judged, it is God's love for humanity, anchored in the covenant of grace, that creates space for God to do something entirely new for the cosmos and for humanity. Election, as an eternal act of God, has ontological signification for both God and humanity. First, in election, God has chosen Godself in Christ to be the "reprobate" human so that sin and the sinner are destroyed in God's own being. This notion that God is never without the "determination" to be for us in this radical way negates any vestiges of divine arbitrariness to God's self-giving love. Second, in election, humanity is already in Christ; therefore our death has taken place in him, and we have already been raised with him into the new creation in advance of our own final resurrection.

Third, rather than God remaining above and distinct from Jesus in his death, as in the second edition of the Romans commentary, now the atonement is shaped by a Christology in which Christ accomplishes reconciliation not apart from or distinct from God but in the unity of his person as both God and man. The unity of the divine and the human in the incarnation means that reconciliation takes place in and through a unitary movement of God toward the human in Jesus Christ.

Fourth, by grounding justification in God's decision in election to be *Deus pro nobis*, Barth maintains Paul's apocalyptic focus on the righteous action of God, upholding it as the backbone to the event of justification insofar as God first of all is consistent with God's self in extending grace and salvation to humanity. Because Barth makes forensicism basic to his theological ontology, he can take seriously

Paul's use of cultic imagery in Romans 3, not giving it pride of place but finding the notion of the ἱλαστήριον to be an outworking, in time, of the covenant of grace.

Finally, because Barth finds the objective and subjective sides of justification to cohere in the person of Jesus Christ, who is himself the event of justification, no dichotomy exists between God's apocalyptic initiative to justify all humanity and the proper human response of faith in God's work of justification. True humanity is realized in obedient human action that corresponds to the lived obedience of Jesus Christ. The active participation of human faith is the true response to God's grace in justifying us in Jesus Christ. On the human side, faith is both an attitude and action that properly corresponds to the divine apocalyptic attitude and action described by Paul as δικαιοῦν.

This chapter has demonstrated that Barth's doctrine of atonement, understood as the objective realization of justification in Christ, provides valuable contributions not only to the cosmic-apocalyptic dimensions of Paul's focus on the cross but also to the key Reformation teachings on justification by faith and the saving power of Christ's alien righteousness. In Barth's hands, we find a unique interplay between Pauline apocalyptic eschatology and the Reformation in that he grounds the concepts of decision and declaration, the central ideas in traditional Protestant doctrines of justification and election, and then makes God's eternal decision basic to theological ontology. The Reformation's hallmark, forensic justification, is made more thoroughly defensible through a theological ontology, which itself offers new depth of meaning to the atonement. In the same way, the cosmic-apocalyptic features of Paul's notion of justification are not divorced from or set over against his forensic ones. Neither is an individual's faith in Christ at odds with God's in-breaking action to put the world aright in the death of Christ. Indeed, the one justified by faith believes that the atonement simply is Jesus Christ and clings to the truth that "Jesus is truly 'Lord' of the cosmos, and the Kingdom of God is made effectively present in his historical person, precisely 'as the happening which determines all history and which embraces all other histories.'"[114]

114. Kerr, *Christ, History and Apocalyptic*, 77.

6

The Aspects of Justification in Barth's Forensic Apocalyptic Doctrine of Justification

> There is no room for any fears that in the justification of man we are dealing only with a verbal action, with a kind of bracketed "as if," as though what is pronounced were not the whole truth about man. Certainly we have to do with a declaring righteous, but it is a declaration about man which is fulfilled and therefore effective in this event, which corresponds to actuality because it creates and therefore reveals the actuality. It is a declaring righteous which without any reserve can be called a making righteous.
>
> —Karl Barth, *CD* IV/1

> Paul's doctrine of justification is more than a logical conclusion; it is the specific Pauline interpretation of Christology in its relation to man and the world. . . . His teaching about justification gives a clear definition of what the apostle understands by the lordship of Christ.
>
> —Ernst Käsemann, "Justification and Salvation History in the Epistle to the Romans"

In this chapter we will endeavor an analysis of the contours of Barth's forensic apocalyptic doctrine of justification as seen in conjunction with his theological reading of Romans 5. At the heart of the classical Reformed doctrine of justification is the idea of acquittal, or a judgment of innocence. For Calvin, such a declaration was made possible because of the double imputation of Christ. Our sin and guilt were transferred onto Christ in his death on the cross. Likewise, the acquired righteousness of Christ, which belonged to him by way of his sinless, human obedience to the will of God, was imputed to us. Calvin's teaching on justification as acquittal was judged by its Catholic detractors as a "legal fiction" because it suggested that God merely declared a guilty person to be innocent when she was nothing of the sort. In order for justification to be true and not some sort of legal fiction, it must be the case that God's verdict not only is based on the alien righteousness of Christ but that *the sinner* is indeed destroyed in Christ's death. What Calvin's doctrine of justification was missing was a true account of how the sinner is made innocent. Calvin understood the sinner to be made more and more righteous until she passes into the glorified state. As this process of sanctification begins with regeneration, we can therefore understand, as later Reformed theologians did, that imputation is a kind of regenerating declaration, which means that God never declares an individual to be righteous without initiating the process by which she is made to be so. In such a scenario, however, there would still not be a true sentence of innocence. A cleaned-up sinner is still a person who has been a sinner, and she can never be a person who is innocent. At the end of the day, then, Calvin cannot completely refute the charge of legal fiction.

Barth's great advantage over Calvin is found in the destruction of the sinner. Unlike Calvin, his use of the term "acquittal" is an accurate description of what results from the destruction of the person of sin and the raising of the elect as new creation. In Barth's account, new creation is not restoration; it is a complete do-over. Forensic justification, as Barth reinvigorates the traditional Reformation doctrine, is the effective, creative, and transformative sentence that, in the first instance, takes place and is complete in Christ. It is a declaration enacted in the death and resurrection of Jesus, first abolishing the old, sinful humanity and subsequently ushering a new humanity in its place. Insofar as humanity is originally in Christ by virtue of election and Jesus is the one true human before God, justification is made to be effective and transformative for us. Insofar as acquittal is pronounced on humanity only as they are in Christ and will be made to be in themselves in the eschaton, forensic justification is not only apocalyptic; it also correlates with Paul's portrayal of the Adam/Christ typology in the second half of Romans 5. Thus there is no basis for the charge of "legal fiction."

In chapter 5 of our study, we learned that Jesus Christ, as the divinely elected fulfillment of both sides of the covenant between God and humanity, accomplishes and is identical to the atonement by humbly coming as the Judge to take our place on the cross as sinners, thereby abolishing sin and sinners by his death, acquitting us as sinners, and objectively accomplishing the reconciliation of the whole world back to God. This chapter, as it explores justification, the twin doctrine to that of the atonement, will further build on that discovery. Just as the doctrine of the atonement specifies *how* justification is objectively accomplished, so the doctrine of justification delineates *what* is accomplished. Likewise, just as this study as a whole argues that Barth's revision of Reformational forensicism, based as it is on the historicized theological ontology that comes to expression in his mature Christology, is apocalyptic in nature, so this chapter will demonstrate the way that Barth employs key elements from Paul's apocalyptic message in Romans 5 in laying out his forensic apocalyptic doctrine of justification. We will also see that Barth's understanding of justification as acquittal is not susceptible to the traditional charge lodged against forensic justification—that it is a legal fiction. Acquittal demands new creation for its accomplishment. For Barth, such new creation is already accomplished in the resurrection of Christ, the event and the person in whom the reality of the future has broken into this world. Furthermore, the human obedience of Christ is made by Barth to be the basis of the new humanity that we will become eschatologically. The net effect of all of this is that the whole of Barth's soteriology is entirely cosmic in scope. At the same time, with the addition of his theological ontology, which is commensurate with forensicism's stress on being as a function of decision and act, Barth's doctrine of justification is more consistently forensic than even that of the Reformers.

Our investigation will first consider the dimensions of Barth's theological reading of Rom. 5:12–21 in *A Shorter Commentary on Romans*, but mostly in *Christ and Adam*,[1] where we will see Barth parsing the particular features of Paul's Christ-and-Adam typology. It will be evident that Barth's reading highlights the apocalyptic eschatology that comes to expression in Paul's typology. Our analysis of Barth's interpretation will be further aided by occasional comparisons with de Boer's reading of this Pauline passage, first discussed in chapter 2 of our study. Having laid the groundwork with Barth's more sustained engagement with Paul's text in *Christ and Adam*, we will next turn our attention to *CD* IV/1, in order to explore the points at which Romans 5 plays a major role in shaping Barth's forensic apocalyptic doctrine of justification.

Barth's Construal of Paul's Apocalyptic Typology of Christ and Adam

Recall that Barth's understanding of justification, as expressed in the second edition of his Romans commentary, sustained a strong emphasis on justification as an eschatological and forensic doctrine. For Barth, justification is a forward-looking sovereign declaration that makes us to be, in a moment's time, that which we are not yet but will be. The eschatological actualization of justification is fleshed out in the role played by faith. Justification is the consequence of the direct act of God on an individual insofar as God creates faith in us, which is then repeated each moment, such that it never becomes a precondition. By faith we learn that our death has taken place in Christ's death on the

1. Barth's exegetical excursus on Romans 5, published in 1952, is material he had omitted from a section on theological anthropology in his doctrine of creation in *CD* III/2.

cross. The unintuitable God is revealed in the death of Christ, whose blood reminds us of the faithfulness of God.

Such a formulation demonstrates that, at that earlier point in Barth's development, Jesus is seen to be a distinct subject from God; he is the locale for the revelation of God's righteousness. Consequently, the forensicism at play in the second edition of the commentary is not yet built on a theological ontology. All of this changed with Barth's revision to the doctrine of election. Henceforth Christology controlled the doctrines treated within the doctrine of reconciliation. Now, Barth urges that the lived obedience of the human Jesus, including his death in God-abandonment, is an event that takes place in the very being of God. This means that the faithfulness of God simply is the faithfulness of Christ. Furthermore, justification does not transpire in us as a consequence of a direct act of God on us, which then creates faith moment by moment. Rather, just as we are elect in Christ, so our justification is objectively accomplished fully and completely in Christ. It is Christ's dying the death of God-abandonment for us and in our place, and his perfectly lived obedience, that justify us. The Holy Spirit awakens us to the truth that, in Jesus Christ, we are justified sinners, in order that we may live more and more in a way corresponding to what we already are in Christ.

Insofar as Barth's revision of the doctrine of election meant that Christology became the controlling factor in formulating his doctrine of reconciliation, it is also the case that he was able more fully to incorporate Paul's construal of humanity in Christ according to Rom. 5:12–21. In *A Shorter Commentary on Romans*, Barth summarizes Paul's argument in the second half of Romans 5 this way: "the whole argument is only meant to be and only allowed to be a reminder of Jesus Christ."[2] He defines the heart of Paul's message according to 5:18: "[t]hrough the transgression of one man came the condemnation of all men, and in the same way, through the righteous deed of one Man, came the acquittal of all."[3] Just as Rom. 5:1–11 describes the assurance

2. *SR*, 37 [73].
3. Ibid.

Christians have regarding the objectivity of God's decision to reconcile them, so 5:12–21 makes clear that this decision is pronounced on all humanity because Jesus Christ has himself "reversed and annulled" the decision made by humanity to be enemies of God.[4] "V[erses] 12–21 are revolutionary in their insistence that what is true of Christians must also be true of all men."[5] Christ is God's love toward us. Therefore God's decision for us and Christ's decisive work, in which he bore our sin for our salvation, are one and the same. In his humiliation, Christ is the reconciling God. Barth frames verses 12–21 in light of 1–11, remarking that Paul puts "the same material in a wider context," as well as making the new point of a "*special* anthropology of Jesus Christ—the one man for all men, all men in the one man—[which] constitutes the secret of 'Adam' also, and so is the *norm* of *all* anthropology."[6] According to Barth, Paul makes such a categorical conclusion regarding all humanity because he sees "Adam not in isolation but in his relationship to Christ."[7] Christ is also, therefore, the true human reconciled to God.

It is crucial that we pause and consider what Barth means by this wider context of Rom. 5:12–21. He specifies that verses 1–11 "only speak of Jesus Christ and those who *believe* in Him,"[8] which, by itself, might cause us to conclude "that for Paul Christ's [humanity] is significant only for those who are united to Him in faith."[9] However, verses 12–21 widen the context from "Church history to world history, from Christ's relationship to Christians to His relationship to all [people]."[10] Barth notes that Paul makes no further mention of faith or the gift of the Holy Spirit and that he switches from first-person plural to third-person plural. Hence "[w]hat is said here applies generally and universally, and not merely to one limited group."[11] When we brought de Boer's reading of this passage in Romans 5 into conversation with

4. Ibid., 36 [71].
5. Karl Barth, *Christ and Adam: Man and Humanity in Romans 5*, trans. T. A. Smail (New York: Harper & Brothers, 1956), 112 [53].
6. Ibid., 36 [9].
7. Ibid., 114 [54].
8. Ibid., 108 [50].
9. Ibid., 109 [50–51].
10. Ibid., 109 [51].
11. Ibid.

Barth back in chapter 2, we saw that he urged that the introduction of Adam is Paul's signal that he is now placing the justifying work of Christ into a cosmic context. More specifically, it is "the cosmological characterizations of sin and death brought into the story of Adam and his trespass in Romans 5:12–21"[12] that marks the shift "from predominantly *forensic* terminology and motifs to predominantly *cosmological* ones."[13] De Boer holds that "Christ and his saving work are placed not only in opposition to Adam and his trespass but also in opposition to the Law as the presumed remedy for that trespass."[14] It is important to point out that Barth sees the origins of the cosmic context of Romans 5 a bit differently from de Boer. In Barth's mind, "Paul does not go to Adam to see how he is connected with Christ; he goes to Christ to see how *He* is connected with Adam."[15] In other words, Barth finds Paul painting a picture of the cosmic horizons of God's reconciling activity based not primarily on the cosmic characterizations of sin and death, however much that plays a part in Paul's typology and his adaptation of the patterns within forensic Jewish apocalyptic eschatology. Rather, for Barth, the cosmic context of Rom. 5:12–21 takes as its point of departure the universal nature of Christ's lordship. Whatever lordship sin and death have over humanity is only a secondary and provisional copy, indirectly witnessing to Christ's lordship.[16]

Barth connects verses 12, 18–19, and 21 in order to focus in on the heart of Paul's message: "[t]here, in Christ, is, for the first time in the true sense, the One who stands, as such, for all others."[17] Forensic justification, expressed in God's righteous declaration of acquittal, has been given to all humanity in Christ. Thus inherent in Barth's formulation of forensic justification is Paul's cosmic horizon, which comes to expression within his christological grounding of God's

12. Martinus C. de Boer, *The Defeat of Death: Apocalyptic Eschatology in 1 Corinthians 15 and Romans 5* (Sheffield: JSOT, 1988), 155.
13. Ibid., 152.
14. Ibid., 158.
15. Barth, *Christ and Adam*, 60 [23].
16. For more on this idea, see chapter 7, footnote 67.
17. Barth, *Christ and Adam*, 42 [13].

reconciliation of the whole world in Christ's death and resurrection. Barth knows that "Paul is not denying that Adam's sin still brings death to all men, but he is affirming that the grace of Christ has an incomparably greater power to make these dead men alive."[18] The "incomparably greater power "[19] of Christ to bring life is the ordering principle that puts "the alien lordship of death"[20] and humanity's enslavement to sin in their proper place.

In no way, however, does Barth downplay Paul's emphasis on death as "an objective and alien power that is now exercising its lordship over man."[21] De Boer rightly stresses that "Paul sees all human history as a monolithic whole in which sin and death reign in tandem as cosmic and cosmological powers."[22] Barth agrees that the whole of human reality is signified, in Adam, as being under "'the dominion of sin and subjection to death.'"[23] But he wants to make clear that Paul's typology is structured around *Christ's* confrontation with the reality of Adam such that both sin and death witness to God's grace and eternal life. "The divine Victor is reflected in our human defeat!"[24] The formal parallel of humanity in relationship to Adam and Christ is deceiving if we stop there. In actuality, "there is really the greatest and most fundamental disparity between them."[25] Barth notes that Paul's procedure is first to emphasize the disparity before bringing out the shared identity. "The parallel between the one and the many, the *heis* and the *polloi*, on both sides in vv. 18–19 is introduced as a corollary of the disparity between them, as the inferential 'then' (*ara oun*) of v. 18 shows."[26]

Moreover, there is no counterbalancing between God's grace and God's judgment, or between the dominion of life and the dominion of death. Indeed, verses 1–11 show that God's love "has . . . not waited

18. Ibid., 50 [18].
19. Ibid.
20. Ibid., 54 [20].
21. Ibid., 53 [19].
22. De Boer, *Defeat of Death*, 173.
23. *SR*, 38 [75].
24. Ibid.
25. Barth, *Christ and Adam*, 48 [17].
26. Ibid., 49 [17].

for us, but has come to meet us and gone before us."[27] Barth's gloss on 5:15a is that "grace is not to be measured by sin."[28] Indeed, God's in-breaking action determines the "primary anthropological truth and ordering principle."[29] Fallen and entrapped humanity, in Adam, is but "a *provisional copy* of the real humanity that is in Christ."[30] "We have to correct and interpret what we know of Adam by what we know of Christ, because Adam is only true man in so far as he reflects and points to the original humanity of Christ."[31] All humanity, in Adam, can only indirectly "witness to the reality of Jesus Christ and to the original and essential human existence that He inaugurates and reveals."[32] Our past enslavement to the power of sin and death has no significance on its own, which is not to say that the situation is not serious. Christ's death on the cross has indeed revealed that "the human predicament is much worse than it appears before or apart from that event."[33] In Barth's words: "'Adam and us,' taken by itself, is an endless chapter which makes completely comfortless reading. But, as we have seen, this chapter is not to be read by itself."[34] Thus the situation can never be seen apart from God's work of redemption in Christ. "The only connection between Christ and Adam is that for Adam Christ died and rose again."[35] Paul does not deny that "Adam's sin still brings death to all men," but the greater reality is that the grace of Jesus Christ is "the grace of *God* and His gift. And so *eperisseusen*, it overflowed, it prevailed, it was greater than sin."[36] The complete incongruity between sin, death, and humanity in Adam, on the one hand, and grace, life, and humanity in Christ, on the other, is sharply characterized by Barth as "radical, final, and irremovable."[37] He calls Christ our Liberator and Head, suggesting that "[b]ecause we know Christ the Conqueror, we

27. Ibid., 31 [6].
28. Ibid., 49 [17].
29. Ibid., 39 [11].
30. Ibid., 46 [15].
31. Ibid., 75 [31].
32. Ibid., 41 [11].
33. De Boer, *Defeat of Death*, 169.
34. Barth, *Christ and Adam*, 70 [28].
35. Ibid., 60 [23].
36. Ibid., 50 [17].
37. Ibid., 50 [17–18].

can also know Christ the Crucified. Because we know Adam and ourselves as men who are acquitted and who are going to share God's glory, we can also know Adam and ourselves as sinners who were once condemned to die."[38]

That the lordship of sin and death, in all their power, does not dictate the terms of divine judgment and condemnation is seen in Paul's construction in verses 15–17. That sin leads to acquittal with the intervention of grace is a logical impossibility. Paul demonstrates this by giving the same grammatical construction to verse 15b and to verse 17. He has already indicated "that where the *dikaiōma* (righteous act) intervenes on the *krima* (judgment), there is no more *katakrima* (condemnation)."[39] But now, Barth suggests, we can say more than this because "the *dikaiōma* is the *dikaiōma* of God."[40] In other words, the invasive action of God to make things right dictates the terms, and, as de Boer follows Paul in 3:21, Christ's death is "the manifestation of 'the righteousness of God.'"[41] Romans 5:12–21 makes it plain that Christ's "death marks God's triumphant invasion of the world under the power of sin to liberate human beings . . . from its destructive and death-dealing power."[42] As Barth understands Paul, what results from this is nothing less than the free gift of acquittal. Paul's πολλῷ μᾶλλον formula, used in verses 9–10 and 15–17, provides the divine logic by which we can understand this. In verses 9–10 we learn of "our reconciliation through the death of Christ when we were still weak, sinners, godless, and enemies,"[43] which makes all the more valid

> our hope of salvation through the resurrection of Christ from the dead. And so both reconciliation and salvation are grounded on the same ordering principle, and both find a common validity in the one work of Christ, in the humiliation and exaltation of this one man. . . . [I]t is because *pollō mallon* first connects the two terms in vv. 9–10, that it can also connect the opposites of vv. 15–17.[44]

38. Ibid., 72 [30], *rev.*
39. Ibid., 55 [20].
40. Ibid.
41. De Boer, *Defeat of Death*, 156.
42. Ibid.
43. Barth, *Christ and Adam*, 58 [22].
44. Ibid., 58–59 [22–23].

Verses 9–10 are already Paul's retrospective account of humanity's past "weakness, sin, godlessness, and enmity," as well as our reconciliation to God "because Christ has thus invaded the world of Adam and claimed it for Himself."[45] Therefore Christ brings our dreadful past "into positive relation with our present and future" because "Christ has challenged the right of sin and death to rule over Adam's world by invading that world and making it His own."[46]

Although Barth and de Boer both highlight the cosmic language Paul uses in casting the particulars of the Adam/Christ typology, they are seeking different end results. As we have just seen, Barth finds the forensic and cosmic elements within Paul's typology to intersect, overlap, and play off of each other, based as they are on Christ's death and resurrection. In contrast is de Boer, who, although he notes that the forensic and cosmic patterns belonging to Jewish apocalyptic eschatology appear in Paul's argument as "Christologically adapted and modified,"[47] ultimately finds Paul to stand closer to the cosmological pattern than to the forensic. He insists that "Christ's death cannot be understood in exclusively forensic terms, since it marks God's triumphant invasion of the world 'under sin' (Rom. 3:9) to liberate human beings (the ungodly) from sin's deadly power."[48] Particularly, he suggests that Paul's typology shows him to be consistently providing not only a cosmological adaptation of forensic material but that "the structure and progression of Paul's argument in Rom. 1–8 suggest that motifs proper to cosmological apocalyptic eschatology circumscribe and, to a large extent, overtake forensic motifs."[49] While Barth never engages in a discussion of the particular patterns of forensic and cosmic Jewish apocalyptic eschatology like de Boer does, what Barth's reading makes clear is that Christ's lordship is the key to understanding both Paul's cosmological and forensic

45. Ibid., 61 [23].
46. Ibid., 61 [24].
47. Martinus C. de Boer, "Paul and Apocalyptic Eschatology," in *The Origins of Apocalypticism in Judaism and Christianity*, vol. 1 of *The Encyclopedia of Apocalypticism*, ed. John J. Collins (New York: Continuum, 1998), 362.
48. Ibid., 366.
49. Ibid., 365.

emphases. Forensic justification is not downplayed or overtaken by cosmic apocalypticism. Rather, Barth understands Paul to be explaining the cosmic import resident in forensic justification as it takes place for all humanity in Christ's humiliation and exaltation.

Christ is superior over Adam and all those who have sinned with Adam. In the midst of the world of sin and death, "He is already King, secretly in His humiliation."[50] He demonstrates this by taking our place, making sin and death his responsibility, pronouncing God's acquittal, removing the condemnation from the world and giving instead "the promise in power."[51] Barth observes that the formal parallel that Paul makes in verses 15–19 between the one and the many in Adam and in Christ has validity because Christ took Adam's place on the cross, and thus he died for the many who had sinned in Adam. "It is because Christ has thus invaded the world of Adam and claimed it for Himself, that Paul can find a connection between the two."[52] Furthermore, it is on the basis of Christ's power to identify himself with Adam (verses 15–17) that the parallel between them in verses 18–19 rests. "Adam is now free to pass into the world of Christ; Christ has removed the barriers and opened the doors and Adam can pass from sin to pardon—from death to life."[53] Again, in making sense of Paul's use of the πολλῷ μᾶλλον in verses 18–19, Barth goes back to the first instance of the formula in verses 9–10, noting first that the second term of the comparison is ζωή and defining it as "the resurrection of Christ, the future salvation it brings us, and our hope of sharing in the glory of God."[54] This ζωή is "'all the more' certain" because the other side of the comparison is our certain reconciliation through Christ's death, which took place "amidst the darkness of the mystery of sin."[55] Our reconciliation is true and real because Christ was humiliated for us and in our place. How much more true, in the light of Christ's resurrection life, therefore, is it that we will also reign in life. De Boer's reading of

50. Barth, *Christ and Adam*, 62 [24].
51. Ibid.
52. Ibid., 61 [23].
53. Ibid., 63 [25].
54. Ibid., 65 [26].
55. Ibid., 67 [27].

Paul offers further support only up to the point of focusing on Christ's death: "the strange—and apocalyptic—import of the gospel is that God destroys the power of sin to effect death precisely at the point at which sin seems to have triumphed, in the crucifixion of Christ. In this event, the condemnation of the whole world to the reign of death is revealed. Yet in this event the whole world is also graciously rectified and placed in the realm of life."[56] Where Barth and de Boer differ is that Barth sees our justification as encompassed by both the death and resurrection of Christ. De Boer, on the other hand, focuses here only on Paul's emphasis on Christ's death, which has the effect of making the event of the cross the basis for new creation.[57] On Barth's reading of 5:9–10, "Christ is raised to die no more. 'New creation' is therefore a function of the resurrection," and "the resurrection is an event of vindication and acceptance, the divine verdict pronounced on the sinless Jesus."[58]

Barth is absolutely convinced that the antithesis in 5:9–10 is no frivolous dialectic. "Men who share the sin of Adam have become men who share the grace of Christ, men who belong to Adam now belong to Christ."[59] Christ's resurrection reveals what was true but hidden in Christ's death on the cross—that Christ had already achieved victory over sin and death, that we have already been reconciled. Here, Barth finds, is the power of Paul's "how much more" clauses. "[I]f the truth in Christ can prove its validity even when it is hidden amidst the sin and death of the world of Adam, 'how much more' does it hold good in the world of grace and life where it properly and originally belongs!"[60]

56. De Boer, *Defeat of Death*, 185.
57. McCormack suggests that Martyn, whose reading of Galatians makes similar moves to de Boer by associating "new creation" with the crucifixion rather than the resurrection, raises more questions than he answers. "Does Paul really limit 'new creation' imagery to an exchange of lords that takes place 'over our heads' so to speak? Is not the re-creation of the human (i.e., regeneration) an event that transforms human life from within? And is this transformation but a foretaste in time of the definitive change that will take place in human beings beyond the limits of history, in the general resurrection of the dead?" See Bruce L. McCormack, "Can We Still Speak of 'Justification by Faith'?: An In-House Debate with Apocalyptic Readings of Paul," in *Galatians and Christian Theology: Justification, the Gospel, and Ethics in Paul's Letter*, ed. Mark W. Elliott, Scott J. Hafemann, N. T. Wright, and John Frederick (Grand Rapids: Baker Academic, 2014), 168. See J. Louis Martyn, "The Apocalyptic Gospel in Galatians," *Interpretation* 54, no. 3 (2000): 259.
58. McCormack, "Can We Still Speak of 'Justification by Faith'?," 174–75.
59. Barth, *Christ and Adam*, 71 [29].
60. Ibid., 73 [30].

Hence our unity with Adam "is less essential and less significant than our true unity with Christ."[61] Christ, although he seems to come second in the typology, actually comes first. Barth reiterates that verses 13–14 and 20 demonstrate "that the formal correspondence and identity between Adam and Christ is based upon their material disparity."[62] Therefore, "[i]n Christ the relationship between the one and the many is original, in Adam it is only a copy of that original."[63] The import of 5:21 is that, through Christ, "grace rules."[64]

Tracing the Impact of Romans 5 on Barth's Mature Doctrine of Justification

When we examine Barth's mature doctrine of justification, in *CD* IV/1, we find that Barth employs the word "justification" in speaking of the entirety of God's work of reconciliation. The divine action of reconciling the world to God in Jesus Christ is one single action. This means that both the objective reality of justification accomplished by and in Jesus Christ in his death and resurrection and an individual's subjective appropriation of it, in faith, by the Spirit, belong to a single, unified movement of the triune God's reconciling activity. Therefore, as the first epigraph to this chapter indicates, for Barth, in justification, we are really made to be righteous. Forensic justification, summed up most basically as a declaration of innocence, or acquittal, is actually filled with a complexity of meaning for Barth. It has not only a negative meaning and content, already fully explored by Barth in the second edition of his Romans commentary, but also a positive one. Justification is an event in the history of Jesus Christ in which the old human is replaced with the new. The negative side is that sinful humanity is abolished in Christ's death. The positive side, proclaimed and fulfilled in the resurrection, is that the human is made to be

61. Ibid., 74 [31].
62. Ibid., 114 [54].
63. Ibid., 75 [31].
64. Ibid., 110 [51].

righteous "before God in Jesus Christ," and "eternal life is already—effectively—ascribed and promised."[65]

As we noted in chapter 4, Barth follows Paul in making the righteousness of God the backbone of justification. Hence the Pauline apocalyptic focus on the otherness and priority of God's action could not be stronger in Barth's forensic doctrine of justification. One way this comes to expression in Barth's mature doctrine of justification is the stress he places on justification as God's act of judgment to restore the covenant of grace established by God with humanity from all eternity. "In the shedding of Christ's blood, i.e., in the offering of His life to the powers of death we have the constancy, the maintenance or the restitution of the covenant between God and man. 'We have peace with God' and *προσαγωγὴν εἰς τὴν χάριν* is how it is put in Rom. 5:1f, and in Rom. 5:10 'we are reconciled by the death of his Son.'"[66] This means that the subjective knowledge expressed in the Christian confession found in Rom. 5:1 is grounded in "the objective knowledge that the gracious justification of man is the work of God's eternal righteousness."[67] Thus the righteousness of God, expressed in God's gracious coming to humanity in Jesus Christ and making atonement, is self-grounding and known only by itself. That it results in our peace with God is not something we could expect. The atonement has taken place solely by God's initiative. It is a sovereign act of God, not owed to God, the world, or humanity, "yet which has in fact taken place and been made manifest."[68] Furthermore, what we receive from the atonement "is our peace, πρὸς τὸν θεόν, not the reverse. And his [Paul's] subject here is the reconciling of . . . the world made by God with Himself,[69] not the reconciling of God with . . . the world. The hurt which

65. *CD* IV/1, 95 [102].
66. Ibid., 252 [277].
67. Ibid., 538 [600].
68. Ibid., 83 [87].
69. Barth's wording here is very important. Note that he states that Paul's subject is the reconciliation of "the world made by God with Himself." In other words, there is no either/or alternative (either God must be reconciled to us or we must be reconciled to God). Rather, God reconciles *himself* to us in that "He made Christ sin" so that we as sinners and sin itself have been abolished in Christ's death. By doing this, God also reconciles us to himself. But the Godness of God in doing that which is necessary to justification will not allow for humanity/the world to be the sole object of God's work as though the object were not also (and in the first instance!) God himself.

has to be made good is on our side."[70] It is important for Barth to stress that Paul does not speak here of the atonement removing an enmity of God against humanity.[71] "God does not need reconciliation with men, but men need reconciliation with Him, and . . . God has made this reconciliation."[72]

Another point Barth makes in tandem with highlighting the priority of God's righteousness is that our reconciliation happens as an act of the free grace of God. As the grace of God triumphs over humanity and in the face of opposition, it does so "miraculously, unilaterally and autocratically—to its own self-glory."[73] Barth's take on Paul's words in Rom. 5:20, "where sin increased, grace abounded all the more," is that the power of God's grace is revealed "only where it shows itself and acts as His free grace to the undeserving, as grace for lost sinners."[74] It is nothing but the sheer mercy of God, who, "without being untrue to Himself . . . is gracious to man, because first He is gracious to Himself, in His own inward being."[75] That God freely crosses the yawning abyss that separates humanity from God is "conceivable only in the fact of His act of power and love."[76] Barth points out that Paul stresses the reality of God's free grace in using the remarkable verb "ὑπερπερισσεύειν (to overflow, to superabound, 5:20)."[77] Furthermore, Rom. 5:5 indicates that the goal of God's reconciling work is that God's love is poured into our hearts, that the world is completely converted to God. The radical message of the gospel is that God has loved first, "not merely before we loved Him, but while we were yet sinners, while we were yet enemies (Rom. 5:8, 10)."[78] God's action in the atonement "consists in the fact that God has given Himself up"[79]

70. *CD* IV/1, 74 [79]. To support his point, Barth adds that in Rom. 1:18 "the presentation of the ὀγρὴ θεοῦ consists solely in a description of the corruption of man to which God has given him up." Idem.
71. Ibid.
72. Ibid.
73. Ibid., 68 [73].
74. Ibid., 69 [73].
75. Ibid., 487 [542].
76. Ibid., 82 [86].
77. Ibid.
78. Ibid., 72 [77].
79. Ibid., 72 [76].

to us who have made ourselves God's enemies. "Jesus Christ fought His enemies, the enemies of God—as we all are (Rom. 5:10, Col. 1:21)—no, He loved His enemies, by identifying Himself with them."[80]

Having established the foundational role played by both the righteousness of God and the free grace of God in justification, Barth next expounds on the role played by the notion of exchange or substitution in the conversion of the world to God, emphasizing first that it is in the person of Jesus Christ that this occurs.[81] This comes as no surprise; we have already seen the apocalyptic focus on the history of Jesus Christ inherent in Barth's forensic doctrine of justification. In considering the particulars of the exchange, Barth first notes Paul's words in Rom. 5:19 that "by one man's obedience many will be made righteous"; he then ponders the significance that God is in Christ and that "what the man Jesus does is God's own work."[82] He stresses the importance of the obedience of Jesus Christ not being alien to God, otherwise it would be impossible for the many to be made righteous "by the obedience of a being which is not properly God."[83] Unlike the reading given by Barth in his second Romans commentary,[84] here we see Barth's mature Christology at play. He highlights that the self-humbling and obedient action of Christ, on behalf of and in place of humanity, is the very self-humiliation and obedience of God. "There

80. Ibid., 244 [268].
81. Ibid., 75 [80].
82. Ibid., 193 [211].
83. Ibid., 196 [214].
84. In the second Romans commentary, Christ's obedience unto death was seen by Barth as an act of the human being. There is no clear explanation of the relation of divine activity to the human self-sacrificial activity of Jesus in the event of the cross. "What is missing is a Christology which could make it clear how a human act, could, at the same time, be a divine act. For a divine act alone can have universal significance and immediate efficacy. At this stage of his development, Barth has no doctrine of the incarnation, no account of the ontological constitution of the Redeemer." Bruce L. McCormack, "Longing for a New World: On Socialism, Eschatology and Apocalyptic in Barth's Early Dialectical Theology," in *Theologie im Umbruch der Moderne: Karl Barths frühe Dialektische Theologie*, Christentum unk Kultur Band 15, ed. Georg Pfleiderer and Harald Matern (Zürich: Theologischer Verlag, 2014), 148n45. For example, Barth comments on 5:19, saying, "But Christ is the 'new' subject, the EGO of the coming world. This EGO receives and bears and reveals the divine *justification* and election—*This is my beloved Son, in whom I am well pleased.* This qualification of man, this appointing as the Son of God, through the power of the Resurrection (i. 3, 4), of Him who was born of the seed of David, is also non-concrete, unintuitable, and non-historical. Flesh and blood cannot reveal it unto us." See Barth, *Epistle to the Romans*, trans. Edwyn C. Hoskyns (London: Oxford University Press, 1933), 181 [160], *rev.*

and then, in the existence of the man Jesus of Nazareth, who was the Son of God, this event [of Christ's being judged in our place] came to pass in the kingly freedom of the God who is holy and righteous in His faithfulness and mercy."[85] The freedom and righteousness of God in justification were already central components in Barth's apocalyptic understanding of justification in the second edition of his Romans commentary. What is added here in *CD* IV/1 is the astounding idea that God's freedom and righteousness are revealed in the fact that God is the subject of the act of atonement "in such a way that His presence and action as the Reconciler of the world coincide and are indeed identical with the existence of the humiliated and lowly and obedient man Jesus of Nazareth."[86] In all freedom and as the expression of divine righteousness "God chooses condescension. He chooses humiliation, lowliness and obedience."[87] What takes place is the divine fulfillment of a divine decree. It takes place in the freedom of God, but "in the inner necessity of the freedom of God and not in the play of a sovereign *liberum arbitrium*."[88] This is a mystery of God's free grace revealed on the cross. Only in this way are we made righteous. That Barth is now able, as we will see, to focus on the positive promise contained in Paul's Adam/Christ typology of our actually being made righteous stems from the fact that he has thought through the being of the triune of God in light of the history of Jesus Christ, in his life, death, and resurrection.

Barth's construal of the exchange that takes place in the event of justification is centered on what happened in the history of the one man, Jesus Christ. Returning again to Paul's arguments in Romans 5, Barth submits that "[a]ccording to Rom. 5:6f it [Jesus' death] happened

85. *CD* IV/1, 223 [245].
86. Ibid., 199 [217].
87. Ibid.
88. Ibid., 195 [213]. A basic problem facing the traditional Protestant doctrine of justification is that it cannot escape the charge that God's decision for us is arbitrary. Even if we were to respond to the charge with God's decision to enter into the covenant of grace with humanity and God's faithfulness to the promises made in that covenant, we would still be unable to answer why God enters into this covenant. Barth's solution to this problem is to "understand God's choices as limited to the *means* he selects for accomplishing an end that he has not chosen but is simply given in what God is (and in how God is what God is)," which results in the "specter of the arbitrary" disappearing. See McCormack, "Can We Still Speak of 'Justification by Faith'?," 176.

at a particular time (κατὰ καιρόν). It was indeed when we were still without strength, sinners (v. 8), even enemies (v. 10), that He died for us (ὑπὲρ ἡμῶν, v. 8), that we were reconciled to God by the death of His Son (v. 10)."[89] Barth references Rom. 5:6 two more times,[90] urging, with Paul, that God in Christ redeemed us, acting for us but without us—"everything depends on this."[91] He clarifies that the event of our salvation took place in the history of Christ's death and resurrection; it "is not a redemptive happening which embraces both Him and us, but the redemptive happening which embraces us in His existence, which takes us up into itself."[92] Again, Barth urges, "[t]he world is not itself capable of this reconciliation."[93] Humanity is absolutely powerless to effect justification.

It is only by looking to the history of Christ that Barth finds the grounds by which to speak of our justification, in both its negative and positive aspects. He notes that the New Testament explicitly sets Jesus' death in relationship to sin, even as the positive side of his death is "always in the background," citing "Rom. 5:9: 'Being now justified by his blood.'"[94] Barth asks after the ontological place of sin in the Bible, suggesting that "[i]n the Bible sin in all its fearful reality is at a disadvantage compared with even the most modest creature in that it has only 'entered into' the world, as we are told in Rom. 5:12. It does not belong to the creation of God. It can be present and active only as an alien."[95] De Boer's analysis, too, finds that Paul, in Rom. 5:12, 14, 17, and 21, personifies sin and death "as alien intruders into the human cosmos."[96] Barth speaks of sin variously as "the obstacle which has to be removed and overcome," "the source which has to be blocked in the atonement," and finally as "the destruction which threatens man, which already engulfs him and drags him down."[97] In the death

89. *CD* IV/1, 224 [246].
90. Ibid., 229, 231 [252, 253].
91. Ibid., 231 [253].
92. Ibid., 229 [251–52].
93. Ibid., 251 [276].
94. Ibid., 255 [280].
95. Ibid., 139 [153].
96. De Boer, *Defeat of Death*, 147.
97. *CD* IV/1, 252–53 [278].

of Christ, God has "spoiled principalities and powers, made a show of them openly (as prisoners), and triumphed over them."[98] Noting that Rom. 5:12 also speaks of death coming into the world by sin, Barth remarks that, in the New Testament, the concept of death "means not only the dying of man but the destruction which qualifies or rather disqualifies it, eternal death, death as the invincibly threatening force of dissolution."[99] While Barth acknowledges Paul's apocalyptic description of death as an "objective and alien power," he primarily understands it spiritually in terms of "God's abandoning of the men who have abandoned Him."[100] Barth follows Paul in speaking of Christ's death as releasing humanity "from an imprisonment"[101] that had resulted from their subjection to sin.[102] It is an imprisonment from which we cannot release ourselves, but from which Christ releases us when he takes our place and judges and destroys sin in his death. "For wrong is an outrage and abomination to God. It has to perish. The right of God confronts it with such majesty. It cannot exist before it. It is taken and burnt up and destroyed by the life of God like dry wood by the fire. This is the event of His righteousness. What takes place in it is the breaking of a catastrophe."[103] God would not be God if sin were not dealt with in this way.[104]

While sin and death are spoken of by Barth as powers by which

98. Ibid., 255 [281].
99. Ibid., 253 [278].
100. Barth, *Christ and Adam*, 53 [19].
101. *CD* IV/1, 256 [282]. Käsemann notes that "for Paul, salvation does not primarily mean the end of past disaster and the forgiving cancellation of former guilt. It is, according to Rom. 5:9f.; 8:2, freedom from the power of sin, death and the divine wrath; that is to say, it is the possibility of new life. He therefore gave a more radical turn to the tradition which he took over." Ernst Käsemann, "The Saving Significance of the Death of Jesus in Paul," in *Perspectives on Paul*, trans. Margaret Kohl (Philadelphia: Fortress Press, 1971), 44.
102. Käsemann highlights that when Paul speaks of salvation as deliverance from the wrath of God in Romans 5, "what is meant is not satisfaction but liberation and release by the act of a change of masters." Ernst Käsemann, "Some Thoughts on the Theme 'The Doctrine of Reconciliation in the New Testament,'" in *The Future of Our Religious Past: Essays in Honour of Rudolf Bultmann*, ed. James M. Robinson, trans. Charles E. Carlston and Robert P. Scharlemann (New York: Harper & Row, 1964), 58.
103. *CD* IV/1, 539 [602].
104. Barth clarifies, as well, that in the New Testament, in contrast to the emphasis on "our redemption from the powers of darkness accomplished in Jesus Christ," the concept of forgiveness "is brought into surprisingly little direct relation to the death of Jesus Christ." Ibid., 255 [281].

humanity is imprisoned and must be released, they are also clearly understood to be no match for the grace of God. "[W]here sin took the upper hand His grace did not cease or retire, but overflowed in the form of avenging righteousness, showing itself to be superabounding (Rom. 5:20)."[105] Here Barth and de Boer give different interpretations, for de Boer characterizes Rom. 5:12 and 21 as putting "sin and death on the one side and grace on the other . . . personified and conceptualized as cosmological rulers in conflict."[106] Barth, on the other hand, agrees that humanity is imprisoned and even speaks of Jesus Christ as the liberator, but he ultimately finds that there is no contest or true conflict between God's grace and the power of sin and death. God's grace is so much more powerful than sin and death. Sin "does not exist in any way on the basis of its own independent right, or even in its dreadful reality by its own independent power. . . . It has its power, but it is the stealthy power of impotence."[107] Moreover, Barth finally understands humanity to be responsible for their imprisonment. Considering Rom. 5:12, Barth writes of human existence imprisoned within a "circle of evil being and evil activity," into which God "makes Himself his liberator in Jesus Christ. But it is still his *peccatum*, the act in which he makes himself a prisoner and therefore has to be a prisoner."[108] De Boer, on the other hand, maintains that "Paul sees all human history as a monolithic whole in which sin and death reign in tandem as cosmic and cosmological powers."[109] He further argues that Paul, in Romans 5, places the "motif of personal accountability or culpability . . . in a new context, a cosmological one. For Paul, the fact that 'all sinned' . . . signifies that all human beings since Adam have been and are, as he has asserted in 3.9, 'under the power of sin.'"[110]

As we have already seen, crucial to de Boer's reading of Paul in Romans 5 is the idea that Paul introduces cosmic apocalyptic motifs into forensic apocalyptic arguments in such a way that the

105. Ibid., 487 [543].
106. De Boer, *Defeat of Death*, 160.
107. *CD* IV/1, 139 [153].
108. Ibid., 500 [557–58].
109. De Boer, *Defeat of Death*, 173.
110. Ibid., 161.

cosmological themes overtake the forensic ones. Barth's reading in *Christ and Adam*, and his references to Romans 5 in *CD* IV/1, in contrast, show priority for both motifs, without either overtaking the other. Barth's doctrine of justification is grounded on a forensic apocalyptic eschatology that is cosmic in scope. What matters for Barth, ultimately, is that each apocalyptic strand is significant only because they have been christologically modified by Paul. As de Boer himself says, "Paul does not preach apocalyptic eschatology, not even Christian apocalyptic eschatology; he preaches the crucified Christ whom God raised from the dead, nothing else."[111] Thus neither cosmic nor forensic apocalypticism is of any importance for Paul, unless they contribute to a greater understanding of the power of God's righteousness, manifest in the history of Jesus Christ, to save.

Where de Boer and Barth do in fact converge in their understanding of the cosmic apocalyptic line in Romans 5 is in regards to Paul's use of the word "all." We have noted that de Boer finds Paul treating "all human history as a monolithic whole." Barth, noting Paul's use of the word "all" in Rom. 11:32; 3:23; and 5:12, suggests that we consider "what we mean by the word 'history.' The verdict that all have sinned certainly implies a verdict on that which is human history. . . . There is, in fact, a history of the world which is grounded on the ignoring and rejection of the will and Word and work of God and determined throughout by this ignoring and rejection."[112] Referencing Paul's "God gave them up" in Rom. 1:24, 26, and 28, Barth concludes that human history is "concluded in disobedience."[113] More importantly, though, humanity is not outside God's control. "The history of the world which God made in Jesus Christ, and with a view to Him, cannot cease to have its center and goal in Him."[114] It is God who has given the name "Adam" to the whole history of humanity. "It is Adamic history, the history of Adam. . . . [T]his is the reason why there can never be any progress—it continually corresponds to his history."[115] Considering Rom. 5:12, Barth

111. De Boer, "Paul and Apocalyptic Eschatology," 368.
112. *CD* IV/1, 505 [563].
113. Ibid., 506 [564].
114. Ibid.

finds that Adam, for Paul, is the one "by whom 'sin entered into the world and death by sin; and so death passed upon all men, for that all have sinned.'"[116] The reason Paul knows this, Barth surmises from Rom. 5:12–21, is that he recognized, in Adam, "quite a different figure" who also "came directly from God, not as a creature only, but as the Son of God and Himself God by nature."[117] Christ represents all of humanity, too, but he was not like them. According to Rom. 5:18–19, Christ "represented them as a genuine leader, making atonement by His obedience, covering their disobedience, justifying them before God."[118] Christ, therefore, is the original Representative of humanity. Adam is only the prophetic type of Jesus Christ (Rom. 5:14). Paul "knew Jesus Christ first and then Adam."[119] Adam is only the negative side of Jesus Christ. In Adam, "God's righteousness and love are victorious by becoming visible and glorious in the figure and parable of human iniquity and enmity."[120] Furthermore, Rom. 5:15–17 indicates that Adam and Christ cannot be compared in substance (*sachlich*), even though they are alike in form. "The former is like the rainbow in relation to the sun. It is only a reflection of it. It has no independent existence."[121] In a corresponding manner, then, "is the relationship between the offence of men in the person and act of the one and the free gift of righteousness and life which comes with the judgment of God in the person and act of this other."[122] What transpires in Christ provides the derivative form of what occurs in Adam. There is no counterbalancing or equality.

Similarly, de Boer points out that the "universality of salvation corresponds to, and addresses, the universal hegemony of sin and death. . . . Unless salvation is universal, sin and death will not have been completely defeated, and God's saving action and thus his sovereignty will remain an extremely limited affair."[123] It is because

115. Ibid., 508 [567].
116. Ibid., 512 [571].
117. Ibid.
118. Ibid.
119. Ibid., 513 [572].
120. *SR*, 37 [74].
121. *CD* IV/1, 513 [572].
122. Ibid.

Barth understands Paul to be making Christ the first and true Adam, from which all humanity has its center and goal, that we find hope that Adamic history is not the end of the story. What is really true of humanity is not who we are in Adam, but who we are in Christ.

> It is beyond the threshold which Jesus Christ has crossed, and every man in Him, that he [Paul] hears in Him the sentence on . . . all men as a Word of God and not of man—a sentence against which there can be no appeal passed on the man of sin, who was every man, but who no longer exists now that God has had mercy on all with the same universality with which He once concluded all in disobedience.[124]

De Boer suggests that Paul's claim of universal salvation is an expression of his theology of the cross, the upshot of which is "that God justifies and thus saves not the righteous but the ungodly. In Paul's view, God saves only the ungodly, those who cannot save themselves, a category that includes all human beings from Adam onward. . . . Salvation is a gift granted by God and takes effect solely at God's initiative."[125] On this point, Barth and de Boer agree. Salvation is a divine gift for the ungodly, an umbrella term embracing all people.

This brings us back around to the positive aspect of justification, achieved in God raising Jesus from the dead as an act of vindication and acceptance of the sinless Jesus. Barth speaks of its essence as "the act of righteousness (δικαίωμα) and obedience (ὑποταγή) of the one man in the power of which the vindication of all men was accomplished as the promise of life (δικαίωσις εἰς ζωήν), in which in the last judgment many will be presented righteous (δίκαιον) in the sight of God and His angels and the whole world (Rom. 5:18f)."[126] In the history of Jesus Christ, the true Representative of all humanity, there is both the end of the old age on the cross and the beginning of the new in the resurrection. As justification is complete in Jesus Christ, he alone is the righteous human who "as the Son of God obedient to the Father in fulfillment of this action of God . . . lived and acted as the one man obedient to

123. De Boer, "Paul and Apocalyptic Eschatology," 373.
124. *CD* IV/1, 513 [572–73].
125. De Boer, "Paul and Apocalyptic Eschatology," 373–74.
126. *CD* IV/1, 272–73 [300].

God."[127] Jesus Christ is the new human, and in him redemption is an actuality. In the same way that Christ's death has completely removed and abolished sin and the sinner, so, too, "the right and life which are before [us] according to the same sentence are [our] whole right and life."[128] Thus in Christ the reality of our future righteousness is already in the present. The reason this is so, Barth says, is the divine declaration of acquittal.

> Again, it is not merely a verbal remission. As pardoning, it is the effectual and righteous alteration of the human situation from its very foundation. . . . The divine pardoning is not a remission "as if" man were not a sinner. As pardoning, it is the creative work of God, in the power of which man, even as the old man that he was and still is, is no longer that man, but is already another man, the man he will be, the new man.[129]

The promise of our complete justification, of being made righteous, "is true and reliable; it cannot fail in anything of its content. As eschatology it is 'realized eschatology.' In and with it, its whole content enters the present of man."[130] God's righteous acquittal of humanity

127. Ibid., 257 [283].
128. Ibid., 596 [664].
129. Ibid., 597 [667]. Barth switches here from using the term *Freispruch*, "acquittal," to using the term *Verzeihung*, "pardon." It is important to put the passage in context to understand what Barth is doing here. He begins by stating that acquittal (*Freispruch*), which is declared in the promise that the reality of our future is already in the present, means that we are *totus iustus*. He then reflects on the promise of our completed justification under the creedal concept of "the forgiveness of sins" by asking after the meaning of the forgiveness (*Vergebung*) of sins. Barth states that it "obviously does not mean to make what has happened not to have happened. . . . The act of the divine forgiveness is that God sees and knows this stain [of our sins] . . . and abhors it infinitely . . . yet He does not take it into consideration, He overlooks it, He covers it, He passes it by, He puts it behind Him. . . . That God forgives means that He pardons (*Gott vergibt heißt schon: er verzeiht*)." Ibid., 597 [666]. What Barth is doing here, in effect, is reflecting on the concept of acquittal in light of the more common Christian confession of forgiveness of sins, but only by considering God's forgiveness as God's pardon (*Verzeihung*). He is trying to avoid the idea that God's pardoning is somehow illegitimate or unlawful (Barth's phrase here is *unrechtmässiges Verzeihen*, which Bromiley translates as "verbal remission") and thus lacking in the power to really alter the human situation. Pardon is thus a work of eschatological acquittal. It is how we experience this acquittal here and now. We are not yet the acquitted persons we will be; we are not yet new creation and, therefore, not yet innocent in ourselves. We are this only in Christ. That God forgives us means that we are given a provisional pardoning for our lives here and now, between the first and second advents of Christ. We can see Barth working with this provisional element of acquittal when he writes: "If God's sentence concerning man is that He will know nothing of this stain, then the stain is washed away and removed, and although man still bears it, in spite of it he is without stain, in spite of his wrong he is in the right." Ibid., 597 [666–67]. Tellingly, in wrapping up this exercise in reflecting on acquittal under the phrase "the forgiveness of sins" (*Vergebung der Sünden*), Barth submits that "[i]t is, however, better not to try to say everything only in this way" (*Es wird aber doch besser sein, nicht Alles nur damit sagen zu wollen*)." Ibid., 601 [668], *rev.*

has altered the very foundation of human history because our acquittal has been pronounced on us as we are in Christ, as Christ has acted for us and in our place as the true, righteous human before God. The foundation of Adamic history is destroyed, and we are "placed in a very definite new situation from which to start."[131] Barth correlates the ontological reality of the new age in Christ with our knowledge of the new age through the eyes of faith. New creation "is real in Christ and nowhere else"; for Christ is our true and only righteousness, in which "we can participate only in faith in Him."[132] Insofar as we receive the promise of our righteousness in Christ, by faith, our justification is already complete. This is the apocalyptic tension between the already and the not yet. As de Boer urges, "the meaning of faith is actually determined by the cosmological-apocalyptic disclosure of God's righteousness and of sin in the crucifixion of Christ."[133] The element missing in de Boer's assessment is, again, the new life made in Christ's resurrection. As we have seen, for Barth "justification—the replacement of the old human with the new—is an event in Jesus Christ prior to and apart from the faith of those for whom it was accomplished. Christian faith embraces the divine verdict, and in so doing the new humanity which justification ushers in is realized in the lives of individuals."[134] In the event of the resurrection, we are pronounced innocent in Jesus Christ and given a new life. "His innocence, the innocence in which He bore and bore away our sin, the innocence which was manifested in His resurrection, was and is our innocence."[135] With the verdict of acquittal in the resurrection of Jesus Christ, God tells the truth about the true being of all humanity, because what we truly are is what God determined for us to be, in election, in Jesus Christ. Hence there is no ground for the charge of legal fiction.

At this point, we have completed our examination of Barth's mature

130. Ibid., 598–99 [668].
131. Ibid., 598 [667].
132. Ibid., 641 [716].
133. De Boer, "Paul and Apocalyptic Eschatology," 366.
134. Adam Neder, *Participation in Christ: An Entry into Karl Barth's Church Dogmatics* (Louisville: Westminster John Knox, 2009), 53.
135. *CD* IV/1, 556 [620].

doctrine of justification in light of his theological interpretation of Romans 5. We have found Barth's doctrine shaped by both the forensic notion of acquittal and the cosmic scope of all humanity in Christ, the true Adam. Following Paul, Barth paints sin and death as enslaving powers over which God's right has conquered. Both sin and the sinner are abolished in the death of Christ. More powerfully still, in the resurrection God's grace overflows for new humanity in the gift of righteousness and life as Christ is seen to be the one true human in which all humanity has been included. In the next two chapters, we will look at Barth's understanding of Romans 7 and 8 and the corresponding doctrines of theological anthropology and eschatology as they are related to justification. We will continue to see Barth work out Paul's apocalyptic notion of new creation in Christ even as we see him repeatedly tie it to the Reformational emphasis, in the forensic doctrine of justification, on the alien righteousness of Christ.

7

The Role of Theological Anthropology in Barth's Forensic Apocalyptic Doctrine of Justification

> The ontological determination of humanity is grounded in the fact that one man among all others is the man Jesus. . . . Theological anthropology has no choice in this matter. It is not yet or no longer theological anthropology if it tries to pose and answer the question of the true being of man from any other angle. We remember who and what the man Jesus is. As we have seen, He is the one creaturely being in whose existence we have to do immediately and directly with the being of God also. Again, He is the creaturely being in whose existence God's act of deliverance has taken place for all other men. He is the creaturely being in whom God as the Saviour of all men also reveals and affirms His own glory as the Creator. He is the creaturely being who as such embodies the sovereignty of God, or conversely the sovereignty of God which as such actualises this creaturely being. He is the creaturely being whose existence consists in His fulfillment of the will of God. And finally He is the creaturely being who as such not only exists from God and in God but absolutely for God instead of for Himself.
>
> —Karl Barth, *CD* III/2

> The dialectic of justification is not that of a to and fro, or an up and down,

> but at every present it is that of a history in which the wrong of the justified man is (in all its reality) behind him and his right before him, in which, therefore, he can have his future only in the movement to his right and his past only in his wrong (in all its reality), in which he can be only on the way from there to here, because that and that alone corresponds to the positive will of God.
>
> —Karl Barth, *CD* IV/1

This chapter takes up the doctrinal theme of theological anthropology in its relationship to Barth's forensic apocalyptic doctrine of justification. If Barth's reconstructed doctrine of election offers a deep recentering of Reformed theology in Christology, his theological anthropology, to borrow a phrase from Emeril Lagasse, kicks it up a notch. By making Christology basic to his dogmatic reflections, Barth offers a new take on the traditional doctrinal understanding of humanity. Jesus Christ alone not only reveals but also establishes human nature. "More than anything else, Barth wants to shake anthropology free from the assumptions that 'being in Christ' is merely one modulation of something more humanly basic, and that human history and activity can be understood without direct and immediate reference to the history and activity of Jesus Christ."[1] Käsemann confirms this take on theological anthropology to be derived directly from Paul: "[*i*]*mago dei* is for him Christ and Christ alone."[2] Barth's approach to theological anthropology derives from the decision made in the doctrine of election that there is no such thing as an independent relationship between creation and God apart from Jesus Christ. "Jesus Christ is the decision of God in favour of this attitude or relation. He is Himself the relation."[3] With the election of Jesus Christ and the fulfillment of his election in history, "a decision has been made concerning the being and nature of every man by the mere fact that with him and among all other men [Jesus Christ] too has been a man."[4]

1. John Webster, "Rescuing the Subject: Barth and Postmodern Anthropology," in *Karl Barth: A Future for Postmodern Theology?*, ed. Geoff Thompson and Christiaan Mostert (Hindmarsh: Australian Theological Forum, 2000), 61.
2. Ernst Käsemann, "On Paul's Anthropology," in *Perspectives on Paul*, trans. Margaret Kohl (Philadelphia: Fortress Press, 1971), 22.
3. *CD* II/2, 7 [5].
4. *CD* III/2, 133 [159].

It is because Jesus Christ alone determines the truth and reality of human nature that Barth describes justification under the forensic rubric of God's unconditional acquittal (*Freispruch*) of humanity. This is "the central event of all human history,"[5] and it refers "to all the men who live both before and after."[6] God's judgment of each person is a "divisive sentence"[7] made in human history, and it is based on God's election and rejection. God's sentence on us contains the whole of our justification. The sentence is "divisive" in that it divides us between the human as the wrongdoer, who is the object of God's rejection, and the human as the elect of God, who is created and called to be God's covenant partner. There is an "unbridgeable gulf"[8] between these two humans—the one is in the past, and the other is in the future. God's divisive sentence "locks up the one in order to free the other."[9] Confirming Barth's sentiment, Käsemann notes that Paul

> does not share our interest in the permanent identity of man with himself and in the continuity of history in its manifold phases. It is hiatus which is the mark of that historicity in which the world of creation is divided from the world of sin, from the world under the lordship of Christ and from the world in the reality of the resurrection; and the breaches are so deep that only the fall of man and miracle can bridge them.[10]

Furthermore, Barth suggests that the divisive sentence of justification—our acquittal—is not a static state into which we enter. Rather, "It is the living Word of the living God in the present of every man."[11] Hence Barth establishes justification as a transition in which we move forward away from our past sinfulness, which requires death, to our right future, which is our new life.

What lies behind the notion of justification as transition is the truth that only in Christ is our justification a completed act. We ourselves live from and to our justification in Christ, which is indeed a completed

5. *CD* IV/1, 568 [634].
6. Ibid.
7. Ibid.
8. Ibid.
9. Ibid., 568 [635].
10. Käsemann, "On Paul's Anthropology," 22.
11. *CD* IV/1, 573 [639].

state of affairs. Our own personal history of justification moves forward only because God has acted decisively for us in the history and activity of Jesus Christ. Jesus Christ, for us and for our salvation, has played out our history of rejection and election in his death and resurrection. Therefore each present moment of our own history contains both this past and this future. Yet, because our justification is totally complete in Christ, in each moment of our present justification, our past rejection is behind us and our future election is before us in the same sequence as the death and resurrection of Jesus Christ. Until the eschaton we are always ever "still the old man and not yet the new."[12] As long as we are in time and consider our own person, Barth says we are *simul peccator et iustus*[13]—both altogether, not half and half, but both altogether, yet *only* in transition and *already* with the future promise of *totus iustus* coming to bear on us in the present. If we are not in this transition, then justification no longer applies to us; for it is only the sinful person who can be pronounced free by God's sentence.

In answer to the question "Who is the person who is justified?" Barth would respond: "[a]ccording to the divine sentence which justifies him he is the man of the history in which there takes place both this turning away and this turning to."[14] In other words, the person who is justified becomes the person "of this history—the history of Jesus Christ. . . . He becomes the man who in every present has both this past and this future . . . in the same sequence as the death and resurrection of Jesus Christ."[15] The key to understanding Barth's description of justification is located precisely in his insistence that

> we are never speaking of a state but of a history, of the transition which does, of course, move in one direction and therefore not in another, . . . and therefore moves from here to there, . . . in which man stands under a twofold determination to the extent that he goes forward from the "before" of his wrong and therefore his death to the "after" of his right and therefore his life.[16]

12. Ibid., 574 [640].
13. Barth, to highlight justification as transition, reverses the sequence of the classic Reformation dictum *simul iustus et peccator*.
14. Ibid., 573 [639].
15. Ibid.
16. Ibid.

The outcome of centering the doctrine of humanity on the history of Jesus Christ is this dialectical pattern of the transition in our subjective experience of justification.

This chapter argues that Barth's theological anthropology shapes his doctrine of justification dialectically in that the justified person not only was and is also still a sinner standing under God's judgment, even as she is already justified and thus made new, righteous, and free for life. In this way, justification is a continual event in the life of a Christian. It is an event that consists of a transition that always begins with acquittal from sin. "Only as it begins there can it and will it be completed in the re-establishment of his right, the renewal of his life."[17] Barth further elaborates: "[t]here is no present in which the justification of man is not still this beginning of justification."[18] It is because Barth's theological anthropology is centered on Jesus Christ that the justification of an individual is understood dialectically as a repeated transitional event consisting of a constant movement away from sin and toward our new life in the Spirit. Insofar as sin and death have been abolished in Christ's death, our justification is always a transition away from sin. And, insofar as Christ's resurrection inaugurates new creation, our justification is a transition toward our new life in the Spirit.

As this chapter explores Barth's treatment of the doctrinal theme of theological anthropology, which arises from Romans 7, it finds some of Barth's most sustained exegetical reflections on a Romans passage in *CD* IV/1. As well, these reflections are very consistent with those in *A Shorter Commentary on Romans*. For that reason, we will integrate our analysis of Barth's theological reading of Romans 7 from both of these sources, as it will afford us a fuller picture of the way Pauline theology informs Barth's elucidation not only of his theological anthropology but also of his apocalyptically cast doctrine of justification. As we investigate Barth's theological exegesis of Romans 7, we will incorporate supporting insights from two scholars of Paul's

17. Ibid., 574 [640].
18. Ibid., 575 [642].

apocalyptic eschatology, Ernst Käsemann and Paul Meyer, which will serve to reinforce Barth's contribution to Pauline apocalyptic scholarship. One important difference between Barth and Meyer, their relationship to the Reformational doctrine of justification, will also be discussed. In conclusion, I will suggest three ways that Barth's theological anthropology, as it is seen in his integration of Pauline apocalyptic eschatology with Reformational forensicism, brings out the dialectical dimensions of an apocalyptically construed doctrine of justification.

Justification as Transition into Liberation in Romans 7

For Barth, more than any other passage in the New Testament, Romans 7 provides a helpful expression of exactly who the justified person is, especially as it keenly illustrates the beginning place of justification. Barth bemoans the fact that so much commentary on Romans 7 has missed the main statement of the chapter: that we have been liberated from the law of sin and death (7:1–6 and 7:24–25), and has instead been preoccupied, unhelpfully, with what he calls Paul's "additional notes in smaller print" in 7:7–12 and especially 7:13–23.[19] Meyer, too, rails against readings of Romans 7 that conclude

> that it is the part of true Christian humility and self-knowledge to find that conflict [between flesh and Spirit] to be "the present design and argument of the apostle," even though there is not a syllable in Rom. 7:7–25 about life in Christ, and even though Paul himself has signaled to his reader in both 7:6b and 8:1–2 that the rest of chap. 7 is to be understood as the antithesis to chap. 8 and not in simple continuity with it.[20]

The latter half of Romans 7 provides a picture of a situation "which can only interest us as our past situation,"[21] as that from which we have been liberated, namely, the law of sin and death. Barth clarifies

19. *SR*, 45 [90].
20. Paul W. Meyer, "The Worm at the Core of the Apple: Exegetical Reflections on Romans 7," in *The Conversation Continues: Studies in Paul and John in Honor of J. Louis Martyn*, ed. Robert T. Fortna and Beverly Roberts Gaventa (Nashville: Abingdon, 1990), 68.
21. *SR*, 45 [90].

that Paul's desire is not to draw our attention to *what* happens in this situation but rather "to the fact that we have been called away from it."[22] The real importance of the realm of sin and death, which Paul describes in 7:7–23, is that "in the faith in the Gospel it is behind us."[23]

We recall from our investigation in chapter 2 that Barth's reading of Romans 7 in the second edition of his Romans commentary stressed the starkest contrast between human striving, summed up in religion,[24] after freedom and the freedom of God to save us. Barth understood a dualism to control the whole realm of religion, with the consequence that sin abounds (5:20) there. Meyer puts it sharply: "[t]he problem with human religion rests not with the 'ungodly' but with those who separate themselves as the 'godly' and in that way seek to establish 'a righteousness of their own' (10:3)."[25] Käsemann, too, understands that for Paul, religion "again and again introduces a process of degeneracy which ruins both man's understanding and his morality, and transforms the world into chaos. It is only under the lordship of Christ that the devout man ceases to make his worship a means of self-justification and self-praise."[26] Christ's death is the means by which we are freed from the limits of human religion and freed for God's possibility. While Barth drops the focus on religion in his subsequent interpretations of Romans 7 in *A Shorter Commentary on Romans* and *CD* IV/1, what is instructive is the element that he carries over from his reading in the second edition of the Romans commentary: "Jesus Christ is the new man, standing beyond all piety, beyond all human possibility. . . . He is—what I am not—my existential I—I—the I which in God, in the freedom of God—I am!"[27] Barth urges that we listen to

22. Ibid., 46 [91].
23. Ibid.
24. Interestingly, Martyn also finds Paul's talk of the law principally to be about religion. "Since God has elected to make things right via the death of Christ, rather than via the Law (2:21), there is now—emphatically for the Galatian situation—a specific antinomy between the cross and circumcision, between the rectifying death of Christ and all religion . . . . And since the Law (*scil.* religion) is in fact impotent to curb the Flesh, it is crucial to see that the true and potent opposite to that monster is the Spirit, rather than the Law." See J. Louis Martyn, "Apocalyptic Antinomies," in *Theological Issues in the Letters of Paul* (Nashville: Abingdon, 1997), 120.
25. Meyer, "Worm at the Core of the Apple," 70.
26. Käsemann, "On Paul's Anthropology," 16.
27. Karl Barth, *The Epistle to the Romans*, trans. Edwyn C. Hoskyns (London: Oxford University Press, 1933), 269 [252].

Paul's words in Romans 7 as not merely descriptive of his situation before his conversion: "[w]e must not deprive this *am* [7:24] of its heavy significance."[28] He reminds us that this is a point the Reformers well understood Paul to be making, namely, that Paul is describing his past, present, and future existence. "Paul is thrust into a dualism which contradicts itself"[29] but into which the grace and freedom of God break through.

Barth's main claim, that the essence of justification is always a transition, is grounded on a strong reading of 7:24–25. Only the person who knows that her justification begins always in the situation of sin, as made clear in 7:7–25, can go forward, almost abruptly, to the good news of 8:1–2, where new life has become an actuality. In other words, it is the justified sinner, in the beginning of her transition, who is described in Romans 7. It is clear that Barth falls in line with Augustine and Luther in seeing Romans 7 as a portrayal of a "spiritual" person. Indeed, he calls 7:7–25 a description of "genuinely spiritual self-knowledge."[30] The key to understanding Barth's commentary on these verses is his emphasis on a person's "self-knowledge," which is, in fact, "most realistic."[31] Only someone confronted by the gospel realizes, by Christ's light, her own captivity to sin. Meyer puts it this way: "Romans 7:7–25 is a theological description, cast in a retrospective and reflective mode, of the destructive power of sin—by one who has himself known it and been delivered from it—and that its antithesis—announced already in the contrasting phrases of v. 6b—is provided by Paul in 8:1–11."[32] Barth, too, clarifies that Paul's "I" is a person still trapped in sin and only at the beginning of justification. Verses 21–23 describe a "strange (*wunderliche*) saint . . . a man rent in two."[33] "[I]n the split of this double existence between desire and achievement . . . is a man who is doomed to death! For what is death if it is not this split life?"[34]

28. Ibid., 270 [253].
29. Ibid.
30. *CD* IV/1, 584 [651].
31. Ibid., 583 [651].
32. Meyer, "Worm at the Core of the Apple," 65.
33. *SR*, 52 [104], *rev.*
34. Ibid., 52 [105].

Barth would thus agree with Meyer that Paul is not giving us a picture of "perfect spiritualness" in the sense of portraying a person who has arrived at the end of Christian perfection.[35] Certainly, 7:14b is most definitely not a description of our whole and perfectly justified life in Christ, but rather a description of a person "in his deepest and innermost being [as] God's enemy and the object of God's wrath."[36] Yet, because Barth understands the lived reality of our justification to be always a dynamic and dialectical process of transition, he cannot simply label Romans 7 as a description of the life of an unbeliever and leave it at that. "Note how the two sections 7:7–12 and 13–23 are dominated by the word 'I.' No sentence beginning with that word could describe man's liberation. The Christian 'I' too, the Christian 'I' particularly, must and shall admit its own state of bondage, its disruption. . . . He who confesses Jesus Christ in particular will know that I shall never be able to leave sin by myself."[37] Barth's aim in describing 7:7–25 as spiritual self-knowledge is to "safeguard the mystery of justification as the transition from wrong to right, from death to life. [Verses 7–25] prevent us from representing this transition as anything but an event and this event as anything but a miraculous act of God."[38] The self-knowledge gained by the spiritual person is that her salvation—her justification—is always an event of pure grace that comes to her while she is still a sinner. The event of grace is God's apocalyptic in-breaking that sets her free even as it puts her to death.

Meyer argues that 6:1–7:6 shows that "God's grace involves a new righteousness and integrity that alter life's previous patterns."[39] In a similar vein, Barth finds a true description of Christian life in 7:1–6. Romans 6 anticipates what Paul now discusses in more detail in chapter 7: "you may not, you cannot sin any longer, because when you yourself, the old man, died with Jesus Christ in his death, the actual 'power' of sin . . . , i.e. the law, lost its dominion over you, because you who

35. Meyer, "Worm at the Core of the Apple," 67.
36. *SR*, 52 [103].
37. Ibid., 52–53 [105–6].
38. *CD* IV/1, 584 [651].
39. Meyer, "Worm at the Core of the Apple," 71.

have died and risen with Jesus Christ are under grace and no longer under the law."[40] By "virtue of our being in the unity of our existence with that of Jesus Christ,"[41] our sinful existence "has taken place in His existence, in His [being put] to death."[42] If we die to our life in the flesh, controlled as it is by the law, we are freed "to bring forth fruit to God instead of to death (v. 4), free for service in the completely new possibility not of the letter but of the Spirit (v. 6)."[43] Christ's death has freed us "from the power of the law, and a new allegiance and a new productive life"[44] has been created for us. Barth argues that Paul's parable in 7:2–3 has one limitation. Paul tells us in 6:2ff. that we have been released from the law of sin and death as we were put to death in the death of Jesus Christ. The parable thus lacks sufficient concreteness to support this point. We have not, Barth urges, "as the wife, merely received the liberty to belong to *just anybody* else. The purpose of that death was that [we] should belong to *someone quite definite*: to the One with whom [we] have died."[45] Jesus Christ, by *his* death, "not just any death (for death as such could only create a vacuum),"[46] sets us free for new life in the Spirit by annihilating both sin and the person of sin.

Interestingly, Meyer locates the problem with Paul's legal illustration elsewhere. He notes that while the example "does not start out as a specific allusion to Mosaic law, its application pertains unmistakably to release from the condemning power that Paul's previous argument has consistently assigned to the Mosaic law."[47] What results is that Paul's argument progressively confuses "the roles of the law and the sin it condemns and discloses."[48] "Ironically, an illustration initially intended to rebut an antinomian argument has suddenly become itself susceptible to an antinomian interpretation, as if God's law and the demonic power of sin are to be identified."[49] That

40. *SR*, 46 [92].
41. *CD* IV/1, 582 [649].
42. Ibid.
43. Ibid.
44. Meyer, "Worm at the Core of the Apple," 72.
45. *SR*, 48 [95].
46. Ibid., 48 [96].
47. Meyer, "Worm at the Core of the Apple," 72.
48. Ibid.

Barth and Meyer have different concerns over Paul's parable in 7:1–6 is telling. Meyer's concern causes him to spend more time illuminating Paul's description of the enslaving power of sin in the second half of Romans 7. Barth's concern, instead, finds him focusing on how Christ's death sets us free, and so he spends more time showing how the event of justification follows the pattern of Christ's dying and rising.

While Meyer emphasizes that 7:1–6 belongs more closely to chapter 6 than to 7:7–25, Barth makes an interesting connection between verses 1–6 and 7–25, remarking that "[t]he problem of vv. 7–25 is the question of the actual death of the first husband and therefore of the legitimacy and truth of our liberation."[50] While Barth would agree with Meyer that the passage "is not autobiographical in any sense that allows it to yield details about Paul's personal life,"[51] Barth does read 7:7–25 as Paul's own self-assessment on discovering that this "first man" is indeed still very much alive, "that his being in the flesh which . . . he has put into the past is still the present."[52] Barth notes Paul's use of the present tense in 7:14–25, concluding that while we cannot simply rule out that this is a recollection of Paul's situation before conversion, neither can we limit it to *just* that. According to Barth, Paul takes justification so seriously that it is "as God's new and concealed miraculous act that he [Paul] not only *saw* it begin once in his earlier life at the very heart of the life of the first man, his own being and flesh, but he continually *sees* it begin again in this way. Every morning and every evening [our] situation is *also* one of departure in the very midst of sin."[53] Käsemann offers further corroboration for Barth's dialectical emphasis here, noting that for Paul "salvation does not simply mean a state; it is an endless path which has been thrown open to us, a path which is ceaselessly characterized by a forgetting of that which lies behind and a straining forward to that which lies ahead."[54] Barth's emphasis on justification as a continual event comes from listening to

49. Ibid.
50. *CD* IV/1, 583 [650].
51. Meyer, "Worm at the Core of the Apple," 64.
52. *CD* IV/1, 583 [650].
53. *CD* IV/1, 583 [651], *revised* and original italics restored.
54. Käsemann, "On Paul's Anthropology," 5.

Paul's focus on the apocalyptically new and disruptive action of God, which is centered in the history of Jesus Christ but must be actualized again and again in our own lives.

Noting the parallel between 6:14 and 7:1–6, Barth suggests that Paul cannot simply go from these statements straight to 8:1 because "[i]f the ensuing description of the freedom created by it [liberation from the flesh and the law of sin] was to have a genuine ring, this could not be stated as a truth which is lightly uttered and easily accepted."[55] Indeed, Paul "evidently suspects that all that has been said in Chapter 6 of the Gospel as man's sanctification might be overshadowed and threatened by the question whether, in spite of the death and resurrection of Jesus Christ . . . the law does not . . . continue to bring sin to life and keep it alive. . . . Is the law still there in this capacity, as this danger to believers?"[56] Barth answers this by suggesting that in the second half of Romans 7 Paul provides two elucidations of his main statement about the law in 7:1–6: "that the law from which we have been liberated is the 'law of sin and death.' Only on this assumption can there be any question of a liberation from the law. It is only from this law that the believer can be free."[57]

Barth notes that another factor in Paul's refusal to move too easily to the actuality of new life in Christ is that he never thought to question "the continuance and validity"[58] of the law. Meyer calls 7:12 "Paul's Q.E.D.: the Mosaic law is not demonic and not to be confused with sin, nor is it responsible for producing sin."[59] Barth lists Rom. 3:21, 31; 8:4; 13:8, 10; and Gal. 3:21 and 5:14 as further demonstration of Paul's support of the valid role of the law of God. "There can be no question of any liberation from this Law or abrogation of it."[60] God's law is the "other man" (7:3) for whom we have been set free. Moreover, this law is the "Law of God" in 7:22 and 25, and its aim is our life (7:10). This law has nothing to do with sin (7:7) and death (7:13). Rather, Barth

55. *CD* IV/1, 582 [650].
56. *SR*, 46 [92].
57. Ibid., 48 [97].
58. *CD* IV/1, 582 [650].
59. Meyer, "Worm at the Core of the Apple," 72.
60. *CD* IV/1, 583 [650].

suggests, "We ourselves in our relation to it [the law of God] have much to do with these [sin and death] but not the law."[61] Barth clarifies that God's law is not denigrated by the Pauline dictum: "we are not under the Law but under grace, and that we are dead to the Law and freed from it. . . . On the contrary, this statement is the most positive indication of the fulfillment of the Law."[62] The problem lies not with the law nor with following the law but with sin and the effect sin has in distorting the good pursuit of humans to follow the law. In fact, Paul makes himself very clear in 8:2: "it is this very Law of God ('the Law of Spirit and life') that liberates man from the law of sin and death."[63]

Barth suggests Paul uses the concept of the law as an instrument for communicating the power of God's miraculous act in the event of justification. But we must be clear on how Paul does this. His usage of the term "law" now has the opposite meaning from the law of God. This law is the "another law" in verse 23, the "law of sin" in verse 25, the "law of sin and death" in 8:2, and the law of the husband back in 7:3. It is this law "from which we are freed on the presupposition of the death of this husband, the destruction of our being in the flesh (v. 4 and v. 6)."[64] This is also the law that still rules in Paul's members (twice in v. 23). Barth calls Paul's decision to use the term "law" to describe the work of sin and death rather bold, but he also thinks it is ingenious in that it serves "to magnify sin as the situation in which justification begins, in order that justification itself may be shown to be truly great."[65] It is because of Paul's insistence that faith be faith in justification alone, not in human understanding or self-control, that he speaks of this second law. "Naturally this law of sin is only a reflection [of God's law] distorted out of all recognition. . . . It is only a poor caricature, an aping of the Law of God. . . . It is the law of anomaly"[66] that, once a person has fallen victim to it, has the power to command and control her such that she cannot escape it. Barth further elucidates the power of sin, stating

61. Ibid.
62. Ibid.
63. *SR*, 49 [97].
64. *CD* IV/1, 584 [651].
65. Ibid.
66. Ibid., 584 [652].

that it "is not something accidental which the man who engages in it can brush off again like a speck of dust from his clothes. Being directed against God, it has in it something of the nature of God to the extent that it acquires, and with it the life of the man who engages in it, a negative logic and necessity which neither it nor the man who engages in it can evade."[67]

Barth sees Paul drawing up such a dire picture of sin in order to force the question of where and how we can find liberation from such a binding law in order that we might be free for fulfillment of God's law. Still, as valuable as the law of God is, Barth does not find Paul stating that the law is where we are to find our freedom. Meyer maintains that the Torah "is not only powerless to prevent what it prohibits but in fact

67. Ibid. An interesting correlation can be made here between Paul's concept of the law of sin and Barth's description of what he terms the lordless powers. See Karl Barth, *The Christian Life: Church Dogmatics IV, 4 Lecture Fragments*, trans. Geoffrey W. Bromiley (Grand Rapids: Eerdmans, 1981), 213–33 [363–99]. Barth describes these powers as "nothing but man's own abilities loaned to his creaturely nature and peculiar to it. For this reason, even though in consequence of man's emancipation of himself from God these abilities emancipate themselves from man and thus acquire the character of entities with some kind of existence and dominion of their own, only a pseudo-objective reality and efficacy can be possessed by them and ascribed to them. If man himself cannot escape the sphere of God's lordship, neither can the alienated forces of man. No matter how bad their effects may be, they cannot be ontologically godless forces. Indeed, God is not just their frontier; he is at liberty to make use of them in the fulfilment of his will. They may pretend to be absolute, but they cannot be so, nor can they be effectively lordless (even their multiplicity forbids this). For God is their Creator, they are his creatures, and they stand at his disposal. Something of the same may also be said of their relationship to man. They are in rebellion against him but even in this rebellion, in their assumed and apparent independence of him, they are still his. There can be no question of an emancipation of these abilities from him that is finally valid, effective, and irreversible. They might play the role of unalterably given presuppositions, of gods or fate, in relation to him, but in the last resort they are not these things even for him. They clearly are not, for they are really given to him and belong to him as his own powers, abilities, and possibilities of life. They derive power and lordship over him because of the disintegration of his relationship to God. He cannot deny their power or shake it off. Nevertheless, it is not ruled out that he can be liberated from them and protect and defend himself against their dominion. Hence they are not necessary determinations of his being and existence. Troublesome though they are, they are only contingent and relative determinations. Related to this relativity of their relationship to both God and man is the obscurity, ambivalence, and unintelligibility of their reality and efficacy. Also related to it is the wraithlike transitoriness with which they manifest themselves, one appearing here and another there, then disappearing or retreating to give place to another, then appearing again. Related to it also is the variety of the forms in which they arise in the different periods and cultural circles of human life and in the lives of individuals. Related to it again is the necessity with which—corresponding to the fact that there always seem to be unknown as well as known powers and possibilities of human life—we have to reckon not only with some very familiar but also with some new and unfamiliar forms of this kind. Related to it finally is the difficulty of finding clear and suitable names and concepts with which to denote them properly and describe them vividly, the truth being that, because they do not and cannot have more than pseudo-objective reality, we can speak of them only in consciously mythological terms." See idem, 215–16 [366–67].

produces the very thing it is supposed to prevent."[68] True freedom is found in the work of God in Christ alone.

> It belongs to God's condescension that in the Law as the form of the Gospel he exposes himself to sin, to human misunderstanding and abuse. It belongs to his holiness that the form of his grace abused by sinful man becomes the instrument of his wrath and judgment of man, the man who is guilty of that abuse, is even in this abused form confronted with God himself, only that he must now experience that God is not to be mocked. And it belongs to God's mercy and omnipotence that in the end he does not acquiesce in the abuse of that form of his grace, that he does not leave it to be abused by man, but that in Jesus Christ he makes the Gospel, hidden in the Law, come out of its profaned shell. Thus he causes the Law to arise again and to be disclosed anew as *his* Law, the holy Law of the Spirit of life.[69]

Romans 7:7–13 shows Paul's horrible discovery that as a sinful person he is not free to either sin or not sin because he is under the law of sin. Such revelation comes, however, from God's law, for "even when it has been used by sin, the law has remained God's and has continued to serve the divine purpose of disclosing and intensifying sin."[70] "Because the Law called me to humility, it was revealed who I am and what I think in contrast to the Law of God. . . . The authority, the power of the law of sin, the aim of that law is this evil awakening of the sinner . . . as it takes place only—but surely—in its confrontation with the Law of God, in the light of His revelation."[71]

In passages such as 7:8b–9a; 4:15; 5:13, and 20, Barth finds examples of sin surfacing "from its anonymous existence when man encounters the self-revealing God and therefore His Law."[72] Yet Paul makes it very clear that sin, not God's law, is at fault in making us slaves to sin. There is "no character or office or function"[73] of the law of God that makes us sinners or delivers us up to death. Rather, "sin takes occasion . . . by the encounter of man with the commandment of God in order that

68. Meyer, "Worm at the Core of the Apple," 73.
69. *SR*, 49 [98–99].
70. Meyer, "Worm at the Core of the Apple," 74.
71. *CD* IV/1, 585 [653].
72. Ibid.
73. Ibid., 586 [654].

by its misuse it might make him the sinner qualified in this way."[74] Meyer, noting Paul's phrase καθ' ὑπερβολὴν in verse 13, calls attention to "[t]he transcendentally demonic nature of sin" with "its power to pervert the highest and best in *all* human piety, typified by the best in Paul's world, his own commitment to God's holy commandment, in such a way as to produce death in place of the promised life."[75] The law of God does indeed reveal the law of sin to the one who is elected and called by God, and that revelation leads to a revelation of one's sin. Yet such self-knowledge, made possible by God's law, will not enable a person to find his freedom from the law of sin and therefore be justified. "On the contrary, when he looks at this relationship, and himself as he exists in this relationship, he will be forced to recognize his obligation to this quite different law [law of sin]—and he cannot possibly regard himself as justified."[76] Put sharply: "[w]hat a person wants is salvation. What he creates is disaster."[77]

It is important to highlight that both Barth and Meyer find sin to be taking advantage of our encounter with God's law, such that "[b]ecause of the dominion of sin in his [sinful man's] eyes, ears and hands, it [the Law of God] becomes that other law from which he has to be liberated and from which he is in fact liberated."[78] Barth sees 7:14–25 as crucial for showing that, in the beginning of justification, the role of God's law is that of revealing the person as subject to the law of sin. Both 7:15–17 and 7:18–20 indicate that "Sin is my owner and lord."[79] "It is clear that the fault does not lie in the law [Torah]. Instead, the self, no longer the agent of its own actions, is controlled by the alien power of sin (vv. 16–17)."[80] The entrapment presented in these verses is that we cannot recognize ourselves in our actual doing or non-doing. We are strangers to ourselves, for it is not we who are at work, but sin dwelling in us (vv. 17, 20). It is at this point that Barth finds the most

74. Ibid.
75. Meyer, "Worm at the Core of the Apple," 74.
76. *CD* IV/1, 587 [654].
77. Ernst Käsemann, *Commentary on Romans*, ed. and trans. Geoffrey W. Bromiley (Grand Rapids: Eerdmans, 1980), 203.
78. *SR*, 49 [98].
79. *CD* IV/1, 587 [655].
80. Meyer, "Worm at the Core of the Apple," 76.

validity in the Reformation claim that this describes Paul the Christian rather than an unbelieving Jew, a Christian prior to conversion, or an unbelieving Gentile. He contends that in these verses Paul "knows that the conflict in which he finds himself, which he has to bear and in which he has to live, is the conflict between Law [Torah] and the law [of sin]."[81] However, unlike Augustine and Luther, who both find in 7:22 the perfect display of righteousness, expressed by Luther's appeal to Augustine's phrase "The will to be righteous is a large part of righteousness,"[82] Barth argues that the hopelessness in 7:22–23 forces Paul to admit that even "his sincere and earnest agreement with the Law of God, his best will to be righteous . . . does not alter in the slightest the fact that in his members in the physico-psychical existence which he sees, this other law is in victorious conflict."[83]

Meyer is quick to clarify that "Paul is not talking about the conflict between the rational and the irrational in the human self, nor about two selves at different levels, as though one were under the power of sin and the other not. Both 'inmost self' (v. 22) and 'members' (v. 23) are but two aspects of the same self that is 'sold under sin.'"[84] Käsemann, however, not wanting to rush past Paul's characterization of human existence as a person in conflict with himself, remarks that Paul does indeed come close "to a dualistic way of looking at things. . . . The truth about ourselves is plain here only in so far as we do not arrive at peace with ourselves by ourselves, as long as we remain, against our wills, restless beings, irritated by a mysterious counterpart within ourselves."[85] Barth, not making as much over the split "I" as many interpreters, remarks on this problem only to the extent that he finds it to be an effect under which all humanity falls, apart from Christ. This is why Paul cries out as he does in 7:24a; he cannot bear to live in his situation of sin any longer. Furthermore, the reality of Christian

81. *CD* IV/1, 588 [656].
82. Quoted in Meyer, "Worm at the Core of the Apple," 67.
83. *CD* IV/1, 589 [656].
84. Meyer, "Worm at the Core of the Apple," 76. Luther makes this same point, stating that it is "this whole man, this person here, [who] stand[s] in this double servitude." See Martin Luther, *Lectures on Romans*, trans. Wilhelm Pauck, Library of Christian Classics (Philadelphia: Westminster John Knox, 1961), 208.
85. Käsemann, "On Paul's Anthropology," 16–17.

existence is also not free of this tension between our old life and new life in Christ. Martyn suggests that the gospel thrusts a person into an epistemological crisis such that one knows herself grasped by God's invasive action in Christ and now "cannot continue to perceive and to know in the old way" but instead "sees bifocally . . . both the evil age and the new creation simultaneously. This bifocal, simultaneous vision is distinctly unbalanced, however, in that, just as God's power is 'much more' than the power of Sin, so God causes the apocalyptic seer to see the powers of the new creation 'much more' than [s]he sees those of the Old Age (Rom 5:12–21)."[86]

Finding Paul, in 7:4, proclaiming that our incorporation into the body of death is already in our past, and then, in 7:24a, telling us that it is still our present, Barth comments that "in so far as all this has not taken place in his own person, but validly and effectively for him in the person of Jesus Christ," he is, "in his own person . . . still in the flesh and therefore is still subject to the law of sin."[87] His daily experience is still one of contradiction, for which he can only cry, "'Who shall deliver me?'"[88] It is "as though we had never read what is stated in v. 4 and he himself had never written it." *As though!* While we can always only be living both by the question of verse 24 and by the answer to this question in verse 25a, Barth stresses that "the two sayings . . . are only meaningful together, the one pointing backwards, the other forwards."[89] The dialectic of justification, the "both at once" of our existence, is not an "unhappy contradiction"[90] but is instead "the history of justification, in that transition as it is really both at once, as indicated in the relationship of the two sayings in v. 24 and v. 25a."[91] Barth proposes that the question of 7:24 is "like the question of Jesus Christ on the cross . . . or like the whole question of Job. . . . All at once there is cause simply to be thankful."[92] He also notices that 7:25a is an

86. J. Louis Martyn, *Galatians: A New Translation with Introduction and Commentary*, AB 33A (New York: Doubleday, 1997), 104.
87. *CD* IV/1, 590 [658].
88. Ibid., 591 [659].
89. Ibid., 589 [657].
90. Ibid., 591 [659].
91. Ibid.
92. *CD* IV/1, 590 [658].

expression of thanks that does not state what act is accomplished. He suggests that this thankfulness, which is characterized not by *what* he is thankful for but rather *to whom* he is thankful, is "the forward leap of the man who is justified by God, the attestation of Jesus Christ raised again from the dead."[93]

Regarding the Reformation: A Key Difference between Barth and Meyer

In the introduction to this study, we noted that Reformation readings of Paul are often quickly dismissed as being highly anachronistic, overly psychologized, and/or inappropriately focused on the role of the individual's faith in salvation. While Meyer's apocalyptic reading of Romans 7 has much in common with Barth's, where he differs is in his purely negative view of the Reformation reading. Meyer believes Paul's depiction of the destructive power of sin has been overshadowed by Augustine's influential decision to read Romans 7 as a description of a spiritual person. He notes that Luther, in particular, picked up on Augustine's reading and utilized it to account for his common refrain, *simul iustus et peccator*, remarking that such a struggle with one's inability to follow the law, in the flesh, can only take place within a believer. Meyer argues that Luther's pastoral concern to offer comfort to believers who struggle with their sin blinded his exegesis. He decries what he finds to be Luther's twisted logic that turns Paul's anguished cry in 7:24a into an expression of perfect spirituality. Furthermore, he notes that Augustine's distinction between the spiritual person and the carnal/fleshly person, which Luther and Philipp Melanchthon both seize on, is based on distorting Paul's distinction in 7:14 about the gulf between God's spiritual law and the fleshly, human person confronted by it. The adjectives are made "to differentiate two classes of *humans*: the religious person who is righteous, wise, understanding, re-born, perfect in self-knowledge and humility, on the one hand and the irreligious, the ungodly, and the sinner on the other, who is utterly

93. Ibid.

devoid of genuine religious impulse."[94] Meyer's real rub with Luther now comes to the fore: "[t]his is the language of binary opposites, used by triumphalistic religion to separate humankind into two groups of people, the saved and the damned."[95] He finds that this thought has been perpetuated in modern times by commentators who draw the conclusion from Paul's text that "the Spirit of God is not at work anywhere outside of the Christian church—even though Paul himself has just stated in unequivocal terms that the (Mosaic!) law is 'spiritual'—and so the inference is drawn . . . that the 'I' of Romans 7 can only refer to the Christian."[96] Meyer points out that Paul's whole argument in Romans has stated that all people, Jew and non-Jew alike, are in the same position of having sinned and fallen short of God's glory. Additionally, it is most especially the religious person who has been sold under the law of sin and is actually possessed by it.

What Meyer's reading betrays is not a faulty view of Paul's text but a failure to understand Luther's main point in his reading of Paul. To be sure, Meyer agrees that Luther's reading explores Paul's design and argument in Romans 7 in such a way as helpfully seeks out "the critical and reforming intent of the text."[97] While Meyer may likely have more of an ax to grind with anachronistic readings of Romans 7 that followed after Luther rather than with Luther himself, at the end of the day, it is the Reformation doctrine of justification that he portrays as resulting from a lack of careful attention to and certain dismissal of Paul's argument. In truth, Luther's commentary shows him to agree completely that Paul has shown all people to have fallen short of God's glory, a point Meyer insists has been missed in subsequent interpretations. In this sense, there is no difference between the "godly" and "ungodly." What Luther is trying to emphasize, which Meyer seems to miss, is that only the person who has come to know God's grace is fully aware of the extent of her sinfulness and therefore has the desire to be delivered from her wretched state. It is only her

94. Meyer, "Worm at the Core of the Apple," 67.
95. Ibid., 63.
96. Ibid., 68.
97. Ibid., 64.

true assessment of her sin, which God's law reveals to her, that Luther and Augustine (and Barth) are upholding as a sign of her spirituality. Luther suggests that her righteousness comes from believing "in Christ whose righteousness covers [her] and is imputed to [her]," but she is a sinner because she does "not fulfill the law and [is] not without sinful desires."[98] To be sure, Luther finds Paul's words in 7:25 to support the idea of *simul iustus et peccator*. In describing this "double existence," he employs the following metaphor: "[t]hey are like sick people in the care of a physician: they are really sick, but healthy only in hope and in so far as they begin to be better, or, rather: are being healed, i.e., they will become healthy. Nothing can harm them so much as the presumption that they are in fact healthy, for it will cause a bad relapse."[99] This metaphor demonstrates that it is the acknowledgement that justification takes place *extra nos*, in Christ alone, a notion that is wholly Pauline, that drives Luther's formulation of the *simul*.

In contrast to Meyer's critique of Luther on this point is Barth's reading. Rather than dismissing the Reformational reading out of hand, Barth assumes the validity of Luther's *simul* but, at the same time, offers an important nuance that actually serves to connect it back to Paul's text more faithfully as well as to bring out the apocalyptic element inherent within Pauline anthropology. As noted above, Barth reformulates the order of the *simul*, putting *peccator* before *iustus*. This fits with Barth's dialectical notion of justification as transition, and it is Barth's reformulation of Luther's phrase that not only strengthens the idea that justification occurs *extra nos* and *solus Christus* but also highlights a key point in Pauline apocalyptic eschatology. And it is here that I make my first point in concluding this chapter.[100] Barth's dialectic of justification supports Paul's apocalyptic concept of the new age being paradoxically present within the old age and thus visible

98. Luther, *Lectures on Romans*, 208.
99. Ibid.
100. I am indebted to my colleague from Princeton Theological Seminary, David W. Congdon, who allowed me to read a copy of his journal article before its publication, "Bonhoeffer and Bultmann: Toward an Apocalyptic Rapprochement," *International Journal of Systematic Theology* 15, no. 2 (2015): 172–95. Congdon helpfully describes"the dialectical nature of the apocalyptic inbreaking as actualistic, paradoxical, and existential " (179). I am borrowing his categories in my analysis of Barth's dialectical notion of justification.

only to faith. By upholding Paul's account in 7:7–25 as containing "genuinely spiritual self-knowledge" Barth confirms that "[t]he apocalypse is . . . a cosmic event in that it decisively changes how one understands the world. It is an event that transfigures the world for the eyes of faith."[101] Here, in Paul's "wretched man," is the correlation between the ontological reality of the new age in Christ and the epistemological knowledge of this new age through faith.

The second way Barth's theological anthropology brings out the dialectical dimensions of an apocalyptically construed doctrine of justification is in its focus on the existential. "The meaning of the apocalyptic invasion cannot be articulated apart from its relation to concrete human existence in the present moment."[102] In other words, God's objectively real in-breaking action is inseparably tied to our own subjective participation in it. The christological reality of what it means to be the justified human must become real in us. It becomes real in us as a turning from sin and a turning toward our new life. This leads us to the third way Barth's theological anthropology complements the dialectical dimensions of an apocalyptically construed doctrine of justification. Just as Barth's reformulation of *simul peccator et iustus* serves to highlight the christological concentration of his apocalyptically cast theological anthropology, so we are reminded that justification is actualized in the particular, historical event in Christ, which is made present to us in the Spirit. As Martyn and Meyer point out, "the guiding theme of Paul's theology is not the law but Christ."[103] Hence the dialectic of justification follows the same sequence as the death and resurrection of Christ. What Christ has already done to perfectly fulfill the will of God in his life, death, and resurrection has to be realized in us again and again as we participate in Christ's history. For this reason, justification is always a dynamic

101. Ibid., 177.
102. Ibid., 179.
103. Meyer, "Worm at the Core of the Apple," 80. Similarly, Martyn remarks that "Paul was firmly of the opinion that the nub of the matter was not the issue of the law, but rather Christology." See J. Louis Martyn, "Paul and His Jewish-Christian Interpreters," *Union Seminary Quarterly Review* 42 (1988): 3.

movement away from our bondage to sin and toward our new freedom and life in Christ by the Spirit.

This chapter has demonstrated how Barth adapts the forensic approach to the doctrine of justification, originally brought out by the Reformers, in light of his understanding of Paul's theological anthropology. Because Jesus Christ alone reveals and establishes human nature in his history and activity, not only is our justification complete in him, but our own lived experience of justification also follows the pattern of the history of Christ's death and resurrection. Barth's description of the dialectic of justification arises from parsing the forensic concept of acquittal in terms of God's divisive sentence on us. Hence, while with Meyer we saw that cosmic-apocalyptic readings of Paul want, at times, to put distance between the Reformation doctrine of justification and Pauline apocalyptic eschatology, Barth's forensic apocalyptic reading does just the opposite: it allows him to formulate a doctrine of justification with stronger ties between the Reformation doctrine and Pauline apocalyptic eschatology.

8

The Eschatological Dimensions of Barth's Forensic Apocalyptic Doctrine of Justification

> The "sufferings of this present time" (Rom. 8:18); the fact that in this time we and all creation look forward with groaning (Rom. 8:19f.) to the redemption and consummation and therefore to the coming of Jesus Christ in His final form; the cry: "O wretched man that I am!" in face of the contradiction in which even the Christian and apostle continually finds himself entangled (Rom. 7:24)—these cannot mean that Christians have cause to complain of an inadequacy of the Spirit who is given them as the pledge and first fruits of the ultimate future, or of His eternal and temporal promise, or of the lights and powers and gifts which are bestowed with it. The promise of the Spirit gives us no grounds for sighing. On the contrary, it is the power of the resurrection of Jesus Christ. There is repeated in it the anticipation of His final revelation. In it all things are already given to us and the world.
>
> —Karl Barth, *CD* IV/3.1

As we begin this last chapter in the main argument of our study, we turn to Romans 8 and the doctrinal theme of eschatology found there, asking after the location of justification in the eschatology of salvation.

As Barth has followed Paul's proclamation in Rom. 1:16–17 that Jesus Christ himself is the gospel—the good news of God's powerful work of salvation—his doctrine of justification has had at its core Jesus Christ as the active subject of reconciliation. This implies that it is the perfect tense that is most decisive in Barth's eschatology of salvation. Jesus Christ is God's efficacious promise of eternal life, and thus amid the now-and-not-yet character of our present reality, our hope is in Christ alone. Justification and sanctification are both oriented to new humanity, which "in its totality is teleologically directed, an eschatological being."[1] Jesus Christ is indeed God's promise of humanity's future, because he is both "the eternally living God" and "also the eternally living man" and so "the pledge of what we ourselves will be."[2] Therefore we are justified and sanctified in Christ so that, by the power of the Spirit, we might "seize this future even in the present and in so doing . . . move towards one's future being, indeed towards Jesus Christ himself—the one in whom this future is already present."[3]

Yet for Barth, in the second edition of the Romans commentary, there was only the "in Christ" element of Romans 8, so completely had he actualized the Spirit's work in our lives. In fact, expounding on 8:24, he famously had this to say:

> Direct communication from God is no divine communication. If Christianity be not altogether thoroughgoing eschatology, there remains in it no relationship whatever with Christ. . . . There is no freedom, but only imprisonment; no grace, but only condemnation and corruption; no divine guidance, but only fate; no God, but only a mirror of unredeemed humanity. . . . Redemption is [unintuitable], inaccessible, and impossible, for it meets us only in hope.[4]

Interestingly, in an illuminating self-critique located in a small-print section at the end of *CD* II/1, Barth recalls these very statements and, after noting "Well roared, lion"[5] to them, then remarks that the

1. *CD* IV/1, 109 [118].
2. Ibid., 115 [126].
3. Adam Neder, *Participation in Christ: An Entry into Karl Barth's Church Dogmatics* (Louisville: Westminster John Knox, 2009), 55.
4. Karl Barth, *The Epistle to the Romans*, trans. Edwyn C. Hoskyns (London: Oxford University Press, 1933), 314 [298].

problem with such statements resides not in their content but rather that in order "to be legitimate exposition of the Bible they needed others no less sharp and direct to compensate and therefore genuinely to substantiate their total claim."[6] In looking back at his early theology, Barth admits that he was most in error when he had "to speak positively about the divine future and hope as such."[7] Yet he continues to stress the utmost importance of the eschatological interpretation of the New Testament and Christianity and even submits, "what the New Testament calls the expectation of the return and the end . . . is indeed the whole truth about God."[8] But he then clarifies that it is precisely for this reason that it cannot "be seized and handled by us as an instrument or weapon. On the contrary, it seizes and handles us. It shows itself at once to be so powerful in its particularity that we cannot tie it, as it were, to this particularity, but have to recognize its inner movement and are compelled to follow this movement."[9] Thus in relationship to the eschatology of salvation, the problem that arose in the second edition of the Romans commentary was that the "tension between the 'then' when we believed and the 'now' of 'disturbing recollection,' a new awareness of Christ's *parousia*, was only a continual tension, having no connection with the tension of two points in time and the time of Church history."[10] As Walter Lowe surmises, "[t]he criterion by which pure futurity is judged lacking is that it fails to do what Barth implies apocalyptic must do: it does not press in upon us."[11]

Barth certainly comes to find more realized eschatology in Romans 8 than what he had allowed for in the second edition of the Romans commentary. That is why, as we look at Barth's treatment of Romans 8 in *A Shorter Commentary on Romans* and his mature doctrine of reconciliation in *CD* IV/3.1,[12] we will see that Barth's new aim is to

5. *CD* II/1, 635 [715].
6. *CD* IV/3.1, 635 [715–16].
7. *CD* II/1, 635 [716].
8. Ibid., 637 [718].
9. Ibid.
10. Ibid., 635 [716].
11. Walter Lowe, "Why We Need Apocalyptic," *Scottish Journal of Theology* 63, no. 1 (2010): 47.
12. It is in this part-volume of the doctrine of reconciliation that Barth takes up a discussion of revelation. He is careful to specify that revelation takes place in and with reconciliation but "in

thoroughly work out *how* Jesus Christ, as God's effective promise of eternal life, is our only hope, and furthermore how hope is a form of our here-and-now participation in the risen Jesus Christ. Under the umbrella of Barth's historicized theological ontology, Jesus Christ is what he does; hence Jesus Christ is himself the event of reconciliation. Jesus Christ himself is thus God's promise of our future. This is not to say that the promise is already fulfilled in us. Barth will never go there. But he now goes farther to embrace that, by the power of the Spirit, our frail human responses to God's work can be offered to God, thereby making that which is objectively true of humanity in Christ to correspond subjectively to who we are, by the Spirit, daily becoming. The Spirit is no longer practically equated with new humanity. Rather, the Spirit is now the active power of God in our lives, confirming and fulfilling what is already true of us in Christ. The Spirit makes us to correspond, more and more, to who we really are. Our obedient actions—our faith, our hope, our love—these are all the realizations of our true humanity that the Spirits empowers in us.

This chapter will show that Barth's theological reading of Romans 8 in *A Shorter Commentary on Romans* and his treatment of eschatology in *CD* IV/3.1 are both grounded on a Pauline apocalypticism that rightly presses in on us—that, as Martyn says, trades on the truth of God's invasion of the present evil age by sending Christ and the Spirit into it.[13] Barth's treatment of Romans 8 in *A Shorter Commentary on Romans* delineates how Christ, in his death and resurrection, by inaugurating new creation and new life in the Spirit, has set us free from our captivity to sin and death and made us free for a life characterized by obedience, hope, and innocence. Our investigation of Barth's theological exegesis of Romans 8 will prepare us to then turn to *CD* IV/3.1, where we will survey Barth's treatment of the middle form

itself and as such" is not reconciliation. Rather, revelation "takes place as reconciliation takes place; as it has in it its origin, content and subject; as reconciliation is revealed and reveals itself in it." See *CD* IV/3.1, 8–9 [7].

13. Expressing Paul's apocalyptic understanding of God's invasion of human history, Martyn writes: "There was a 'before,' the time when we were confined, imprisoned; and there is an 'after,' the time of our deliverance. And the difference between the two is caused not by an unveiling, but rather by the coming of Christ and his Spirit." See J. Louis Martyn, *Galatians: A New Translation with Introduction and Commentary*, AB 33A (New York: Doubleday, 1997), 99.

of the one event of Christ's parousia and the role of the Spirit in it. Though never spelled out, the apocalyptic eschatology of Romans 8 lies just beneath the surface of Barth's eschatology of the time between the times. Barth infers a missional calling from Paul's understanding of the new life in the Spirit of the adopted children of God that has resulted from God's invasive, reconciling activity in Jesus Christ. The chapter will conclude with a discussion of the difference between the Reformation theology of Calvin and Barth in this matter of the middle form of Christ's parousia and will suggest that Barth's attention to the apocalyptic eschatology of Romans 8 constitutes a gain made by Barth over against Reformation theology in this instance.

New Life in the Spirit in the Eschatology of Romans 8

If Barth's reading of Romans 8 in the second edition of his Romans commentary was void of the mere hint of realized eschatology, his rereading of it in *A Shorter Commentary on Romans* has, with important qualifications, learned to make some room for it. Taking the proclamation in 8:1 that there is no condemnation for those in Christ Jesus as the theme verse of the chapter, Barth provides a thorough reading and analysis of the chapter, which he says aims at teaching *how* condemnation has been abolished for sinful humanity. Barth reaches back to the truth established about all humanity by Paul in Romans 5, that "[t]he man who as Adam's child does what Adam does is condemned," as well as to the misappropriation of God's law by the power of sin in Romans 7, in order to highlight the significance and climax of God's work in establishing "anew and more than ever" his "Law in Jesus Christ, by obtaining for it due respect and observance through Jesus Christ and thereby making his grace triumphant with and *for* everyone who believes in Jesus Christ."[14] In the giving of the Spirit to those who believe God establishes his law, such that "already *here* and *now*" justification is "authenticated and the reconciliation, sanctification and liberation of man is completed" by the Spirit.[15] Keck

14. *SR*, 55 [107].
15. Ibid.

argues that, for Paul, "the Spirit is not just a lively attitude; it is essentially the name for *God's power experienced immediately* (without mediation). The presence of the Spirit both confirms what the gospel announces about God's act in Christ and obligates as well as enables the recipient of the Spirit to live in accordance with the new freedom."[16] Liberation from sin and death is thus liberation for this new life under the Spirit's domain, which is already characteristic of the new life given to those who believe.

Barth urges that the fundamental point in the first section of the chapter, which he finds to be contained in Rom. 8:1–11, is that the "condemnation of man by the law of sin and death" does not affect those who are in Christ Jesus, because as such they have been "released, *liberated* from that Law" by the law of the Spirit of life.[17] Barth thus concludes that to be "in Christ" in the present is nothing other than to be subject to this "different Law," or an "entirely new reality of human life," which Paul first signaled in 7:1.[18] The new reality, in stark contrast to the picture drawn in Rom. 7:7–25, is one in which a person is "allowed to start with Jesus Christ instead of with 'I'" because the Law has liberated "*itself* from abuse by sin" and "shown itself in its true form as the Spirit which moves this [person] to seek God's grace."[19] Similarly, Meyer argues that the key contrast in 8:1–17 is between the ineffectiveness of the law under the power of sin to renew life, and the power of God's Spirit to do just that. "The law itself is not demonic; to link law with Spirit instead of sin is the logical sequel to the argument of chapter 6 that freedom in Christ is aimed at the reshaping of human life, both individual and corporate, according to the good that God wills for it."[20] Barth's reading places a stress on God's own vindication of his law as well as on the revelation, achieved "by what God brought about in Jesus Christ," of the law's true form as the Spirit who moves us to seek God's grace. In other words, what God

16. Leander E. Keck, *Romans*, Abingdon New Testament Commentary (Nashville: Abingdon, 2005), 218.
17. *SR*, 55 [108].
18. Ibid., 56 [109].
19. Ibid.
20. Paul W. Meyer, "Romans: A Commentary," in *The Word in This World: Essays in New Testament Exegesis and Theology*, ed. John T. Carroll (Louisville: Westminster John Knox, 2004), 189.

accomplished in the perfect tense of salvation by Christ's humiliation (8:3) has made possible our participation "with him" to "live another life, a new life" (8:4).[21] In walking after the Spirit God's law is fulfilled, for walking after the Spirit is defined as becoming "*obedient* to God's *grace* which has appeared with compelling power in Jesus Christ."[22] Barth cannot reiterate enough the strong identification Paul creates between the Spirit and "the power of the Law of grace established by the sending of the Son of God over those who believe in him, because he has died and risen for them."[23] So too Meyer draws attention to the "free interhangeability of a whole series of phrases: 'belonging to Christ' (v. 9b), 'being in the Spirit' (v. 9a), 'God's Spirit dwelling in you' (vv. 9a, 11b), 'Christ's Spirit' (v. 9b), 'Christ in you' (v. 10), and 'the Spirit of the one who raised Jesus from the dead' (v. 11). Each interprets the others and is interpreted by them."[24] The Spirit "is the power of the risen Jesus to take men and women into his power and reshape life to make it well pleasing to God—thus doing what the law could not do and reversing the power of sin."[25]

Although the existence of that "strange saint" of Romans 7, "who allows himself to be deceived by sin through the Law and for whom the law of sin must ever become the law of death,"[26] still resides in them, those who believe in Jesus Christ are not torn between life in the flesh and life in the Spirit because they already belong to the Spirit and have turned away from "their existence dominated by sin."[27] This new existence is not something brought about by human striving, activity, or participation. It is true for them only by the fact that *in* Jesus Christ God's law has been established for and over them. Keck clarifies that, for Paul, the plight of the human condition is replaced

21. *SR*, 56 [110].
22. Ibid.
23. Ibid., 56 [110–11].
24. Meyer, "Romans: A Commentary," 190.
25. Ibid.
26. Barth would thus agree with Martyn's appraisal of Paul's apocalyptic perspective as one that finds the world not yet fully subjected to God even as the eschatological subjection has indeed begun, giving glimpses into the awaited end. See J. Louis Martyn, "Apocalyptic Antinomies," in *Theological Issues in the Letters of Paul* (Nashville: Abingdon, 1997), 113.
27. *SR*, 57 [111].

by solidarity with Jesus, God's eternal Son, "through whose death God condemned sin in the flesh, and by the residence of God's Spirit, whose work will be completed by the resurrection of the body."[28] Because of the Christ event, in other words, the power of sin has been undone, its condemnation not just pronounced but actually carried out in the present tense. The only way we can talk of our new life is to speak of it as "the Spirit of God and of Jesus Christ . . . who has transferred [us] into the righteousness of a [person] who only desires to live by grace."[29] Barth notes that for Paul, the Spirit's presence combines the "already" and the "not yet" of our existence. Human existence, even as it has been condemned and abolished in Christ's death, is intended, by God, for true restoration to us in a redeemed form. God "does not take our 'I' without restoring it to us in Jesus Christ."[30] In the present, however, we must "be content here and now to live in the Spirit of God and Jesus Christ, but to see . . . ourselves hastening towards death"[31] even as we know death has been conquered on the cross.

As we await our redemption, our life in the Spirit of God and Jesus is to be characterized by obedience. This is what Barth finds Paul describing in 8:12–16. Indeed, he finds the essence of what Paul means by being in Christ to center on being "led, moved and drawn by the Spirit of God (8:14)."[32] As our justification is complete in Christ, we are made to be God's children by the Spirit of adoption and so can fulfill God's will for us (8:15). The Spirit thus creates the relationship of the Christian to Christ. "Obedience is not finally the work of the self but the result of the Spirit's leading."[33] Keck notes that the imagery in these verses aligns with Paul's theology quite well since "adoption confers on the 'son' a new status to which he has no right but which he receives solely because of the father's decision—theologically, adoption is an act of grace."[34] The Spirit gives testimony "again and again . . . that

28. Keck, *Romans*, 209.
29. *SR*, 57 [113].
30. Ibid., 58 [113].
31. Ibid.
32. Ibid., 59 [115].
33. Meyer, "Romans: A Commentary," 190.
34. Keck, *Romans*, 206.

consequently we may tell ourselves: we are God's children!"[35] The one good work we are asked to do is nothing other than crying out, as prodigal children, to God, "and so performing the one act of *obedience* demanded by the Law."[36] While there is no other work of obedience that is to be added to this, all other acts of obedience are included in it. The law of the Spirit is the law of grace, and therefore "the fulfillment of God's Law (8:4) will primarily and finally always consist in that which these verses define as *the* gift of the Spirit."[37] Barth's reflections here, in comparison to those of the second edition of the Romans commentary, demonstrate a deeper ability to take seriously this dimension of new life in the Spirit, which we have by adoption. God's initiative—God's grace—is the heartbeat of new life in the Spirit. But, just as surely as God is Spirit, so there is really new life in the Spirit.

Turning to the large central section of the chapter, Barth notes that 8:17–27 provides us with the perspective of hope. In the present, we live "here and now," not only in the light of the cross but also amid the shadow of death hanging over "our whole human condition. This condition has been judged and put to death on the cross of the Son of God; now it can only learn, and must in fact learn, that it has been judged and killed there. Its further existence can only be temporary."[38] In 8:17 we find a counterpart to the person subjected to the law of sin and death as described in 7:7–23. Those in Christ Jesus, living here and now under both the promise and the "inexorable fatality" of the shadow of death cast by the cross, are also God's heirs. This means we have expectations of sharing in what belongs to God, even as our present existence, "which precedes that future with him, can obviously only be one that is determined by his suffering."[39] Yet the suffering cannot outweigh the future glory to be revealed. "Paul regards that which is to be suffered as an inevitable effect of the death of Christ (in which truly an end has been made of all idealism and optimism):

35. *SR*, 59 [116].
36. Ibid.
37. Ibid., 60 [117].
38. Ibid., 60 [118].
39. Ibid., 60 [119].

for this reason, and only for this reason, he can see the sufferings of this time far outweighed by the glory to come."[40] Connecting the perfect-tense reality of the salvation accomplished in the death and resurrection of Christ to our present experience, Barth urges that Paul views the "temptation of Jesus Christ before his death and our own" from the "all-controlling" place of the resurrection so that the former is "only heard for a moment to fade away in what follows."[41]

Likewise, 8:19–22 tells of the whole of creation[42] heading for the same renewal from the coming glory of God, even as 8:23 speaks of the groaning for redemption of the whole world, including Christians.[43] "The gift of the Spirit is not a partial resurrection or a certificate of exemption from the world's suffering."[44] Barth explains the necessity of the subjection spoken of in 8:20 this way: in his death, Jesus Christ has made an effective end to the world, having "pronounced and executed his verdict," such that here and now "there is only dying life . . . only . . . a groaning creation. . . . But since Jesus Christ subjected us, it is a subjection 'in hope' (8:20)."[45] Hope, "as certainty about God's future, . . . makes meaningful connections between God's salvation and the miserable realities of the present world."[46] The promise given to God's children, however, offers the world a picture of "*what* man and with him all creation is groaning for, *what* they lack, *what is* the liberty corresponding to that subjection and vanity."[47] Indeed, the groaning for liberty is not in vain. Barth connects the dots of Paul's cosmic

40. Ibid., 61 [120].
41. Ibid.
42. Eastman has shown that while most commentators believe κτίσις in this section refers to the natural order of creation apart from humanity, to "exclude a human voice from the groaning of 'creation' . . . is as erroneous as to exclude the natural world. Rather, Paul assumes the unity of 'the whole creation,' which groans and suffers the pangs of childbirth together—that is, as one. The unity of the suffering points to the unity of redemption." See Susan Eastman, "Whose Apocalypse? The Identity of the Sons of God in Romans 8:19," *Journal of Biblical Literature* 121, no. 2 (2002): 274.
43. Cousar submits that "[t]he Spirit makes believers participants in the eschatological anguish as creation and community together experience the birth pangs of the new order." See Charles B. Cousar, "Continuity and Discontinuity: Reflections on Romans 5–8," in *Pauline Theology*, vol. 3, *Romans*, ed. David M. Hay and E. Elizabeth Johnson (Minneapolis: Fortress Press, 1995), 206.
44. Meyer, "Romans: A Commentary," 192.
45. *SR*, 62 [122].
46. Meyer, "Romans: A Commentary," 192.
47. *SR*, 62 [122].

horizons. "Because that judgment applies to the whole world, the whole world has been given this future, the whole world has been promised this answer to its groaning: this new birth as the fruit of its travails."[48] Connecting 8:21 to 8:19, Barth urges that the future of God's children is "a guarantee for the future which all men and all things have before them."[49] Yet even the revelation of the right and inheritance as God's children is still to come. Hence Barth finds we must put equal stress on the two aspects—"in hope" and "we were saved"—of Paul's words in 8:24. "Nothing needs to be added to our salvation, which has taken place in Jesus Christ."[50] What is lacking is that this finished work of salvation is "as yet *hidden, is* as yet *not visible.*"[51]

Our hope, insofar as it is concerned with the revelation of the final consummation, is also faith, which consists in waiting patiently for the fulfillment of the promise (8:25). Gaventa notes that Paul has painted a picture of humanity and all of creation together in the process of giving birth, yet without birthing a baby. "Instead, there is adoption and redemption, activities that are carried out not by creation but by God. What creation longs for is God's action, not its own."[52] Our patience, Barth writes, has, however, been made easy since "Jesus Christ himself is our hope; we need no longer wait for anything save the revelation of that which he has already finished, for our waiting as such is already full of the presence of that for which we are waiting."[53] And so, finding an analogy to the explanation in 8:16, Barth says that Paul writes 8:26–27 to emphasize again that during this present time, we are not left on our own.[54] We are to carry on the work of calling on God, which the Spirit helps us do. God makes intercession on our

48. Ibid.
49. Ibid., 62 [123].
50. Ibid., 63 [124].
51. Ibid.
52. Beverly Roberts Gaventa, "The Birthing of Creation," in *Our Mother Saint Paul* (Louisville: Westminster John Knox, 2007), 57.
53. *SR*, 63 [124].
54. Likewise, Meyer urges that "[h]uman beings are not left to their own resources, even to the inadequacies of their praying, to bear the burdens of this time, for the Spirit's intercession is authorized by God himself." See Meyer, "Romans: A Commentary," 193.

behalf, making "himself our advocate with himself . . . so that he will surely hear what we ourselves could not have told him, so that he will accept what he himself has to offer."[55] This is the secret of our hope and our patience.

Barth suggests Paul's final section of the chapter, 8:28–39, describes life under God's law as a life of innocence. Likewise noting the forensic framework of the section, Meyer titles 8:31–39 "Justification as Vindication by the Love of God in Christ."[56] Only Jesus Christ has the right to pronounce guilty those who are in Christ Jesus. Yet as the eternal Judge and measure of all righteousness, he has pronounced us innocent. The "ultimate accuser in the heavenly court is now the one who has taken their side in Christ Jesus."[57] The chapter ends the way it began (8:1).

As he did earlier, Barth draws on the Spirit's work of intercession in 8:26–27, now bringing it into the courtroom scene of 8:31–34. "The Spirit is God's grace triumphant in their faith over their whole bondage to sin and death. This Spirit is the counsel for the defense, who acquits them because he is also their Law and their Judge."[58] Continuing to focus on the work of the Spirit, Barth suggests that those who love God (8:28) do not do so by their own will. "Paul is speaking of the living power of the Spirit, of the Law of life established at Golgotha. Those who love God are the ones whom God from all eternity, according to his free will, has destined and in due time called to such love."[59] Paul states, as an eternal, prehistorical fact, that God has "on their behalf dealt with them (8:29–30). . . . From eternity he has given them their purpose for their temporal existence. By the love with which God loves his own Son they have been destined to be his children and therefore to love him in return."[60]

It is because of this very love of God that God does not accuse them (8:31–39). God is for them. That "is the secret of their love. God is for

55. *SR*, 63–64 [125].
56. Meyer, "Romans: A Commentary," 193.
57. Ibid.
58. *SR*, 64 [126].
59. Ibid., 65 [128].
60. Ibid.

them."[61] Keck and Meyer both find this to be central to Paul's message. "God's being 'for us' . . . sums up the thrust of the whole argument since 3:21."[62] It is "the very heart of Paul's teaching on justification."[63] In Jesus Christ, God has not spared himself. Gaventa suggests that here in this last section of Romans 8 Paul reaches all the way back to the argument in Rom. 1:18–32, but that now "there is a kind of reversal . . . of the situation depicted in chapter 1."[64] Barth, too, notes that Paul picks up the expression thrice repeated in 1:24, 26, and 28 when he writes that in Jesus "God has 'delivered himself up' so that their eternal predestination should be accomplished and fulfilled."[65] The divine delivering of humanity to sin and death is thus done "for their sake, so that this infamy should be taken away from them and no longer be theirs."[66] This is why there is no doubt of our innocence, even as Paul does not deny that we have deserved damnation, condemnation, and rejection. But who executes it? Jesus Christ has executed it "once and for all for us . . . by bearing it himself and dying as its bearer."[67] More than that, Christ has been raised from the dead and now makes intercession for us (8:34). This intercession, Barth notes, is the same expression Paul uses in 8:27 for the Spirit. Such a reality, for those under the law of God, means that no one and nothing can separate us from the love of Christ (8:35–37). Even so, we face persecution and are "in danger of losing [our] innocence, of losing sight of the Law of life under which [we] live."[68] Yet as the quotation from Psalm 44 testifies, because we live under God's law "as it was established at Golgotha—in the same way as all the suffering of the whole creation is secretly the radiation of the suffering of the Son of God," it is "therefore a suffering in hope."[69] Meyer points out that while the psalm was originally a lamentation to God over the attacks

61. Ibid., 66 [129].
62. Keck, *Romans*, 219.
63. Meyer, "Romans: A Commentary," 193.
64. Gaventa, "Birthing of Creation," 59.
65. *SR*, 66 [130].
66. Ibid.
67. Ibid.
68. Ibid., 66 [131].
69. Ibid., 67 [132].

of Israel's enemies, Paul has universalized it as "an apocalyptic truism that God's faithful are always exposed to violent death."[70]

Barth closes by pointing out how in 8:38–39 Paul apocalyptically visualizes, in very personal forms, "a whole upsurge of spiritual realities, a whole agitated sea of hidden rebellion of which the persecution of the Christians is merely a symptom."[71] He does so in order to urge that these, too, will not be able to separate us from God's love because, as 8:39 mentions and 1 Cor. 8:5 reiterates, "they are only creatures, only 'so-called gods,' who "in their most evil work . . . were in no way able to act as gods and lords in their own right but ultimately only as servants of the One who by the cross that they erected has brought to light the innocence of those who believe, in such a manner that they are now too late if they still want to take it from them."[72] The good news of 8:1 stands. The love of Christ is the love of God himself; "that is the meaning for this life of calling Jesus of Nazareth, crucified and raised, 'Christ Jesus our Lord.'"[73]

The New Coming of Jesus in the Present Time: The Promise of the Holy Spirit

While Barth has been criticized for leaving behind the eschatological perspective of his earlier theology,[74] our investigation of a portion of *CD* IV/3.1, in which Barth describes the relationship between the prophetic history of Jesus Christ and our sphere, will show this to be anything but the case. Jesus Christ is the prophet of the reconciliation he has achieved.[75] "As He lives, Jesus Christ speaks for Himself, . . . He is His own authentic Witness."[76] Whereas in the second edition of the Romans commentary, revelation was reconciliation, Barth's mature

70. Meyer, "Romans: A Commentary," 193.
71. *SR*, 67 [132].
72. Ibid., 67 [133].
73. Meyer, "Romans: A Commentary," 193.
74. See Jürgen Moltmann, *Theology of Hope: On the Ground and the Implications of a Christian Eschatology*, trans. James W. Leitch (London: SCM Press, 1967), 39–40.
75. For a particularly fine treatment of this material see John Webster, "Eloquent and Radiant: The Prophetic Office of Christ and the Mission of the Church," in *Barth's Moral Theology: Human Action in Barth's Thought* (Grand Rapids: Eerdmans, 1998), 125–50.
76. *CD* IV/3.1, 46 [49].

doctrine of reconciliation makes clear that reconciliation is revelation.[77] Not only does Jesus Christ accomplish and is in himself humanity's reconciliation with God, but he also discloses this truth about himself as this victorious mediator between God and humanity.

It is important to understand that Barth defines the term "eschatological" as the time of human and world history that has an end set for it by the death of Jesus Christ and that is currently marching toward this appointed end.[78] That which is eschatological is thus not merely connected to the final return of Christ. The one event of Christ's coming again is constituted by three different forms, which are each thoroughly eschatological. The Easter event is the first eschatological form of Christ's coming again. "What took place on Easter Day was already the end of the being of the world and man in its previous form of death and the beginning of their being in the new and eternal form of life given them in God."[79] The time of our present existence, which is the time between Easter and the final consummation of all things, is the second eschatological form of Christ's coming, characterized by the promise of the Holy Spirit.[80] Barth's description of the three forms of the one event of Christ's parousia lines up nicely with the three foci of Paul's apocalyptic perspective on time, described by Martyn as: "Christ's future coming, Christ's past advent (his death and resurrection), and the present war against the powers of evil, inaugurated by his Spirit and taking place between these two events."[81]

In order to understand the purpose of the present time as the time of the coming of the Holy Spirit, Barth begins by setting up the problem that the Spirit's coming addresses. In terms of Romans 8, Barth is asking after the reason for the longing of all creation as well as the

77. The main features of Barth's treatment of Christ's prophetic office can be helpfully summarized as follows: "Jesus Christ, risen from the dead, victorious over the powers and principalities, manifests himself in the power of the Holy Spirit, glorifies himself, makes himself known, reveals himself as the reconciler of the world, and creates a confessing community that witnesses to him as Lord." See Neder, *Participation in Christ*, 75.

78. *CD* IV/3.1, 295 [340].

79. Ibid., 316 [364].

80. For a helpful discussion of Barth's doctrine of the Holy Spirit see George Hunsinger, "The Mediator of Communion: Karl Barth's Doctrine of the Holy Spirit," in *Disruptive Grace: Studies in the Theology of Karl Barth* (Grand Rapids: Eerdmans, 2000), 148–85.

81. Martyn, *Galatians*, 105.

cosuffering of Christians with Christ, taking seriously the tension that arises between the "now" of the time of the Spirit and the "not yet" of redemption. In fact, he asks, as he says Paul himself does,[82] why, if the Easter event has already made present the future of the reconciled world, we must speak "in terms of 'only' and 'still' and 'not yet'?"[83] "How was it possible that the world's future already made present there in that [Easter] event should not at once engulf the whole world like a tidal wave, engulfing with its presence all the men of all times and places whose future had become present there in the appearance of the risen Jesus?"[84]

Barth affirms the validity of the unrest and impatience felt in light of the resurrection, as they indicate the reality that the power of the resurrection is so great that it points beyond itself, anticipating "that other, all-embracing and conclusive event,"[85] i.e., the final form of Christ's coming again. The fact that we ask questions having to do with the contradiction of what we still see remaining in this world and the truth we know, only by faith, of the restoration and newness that has come with Christ's work of reconciliation has its grounding in the Easter event itself. "We know that the contradiction itself is light and not darkness. . . . We are basically forbidden to try to escape the unsettlement caused by these questions, i.e., the necessity of looking from the one Easter Day to the very different one, to the day of the Lord."[86] It is in this contradiction that the living Jesus Christ "expresses, reflects, declares and reveals Himself,"[87] both giving the answers and asking the questions, because "[a]s the Revealer of His work He has not yet reached His goal."[88] Barth's focus on the contradiction that arises from the Easter event represents the type of

82. Gaventa observes that Paul, in Romans 8, "plunges his audience even more deeply into the present. Where he might have taken them out of the world to reorient their angle of vision, he instead touches on the future but then returns to the present situation of conflict, in which threats come from circumstances of persecution and deprivation as well as from the Powers themselves." See Gaventa, "The Apocalyptic Community," in *Our Mother Saint Paul*, 141.
83. *CD* IV/3.1, 320 [369].
84. Ibid., 316 [365].
85. Ibid., 324 [374].
86. Ibid., 325 [375].
87. Ibid., 326 [376].
88. Ibid., 327 [377].

hard realism present in Romans 8.[89] His language, at this point, takes on a decidedly apocalyptic tone, as he ponders the "reason for the incompleteness of [Christ's] conflict."[90]

He emphasizes that it is first and foremost Christ himself—"the One in whom reconciliation is already accomplished"[91]—who is in the conflict, not the world. Much more than us, Christ himself is startled and displeased by the reality that "all creation is still bound and tortured."[92] With a pity that is "active, angry, militant, aggressive and therefore genuine," Christ himself "bears the burden of persisting wickedness, the resultant evil and the death which darkens everything."[93] "He first, who alone is a match for and superior to this enemy even in the last round of the conflict, sighs and weeps and entreats and prays, as He previously did, in the open battle which has not yet been carried through to final triumph."[94]

By emphasizing the involvement of the living Christ in the current darkness and remaining conflict of the world, Barth offers a description of the external form of the relationship between Christ's prophetic history and the "not yet" reality of our present time. The first element of the description is that in order for Jesus to prove himself the Victor over the already-defeated enemy, he gives himself "time and place for combat."[95] Thus referencing without explicitly citing Romans 8, Barth urges that our "sigh[ing] and long[ing] for the liberation of the children of God"[96] is done in company with Christ rather than Christ in company with us.[97] The second element of the

89. "It is indeed a fact that the world reconciled to God in Him is far from being a redeemed and perfected world, that wickedness, evil and death are still rampant in it and in each individual, that there is still within it a whole sea of 'deserved' and 'undeserved' suffering, that we must still fight, and can only fight, under so many errors and in so much weakness. Who can overlook or deny this?" See ibid., 328 [378–79].
90. Ibid., 328 [379].
91. Ibid.
92. Ibid.
93. Ibid.
94. Ibid., 329 [380].
95. Ibid., 330 [381].
96. Ibid., 329 [380].
97. "On the contrary, the 'not yet' in which the world, the community and we all exist has its basis in the fact that it is the good will of Jesus Christ Himself to be not yet at the goal but still on the way, so that the rest of creation has no option but to participate in and adapt itself to His situation. It is not because darkness is still there, and the defeated enemy still has power and opportunity to

description of the external form of the relationship between Christ and the "not yet" follows from the first. Namely, it is the "good will" of Christ that creation, though already reconciled in Christ, might also have the "time and space, not merely to see, but actively to share in the harvest which follows from the sowing of reconciliation."[98] In making space for us to be free to speak "as independently active and free subjects" before Christ speaks "His last and decisive Word," he allows us to participate in his work, which is the original purpose of our election in him.[99] As Martyn surmises, as Paul found the "cosmos in which he had been previously living" coming to its end in God's apocalypse of Jesus Christ, his gospel mission was birthed.[100]

Barth's next move is an identification of the external conditions of the relationship between Christ's prophetic history and our present time. Barth describes these conditions in terms of both the distinction and the solidarity between Christians and non-Christians. Again, without explicitly referencing Romans 8, we can see elements of Paul's own logic at play in Barth's formulations. A few points are worth highlighting. First, in terms of the solidarity between Christians and non-Christians, Barth says two things. The first is that they both exist under certain positive conditions, provided by the fact that "according to the revelation made to all and valid for all they are reconciled to God in Jesus Christ."[101] The positive side of Paul's Christ/Adam typology, which is the foundation for his discussion of life in the Spirit and the hope of redemption in Romans 8, is in the background here.[102] The second similarity between Christians and non-Christians is the critical

lash out in its death-throes, that Jesus Christ is forced to fight him as the Protector of the peace made by Him . . . until He is finally pleased to put an end to the struggle. . . . On the contrary, it is because Jesus Christ . . . is the victorious Aggressor, and because it is His good will to act and show Himself as Victor in the fight against darkness . . . that power and opportunity are given to the enemy to make his fatal resistance, that darkness may exist, that the conflict of light against it is not ended." See ibid., 329–30 [380–81].

98. Ibid., 331 [383].

99. Ibid., 332 [383].

100. Martyn, *Galatians*, 99.

101. *CD* IV/3.1, 336 [387].

102. As Gaventa emphasizes: "The contrast Paul sets forth between the death accomplished by Adam and the life accomplished by Jesus Christ only works if both actions include all of humanity. Where there had been condemnation for all, now there is rectification and life for all (5:18)." See Gaventa, "Apocalyptic Community," 145–46.

conditions under which they both exist. Barth describes the power of evil, which, although broken in the reconciliation accomplished by Christ, can "still mount its assaults and temptations and acts of violence. The defeated enemy is still capable of attack in his dangerous death-throes, and we for our part are still vulnerable to his efforts."[103] Here again is the hard realism of Paul's insistence that the powers of evil are bent on separating us from God, even as he insists that they shall not prevail.

In terms of the distinction between Christians and non-Christians, Barth points out that while non-Christians are indeed made free for life with Jesus through the reconciliation achieved by, through, and in him, they do not know this. Thus they can exercise their freedom for life only in bondage—moving "only with the sorry freedom of prisoners, thinking and speaking and acting at random."[104] This is the main distinction between Christians and non-Christians. Even so, Christ is still the hope of non-Christians. But more can be said about Christians. They are, as Paul points out in Rom. 8:1–11, "under the law of a new and different world established in the accomplished reconciliation."[105] They live already "in the power of the kingdom of God drawn near."[106] Yet, the freedom in which Christians already live is to be characterized by solidarity with non-Christians, still in bondage.[107] The truly distinguishing feature of Christians is their knowledge: "we know that Jesus Christ Himself, and He alone, is our hope as well as theirs, that He died and rose again for those who are wholly or partially non-Christians, that His overruling work precedes and follows all being and occurrence in our sphere, that He alone is the perfect Christian, but

103. *CD* IV/3.1, 336 [388].
104. Ibid., 338 [390].
105. Ibid., 340 [392].
106. Ibid.
107. Likewise, Furnish acknowledges that Paul "does not summon his converts to withdraw from society" and "specifically encourages believers to include all people within their circle of concern." See Victor Paul Furnish, "Uncommon Love and the Common Good: Christians as Citizens in the Letters of Paul," in *In Search of the Common Good*, ed. Dennis P. McCann and Patrick D. Miller (New York: T&T Clark, 2005), 64. Gaventa adds an important theological point, stating that "if it is God who calls, then clearly the boundaries also belong to God, so that the believing community has an obligation not to treat these boundaries as human property." See Gaventa, "Apocalyptic Community, 146.

that He really is this, and is it in our place."[108] This correlates with what Paul writes in 8:18–30 of our hope and knowledge, which are both brought about in Christians by the work of the Spirit. As Kerr narrates it: "What emerges from within an apocalyptic perspective . . . is the requisite existence of a people who celebrate Christ's lordship by sharing in his mission, by being broken for the world as he was broken, by being poured out in sacrificial love for others."[109]

In concert with Eastman's point that Paul's movement in Romans is "from the present to the future 'apocalypse of the sons of God' [8:19] . . . to the salvation of 'all who believe' as promised in 1:16,"[110] so Barth urges that Christians see, in the Easter event, this very goal, "i.e., the presence of the future of salvation of their own and all existence."[111] For this reason, Christians are called to continually follow the way of Christ's own prophetic work in their own limited way by attesting, in the power of the Spirit, Jesus Christ in the world.[112] As this creates a heavy burden for Christians, so too, as for non-Christians, Jesus Christ is their only hope. "That He is the hope of all means that wittingly or unwittingly all move towards His appearing and judgment. Whether known now or unknown, He is the future of all."[113] And as the future of all, he is "the hope which shines here and now, among and in them, at the point where they exist."[114] Thus the startling truth is that there is no gap between the Easter event and Jesus' final return.[115] This middle time, and the second form of Christ's coming, "in which it is His coming

108. *CD* IV/3.1, 342 [395].

109. Kerr, *Christ, History, and Apocalyptic*, 16.

110. Eastman, "Whose Apocalypse?" 263–77.

111. Barth, *CD* IV/3.1, 343 [396].

112. Kerr makes an instructive point in this regard, clarifying that "the church is this mission as that people for whom Christ's lordship over history is not an assumed and static *given*, but a dynamic *gift*, to be received ever anew in the mode of engaged and embodied action. It is precisely by way of such missionary reception that a certain Spirit-empowered . . . mission emerges as a sign of the gift and reality of God's ongoing apocalyptic action in Christ." See Nathan Kerr, *Christ, Apocalyptic, and History: The Politics of Christian Mission* (Eugene, OR: Cascade, 2009), 16.

113. *CD* IV/3.1, 346 [399].

114. Ibid., 348 [402].

115. Martyn offers helpful insight into Paul's understanding of the relationship of the three forms of Christ's parousia: "If Paul is sure that Christ's parousia will bring the final victory of God over all his enemies (1 Corinthians 15), he is no less sure that Christ's advent has commenced the war that will lead to that victory. Thus, in an anticipatory but altogether real sense, Christ's advent is that victory, even if its victorious character can be seen only in the bifocal vision of apocalyptic. Christ's advent has already changed the world, commencing God's war of liberation in a way that

to us in our intervening sphere" is Christ's "coming in the promise of the Spirit. This is His direct and immediate presence and action among and with and in us. In it He is the hope of us all."[116]

With this move, Barth has landed squarely in the midst of Paul's discussion of the Spirit in Romans 8. As he does in *A Shorter Commentary on Romans*, Barth connects the work of the Spirit to Christ's work of reconciliation, specifying that the "Spirit is the particular mode of the coming again and therefore the presence and action of Jesus Christ in the place and time between His resurrection and His final appearing."[117] As Keck speaks of the Spirit in Romans 8 combining the "already" and the "not yet," and Meyer finds that the Spirit "confirms the gap between present and future, but at the same time sustains the expectation and turns it into a certain hope,"[118] so Barth speaks of the twofold pledge of the Spirit, who acts and speaks in the power of Christ's resurrection. The first pledge is the promise of Christ's coming as Redeemer and "of the new cosmic form to be inaugurated by Him as the future of the world and their own ultimate future," and the second is the promise of Christ's presence and help "in their temporal future, in the world which has not yet reached its goal but is only moving towards it."[119] As adopted children of God Christians are the "bearers and possessors of the promise given by the Holy Spirit."[120] The liberation for a new life of obedience, made possible in the Spirit, and described in the first half of Romans 8, is what Barth describes as the assistance of the Spirit permitting, commanding, and helping Christians "to become and be Christians step by step . . . bestowing on them in the twofold form and strength of His promise the gifts and lights and powers which they need for this purpose."[121]

As we see a dialectic at work in Paul's description of the "already" and the "not yet" in Romans 8, so we find Barth describing the tension

can be celebrated in 'enthusiastic' terms, without forgetting the future of Christ (Gal 5:5)." See Martyn, *Galatians*, 105.

116. *CD* IV/3.1, 350 [405].

117. Ibid., 351 [405].

118. Meyer, "Romans: A Commentary," 192.

119. *CD* IV/3.1, 351 [406].

120. Ibid., 352 [407].

121. Ibid., 353 [408].

created in this dialectic. He cannot leave lightly aside Paul's description of the hardships of our life and the powers aligned against us. He again describes the reality of our present existence as one in which "the earth is covered, as once before the flood, by so much merited and unmerited suffering," "when no moment passes in which death does not make what seems to be an irrevocable end of some human life," and as "a day of the devil and demons, of yielding but still resisting darkness."[122] And again, he states that it is most especially the Christian, who has received the promise of the Spirit and knows Jesus Christ is the hope of the world, who is also painfully aware of the "dominant darkness around and in him . . . by the contradiction in what is already true but not yet actual, by the manifest dominion of sin and death, by the constantly renewed resistance of the evil in whose service he again and again finds himself."[123]

Barth asks what our response to this should be and submits that "[w]e do well not to say anything more or better than what Paul said in Rom. 8:31: 'If God be for us, who can be against us?'"[124] Thus the dialectic is not an end in itself but has its foundation and goal in the good news that God has decisively accomplished the reconciliation of the world in the history of Jesus Christ. Hence our longing and waiting in expectation for the redemption of all things, our "vale of tears,"[125] is not, in God's salvation history, a negative thing, but instead "a specific form of the greatness of the pitying love of God."[126] The "riddle of our existence in transition, in the time of the 'still' and 'not yet,'"[127] is answered in the fact that "Jesus Christ Himself is in transition . . . so that it cannot be to our hurt that He is present in the form of the promise of the Spirit, but to our full salvation."[128] Thus our hope is that "the coming is not just ahead but is *already an event*."[129]

122. Ibid., 362 [418].
123. Ibid., 366 [423].
124. Ibid.
125. Ibid., 359 [415].
126. Ibid., 361 [417].
127. Ibid.
128. Ibid., 361–62 [418].
129. Karl Barth, *The Christian Life: Church Dogmatics IV, 4 Lecture Fragments*, trans. Geoffrey W. Bromiley (Grand Rapids: Eerdmans, 1981), 247 [427].

Martyn points out that Paul "uses the noun *apokalypsis* and the verb *apokalyptô*," and then proceeds to read Paul as saying that "his gospel came into being when God apocalypsed Christ to him."[130] What Martyn's reading highlights is "that in some very real sense the longed-for transformation has already occurred; in a real sense the apocalypse has already happened! It lies 'behind' us as it were."[131] Barth finds Tertullian's statement that "'In the gospel Christ Himself is the kingdom of God' (*Adv. Marc.*, IV, xxxiii, 8)"[132] to say it just right. Our hope is set on Jesus himself, who has inaugurated a new world and a new creation in his death and resurrection.

> He comes and creates righteousness . . . as the right order of the world that belongs to him. He comes and creating righteousness he abolishes the unrighteousness of people both in their relationship to him and also in their relationships to one another. He comes and sets aside not only unrighteousness but also the lordship of the lordless powers . . . restoring to man the freedom over his abilities of which they had robbed him. . . . He comes and with him comes that "peace on earth among men with whom he is pleased." . . . This peace on earth, actualized when God himself comes as King and Lord and creates and establishes it, is the kingdom of God.[133]

Together the resurrection of Christ from the dead and the pouring out of the Spirit are the eschatological events that proclaim Jesus as Lord of all and awaken us to the truth that our future is enclosed in the future of Jesus Christ. They enable us to turn "from the past of the history of Jesus Christ and the coming of God's kingdom to [our] future."[134]

This middle time between God's in-breaking action in Jesus Christ and the end time of his returning is our time in "the presence of Jesus Christ in the Holy Spirit . . . the space for gratitude, hope, and prayer, and also . . . responsibility for the occurrence of human righteousness."[135] Such human righteousness, little, derivative, and limited though it is, is to correspond with God's action in Jesus Christ

130. Martyn, *Galatians*, 99.
131. Lowe, "Why We Need Apocalyptic," 52.
132. Barth, *Christian Life*, 252 [435].
133. Ibid., 237 [405].
134. Ibid., 256 [443].
135. Ibid., 264 [457].

and therefore must "reflect . . . God's being and acting for man . . . by making man the special object of their own interest."[136] The continuing existence of non-Christians is to be the main concern that occupies us in the time that remains. "Their existence is a reminder of the darkness which resists [the prophecy of Jesus Christ]. It is for their sake that [time] must go forward, that Jesus Christ as the living Word of God is still on the way to-day."[137] The in-breaking, reconciling activity of God in Jesus Christ thus presses in on the Christian in the present time by the power of the Spirit. The Spirit makes us to correspond to our true status of adopted children of God by making us "to be not merely an object in [Christ's] work but a subject in His service."[138] The Spirit equips us to be not just hearers of the word of God in Jesus Christ but witnesses of this word. The Spirit makes the life of the Christian to be "from the very first . . . one long calling upon God."[139]

One way to frame Barth's interpretive move in describing the Christian's life in the Spirit as a missional life of witness is to return to Paul's words in Rom. 8:17. There Paul uses the term "heir," a legal image meaning "one whose entitlement is firmly established even though actual possession remains outstanding."[140] With this term Paul links the certainty of new life in the Spirit "to the still unrealized future consummation of God's deliverance."[141] Certainty and hope, Meyer suggests, are both based on the central element of Paul's gospel, "the inclusion of all in the one destiny of Jesus Christ."[142] Therefore Barth's move to speaking of the mission of the Christian as that of witnessing to the reconciliation accomplished for all in Jesus Christ is a way of giving concreteness to Paul's "heir" language in 8:17. The present suffering of Christ consists in his prophetic work to reveal the light of his reconciliation for all in spite of the surrounding darkness. Thus the

136. Ibid., 267 [462].
137. *CD* IV/3.1, 364 [421].
138. Ibid., 367 [424].
139. Ibid.
140. Meyer, "Romans: A Commentary," 191.
141. Ibid.
142. Ibid.

call to witness to this reconciliation is how we are to share in Christ's suffering.

One of the major lines of argument throughout this study has been to demonstrate how Barth's revision of Reformational forensicism according to Pauline apocalyptic eschatology safeguards his doctrine of justification against some of the criticisms commonly brought against forensicism, even while making his soteriology more consistently forensic than that of the Reformation. In this chapter this component of the argument has played out in a rather different way from what we have seen up until now. First of all, we have moved away from a direct discussion of justification and into a discussion of the eschatology supported by Barth's forensically construed doctrine of justification. In dealing with eschatology, however, Barth's relationship to Reformation theology is better characterized as a corrective rather than a mere deepening. Barth understands the prophetic activity of Jesus Christ, given in this middle time in the promise of the Spirit, as a work of drawing all people and creation to himself. Likewise, he portrays the missional calling of the Christian, in the power of the Spirit, as witnessing to the truth of Christ as the hope of all. While Barth acknowledges that the theology of the Reformation, and more specifically, the theology of Calvin, was the first to give due attention to the prophetic office of Christ in relationship to the doctrine of reconciliation, Barth questions "to what degree the meaning, importance and relevance" of the third problem of the doctrine of reconciliation was grasped by Calvin, since "in detail there seem to be all kinds of obscurities."[143] Barth concludes that Reformed theology's doctrine of double predestination especially proved to be a major barrier "between the people of God, as the elect and exclusive recipients of the witness of the Spirit, and the world."[144]

Barth implores that we must take seriously the prophetic dimension of the act of reconciliation accomplished in Christ and "consider that

143. *CD* IV/3.1, 14 [13]. Within this small-print section, Barth delineates five uncertainties regarding the formulation of Christ's prophetic office in Calvin's theology and the Reformed theology following after him. See ibid., 13–18 [13–18].

144. Ibid., 18 [17].

in sending Him God loved the world and that in Him He has reconciled the world to Himself, so that the specific history of those who hear the voice of the Good Shepherd as distinct from others cannot be the final end of His prophetic work, but can be fulfilled only in the special existence and history of the people of God."[145] He hastens to add that, given its limitations, there is no point in attempting a reconstruction of the older doctrine of Christ's prophetic office. Instead, his suggestion is that we "carefully and respectfully but boldly and resolutely transcend" it.[146] As we have seen, Barth does this by bringing those who have received the firstfruits of the Spirit into the apocalyptic drama of the conflict Christ engages in as part of his prophetic office, suggesting that their missional calling is to witness to Christ's perfect work of reconciliation to a world still threatened by the powers of darkness.[147] Moreover, the Spirit's work in liberating Christians for this new life is how their perfect justification in Christ is made subjectively true in the present time, even as they await the full realization of their new humanity and that of all creation on Christ's final return.

145. Ibid.

146. Ibid., 18 [18].

147. Kerr aptly observes that "[t]his in-between time is the time within which Christ's own cosmic victory over the powers is *performed* (through the power of the Spirit) with respect to the contingencies and particularities of our own histories. It is by way of this performance that Christ's apocalyptic historicity is made real and visible as constitutive of the very meaning, or 'truth,' of history itself. Christian apocalyptic articulates history itself as nothing less than the time of the Spirit's ongoing focal disclosure in our lives of Jesus Christ's death and resurrection, of his cosmic 'independence' from the powers and principalities, until this world's final consummation in glory." See Kerr, *Christ, History, and Apocalyptic*, 14.

9

Conclusion

> It must be asserted with the greatest possible emphasis that both historically and theologically Paul has to be understood in the light of the Reformation's insight. Any other perspective at most covers part of his thinking; it does not grasp the heart of it.
>
> —Ernst Käsemann, "The Saving Significance of the Death of Jesus in Paul"

> [W]hen you read Barth on Romans, whether you agree with his interpretation or not, you know you have confronted someone who understands Paul. It reminds one, again, of Augustine or Chrysostom.
>
> —Brevard Childs, "Karl Barth as Interpreter of Scripture"

This study has sought a closer connection between Paul and Reformation theology by offering a thorough analysis of Karl Barth's forensic apocalyptic doctrine of justification. It has had a twofold point of entry in the form of (1) a dialogue between Barth's theology and Pauline apocalyptic eschatology as it comes to expression in Romans and (2) a more sustained, accurate, and theologically complex analysis of Barth's mature contribution to the question of a Pauline theology of justification. Guided by the conviction that significant theological development occurred for Barth following the publication of the second edition of his Romans commentary, which resulted in his moving beyond the earlier theological perspectives that dominated the second edition of his Romans commentary,[1] this study has sketched out the form and content of Barth's forensic apocalyptic understanding of justification that emerges out of his mature Christology in his doctrine of reconciliation in *CD* IV and later readings of Romans both in the *CD* and *A Shorter Commentary on Romans.*

In chapter 2's analysis of the cosmic-apocalyptic features of the second edition of the Romans commentary, we discovered two things: (1) Barth's theological interpretation contains important cosmic-apocalyptic strands that he later integrates into his revision of a forensic doctrine of justification; and (2) Certain key elements in Barth's subsequent readings of Romans and explication of justification in the *Church Dogmatics* are missing in this early stage of his theology.

In chapter 3, we saw how the development in Barth's knowledge and understanding of the Reformation, coupled with the revisions that he would make to his doctrine of election in *CD* II/2, created the necessary groundwork for him to adapt and intensify the forensic reading of Paul's theology of justification, which heretofore had been carried out by the Reformation. We noted that Barth's development of a historicized theological ontology changes the way in which his mature doctrine of justification is apocalyptic. That both the being of God and humanity are established through God's self-determination to be God for us in Jesus Christ means that God's justification of sinful humanity has a historical ontological ground. Barth comes to explain justification as an event between God and humanity. Even more, justification is a history that involves a movement from death to life. The history of Jesus Christ is the unfolding history of the movement and event of the justification between God and humanity. And because this justification

1. Most notably, that the death of Jesus is a death to all *human* possibilities as an act of a human being but was not the annihilation of the being of sin as an act of the God-human, Jesus Christ. Barth's theology in the second edition of the Romans commentary is missing a Christology that expresses how the death of the human Jesus could, at the same time, be a divine act of God. See Bruce L. McCormack, "Longing for a New World: On Socialism, Eschatology and Apocalyptic in Barth's Early Dialectical Theology," in *Theology im Umbruch der Moderne: Karl Barths frühe Dialektische Theologie*, ed. Georg Pfleiderer and Harald Matern, Christentum unk Kultur Band 15 (Zürich: Theologischer Verlag, 2014), 147–48.

of God and humanity in Jesus Christ is the result of the eternal decision of God, in which God elected that both our being and God's own being would be constituted in the history of the life, death, and resurrection of the God-man Jesus, the main thrust of Pauline apocalyptic eschatology—God's in-breaking action to put the world aright—is upheld. With this historicized theological ontology in place, the classical Reformation emphasis on the forensic nature of justification takes on new meaning. Using the central idea found in a forensic (judicial) doctrine of justification, namely that of decision/declaration, Barth grounds it in election by making God's eternal decision in election basic to his theological ontology for God and humanity. Not only does this move lend itself to a faithful treatment of Paul's apocalyptic gospel, but it also creates a framework of apocalyptic forensicism that then shapes all of the doctrines interrelated to justification.

Throughout the investigation into Barth's forensic-apocalyptic doctrine of justification (chaps. 4–8), I have argued two things: (1) Barth's attention to Paul's witness to God's saving action for the world in the death and resurrection of Jesus Christ allows him to highlight the real connection between a revised understanding of forensic justification and Paul's apocalyptic witness to the subject matter of the biblical text—Jesus Christ; and (2) Barth's radical restating of justification is a result not only of grounding the forensic concept of God's decision/declaration in election, establishing a historicized theological ontology, but also of working out a mature Christology based on the history of Jesus Christ, the God-human, in his life, death, and resurrection.

In chapter 4, which considered the theme of revelation as it comes to expression in Barth's reading of Romans 1, we saw Barth reversing his emphasis on the relationship between revelation and reconciliation. In the mature Barth, reconciliation is revelation, full stop. To put it this way is to suggest that the doctrine of revelation is no longer his principal concern, reconciliation is. The difference this makes is that humans are not saved simply because they have received revelation.

Revelation does not, as such, save. The reconciling work of Jesus Christ, which Barth now understands as the history of Jesus' obedience unto death and exaltation to God's "right hand," is what saves. Revelation is now made a function of that very reconciling activity of the triune God. To say, however, that reconciliation is revelation does not require an alteration of the basic structure of revelation. It is still an apocalyptic event. But now that apocalyptic event has been grounded in a divine decision that is basic to Barth's revised forensicism.

We looked, in chapter 5, at Barth's treatment of Romans 3 in relationship to the doctrinal theme of atonement and found that, in his mature doctrine of reconciliation, the atonement functions to provide the objective realization of humanity's justification in Christ. Barth maintains that in the death of Christ, Jesus Christ caused sin and sinful humanity to be utterly abolished in his own person, thereby saving us from destruction and rescuing us from eternal death. We discovered five ways in which Barth's doctrine of atonement provides valuable contributions not only to the cosmic-apocalyptic dimensions of Paul's focus on the cross but also to the key Reformation teachings on justification by grace through faith and the saving power of Christ's alien righteousness. In Barth's hands, there is a unique interplay between the theologies of Pauline apocalyptic eschatology and the Reformation. Barth makes decision and declaration, the central ideas in traditional Protestant doctrines of justification, to find their eternal ground in election and then makes that eternal decision basic to a historicized theological ontology. The Reformation's hallmark, forensic justification, is more thoroughly connected to Scripture's subject matter, Jesus Christ, by pairing it with a historicized theological ontology, which itself offers new depth of meaning to the atonement. In the same way, the cosmic-apocalyptic features of Paul's notion of justification are not divorced from or set over against his forensic ones. Paul's forensic apocalyptic emphasis on faith—that an individual's Spirit-empowered faith in Christ is her obedient, subjective response to her objective justification in Christ—is not at odds with his cosmic-apocalyptic stress on God's in-breaking action to put the world aright in the death of Christ.

In chapter 6 we investigated the ways Barth's mature doctrine of justification is shaped by his theological interpretation of Romans 5 and found two key emphases at play: the forensic notion of acquittal and the cosmic scope of all humanity in Christ, the true Adam. Following Paul, Barth paints sin and death as enslaving powers that God's righteousness has conquered. Both sin and the sinner are abolished in the death of Christ. More powerfully still, in the resurrection God's grace overflows for new humanity in the gifts of righteousness and new life as Christ is seen to be the one true human in which all humanity has been included.

Chapter 7 considered Romans 7 and the interrelated doctrinal theme of theological anthropology, and demonstrated how Barth adapts the forensic approach to the doctrine of justification in light of his understanding of Paul's theological anthropology. Because Jesus Christ alone reveals and establishes human nature in his history and activity, not only is our justification complete in him, but our own daily experience of justification also follows the pattern of the history of Christ's death and resurrection. Barth's description of the dialectic of justification arises from parsing the forensic concept of acquittal in terms of God's divisive sentence of us, which ultimately allows him to formulate a doctrine of justification with stronger ties between Reformation emphases and Pauline apocalyptic eschatology.

Finally, chapter 8 brought us around to the doctrinal theme of eschatology, as explored by Paul in Romans 8. We found Barth working out *how* Jesus Christ, as God's effective promise of eternal life, is our only hope, and furthermore how hope is a form of our here-and-now participation in the risen Jesus Christ. We saw Barth highlighting, with Paul, that by the power of the Spirit our frail human responses to God's work can be offered to God, thereby making that which is objectively true of humanity in Christ to correspond subjectively to who we are by the Spirit daily becoming. The Spirit's work in liberating Christians for this new life is how their perfect justification in Christ is made subjectively true in present time, even as they await the full realization of new humanity and that of all of creation on Christ's final return. We learned that Barth worked especially at transcending the older Reformation limitations of Christ's prophetic office. He did this by bringing those who have received the first fruits of the Spirit into the apocalyptic drama of the conflict in which Christ engages as part of his prophetic office. Barth suggests that the missional calling of Christians is to witness to Christ's perfect work of reconciliation to a world still threatened by the powers of darkness.

Thus throughout chapters 4–8 I have demonstrated how Barth's revision of forensicism, based as it is on the historicized theological ontology that comes to expression in his mature Christology, is apocalyptic in nature. We have noted that insofar as Barth's mature Christology is apocalyptic in nature, his later reading of Romans takes up some of the same concerns as the cosmic-apocalyptic readings of Paul, if on slightly different grounds. It has become apparent that because Barth revises Reformational forensicism according to Pauline apocalyptic eschatology, his doctrine of justification is not susceptible to the same criticisms commonly brought against forensicism, even while his soteriology becomes more consistently forensic than that of the Reformation by making forensicism a framework for his historicized theological ontology. We have seen how Barth's attention to Paul's apocalyptic witness to Jesus Christ in *A Shorter Commentary on Romans*, *Christ and Adam*, and *CD* IV allows him to highlight the real connection between a forensic doctrine of justification and Paul's apocalyptic eschatology in Romans. The theology of justification in the later Barth is an integration of Reformational forensicism and Pauline apocalyptic eschatology.

Where does this leave us? This study's attempt to lessen the gap between Pauline apocalyptic eschatology and the Reformation doctrine of justification has demonstrated, through its analysis of Barth's theology and theological interpretation of Romans, that discussions about the relationship between Pauline apocalyptic eschatology and the Reformation doctrine of justification must take a different approach. For Barth, it was never a question whether the Reformers, or their doctrine of justification, were at odds with Pauline theology. He found the Reformers to be eager pupils of Paul. By allowing Paul's witness to the gospel to shape their articulations of doctrine for their own day, Barth found an example in them he desired to emulate. Yet, this did not mean he was above critiquing their theology, or even, when it came to articulating Christ's prophetic office, carefully transcending the limitations he found in them.

In the index volume to the *Church Dogmatics*, Martin Luther and John Calvin, respectively, receive the longest and second-longest entries of any other cited theologians. Although explicit reference to their work is not the sole indicator of their influence or importance for Barth, it does point us to Barth's extensive engagement, both favorable and critical, with them. George Hunsinger has noted that one of the axioms of Barth's theology is that "the No is always spoken for the sake of the Yes" and "also that the No itself is always finally contained by a larger Yes, even when that Yes remains unspoken."[2] He suggests that this axiom is often employed in Barth's practice of theological criticism. Therefore, in summarizing what Barth learned from Martin Luther, Hunsinger argues that Barth "goes beyond Luther only by building on him," not contradicting Luther so much as developing and cultivating "the quintessence of Luther's Reformation breakthrough."[3]

Barth's theology of justification and reading of Romans, therefore, constitutes not a departure from Protestant theology but a radical recentering of it on the subject matter to which it must be beholden. Barth maintains that Christology is the climax of the doctrine of justification, and he finds Paul's writing testifies most explicitly to this truth.[4] Furthermore, for all of his critical engagement with the Reformers' theology, he extolls them particularly in relationship to the doctrine of justification and their understanding of Paul's theology.

The strength of the Reformation exposition of righteousness by faith

2. George Hunsinger, "What Karl Barth Learned from Martin Luther," in *Disruptive Grace: Studies in the Theology of Karl Barth* (Grand Rapids: Eerdmans, 2000), 280.
3. Ibid., 304n40.
4. *CD* IV/1, 637 [711].

> alone consisted in a word in this, that it saw and made plain that *the living Jesus Christ—and His righteousness as man's righteousness—*is the scarlet thread which runs through Galatians and therefore through the rest of Holy Scripture. . . . That is why in the *substance* of our understanding of this matter we definitely have to take our stand with them.[5]

Along this same line, Käsemann upholds the correctness of the Reformers in appealing to Paul for understanding "evangelical theology as a theology of the cross."[6] Furthermore, he finds Barth (along with Adolf Schlatter and Bultmann) as offering properly provoking interpretations of Paul's theology of the cross. He commends Barth's work on Paul's theology for the way it upholds the original controversial stance of Protestantism—"the 'through Christ alone, through faith alone,'"[7] which, of course, derives directly from Luther's work. Käsemann's point is to emphasize that a "theology of the cross" is always to be polemical, "always a critical attack on the dominating traditional interpretation of the Christian message."[8] It was not by chance, Käsemann points out, that Paul's theology of the cross "characterized Protestant beginnings."[9] I would suggest that Käsemann's talk of Paul's theology of the cross here is simply another way of describing Paul's apocalyptic eschatology—his witness to the in-breaking action of God, which calls all human action into question and is seen most decisively in the history of Jesus's life, death, and resurrection. Cross theology—or Pauline apocalyptic eschatology—centers not only on an epistemology in which God has revealed himself in Christ crucified. It is also founded on an eschatological perspective that sees God's action in Christ as always moving out of death toward new life.[10]

Käsemann finds not only the Reformers' theology but also Barth's

5. Ibid., 642 [717] (emphasis mine).
6. Ernst Käsemann, "The Saving Significance of the Death of Jesus in Paul," in *Perspectives on Paul*, trans. Margaret Kohl (Philadelphia: Fortress Press, 1971), 32.
7. Ibid., 34
8. Ibid., 35.
9. Ibid.
10. For a thorough examination of cross theology as well as a treatment of Barth as a theologian of the cross, including a discussion of his relationship to Luther on this issue, see Rosalene Bradbury, *Cross Theology: The Classical* Theologia Crucis *and Karl Barth's Modern Theology of the Cross* (Eugene, OR: Pickwick, 2011), 149–301.

to be faithful to Paul's provocative and polemical message, yet he is concerned with the ways he sees Protestant theology and churches moving away from Paul's message in favor of the illusion of a modern view of the world and self-understanding. "Once more Paul proves to be of lasting and fateful significance for Protestantism, since his Christology brings us inevitably to a crossroads."[11] Furthermore, he finds the history of Pauline interpretation to be nothing more than the history of the apostle's "ecclesiastical domestication."[12] Paul's message of humanity's salvation in Jesus' death on the cross challenges us because it tells us who God and humanity really are.

> The dying son of God does not give life without killing; he pardons, but as judge; he glorifies us by humbling us to the deepest degree; he illuminates by confronting us inexorably with the truth about ourselves; he heals by placing us among the poor in spirit. . . . All this can be brought down to a common denominator: the justification of the ungodly is for Paul the fruit of Jesus' death, and nothing else. And this means *regnum dei* on earth.[13]

As Käsemann sees things, we are engaged, as theologians and church members, in what he calls "jungle warfare" over the dilemma that Protestant churches now seem to understand Paul's theology as anything but the cruciform theology of the Reformers.[14] "It is not entirely by chance," he surmises, "that contemporary Protestantism feels itself more at home with Orthodoxy and Roman Catholicism than with . . . a radical Reformed theology of the cross."[15]

The challenge issued by Käsemann is to "learn again to spell out the question: who is Jesus? Everything else is a distraction. We must measure ourselves against Jesus, not measure him against our churches and dogmas and devout church members."[16] As Käsemann himself has indicated, and, I would submit, as this study has demonstrated, Barth's theology of justification holds up under this challenge. And, insofar as Barth's allies, scholars of Pauline apocalyptic eschatology, also align

11. Käsemann, "Saving Significance of the Death of Jesus," 36.
12. Ibid., 47.
13. Ibid., 46.
14. Ibid., 48.
15. Ibid., 49.
16. Ibid., 53.

themselves with Käsemann's call, the potential not only for fruitful dialogue but also for a refreshed approach to the question of Paul's theology of justification is promising. Yet I would venture two suggestions in relationship to this dialogue and the idea of a new approach. First, while it is clear that critiquing, deepening, and radicalizing the theology of justification of the Reformers is to be expected and welcomed, especially if its aim is to connect the theology of justification more closely to Paul, we do ourselves, as Protestants, no favors if we only critique the doctrine, especially if the critique is based more on a caricature or the misguided representations of Reformation theology often perpetuated in our churches. Indeed, the road taken by Barth and Käsemann provides an example worth emulating in this regard. Above all, what we must avoid is the impulse, seen, for instance, in Harink, to move "beyond Protestantism"[17] and to conclude, full stop, that the Reformation doctrine of justification is "neither necessary nor warranted" "on the basis of fresh examinations of some Pauline texts and with the help of recent Pauline scholarship."[18]

Second, we must not let the inevitable discipline-specific differences of approach between theology and biblical studies prevent us from working together toward the same goal. A theologian's approach to Paul's apocalyptic theology of justification and a biblical scholar's approach are bound to treat different angles and prioritize things differently. We each must remain true to our discipline while at the same time challenging ourselves not to get bogged down by methodological disagreements, thus missing the opportunity to work for something greater together. At the same time, if we find ourselves coming back to the same arguments about how to frame our discussion of justification in light of Pauline apocalyptic eschatology, each party must do its work to answer the objections of the other, allowing for the possibility that the other discipline may have an insightful corrective to offer. In this regard, I would highlight two important avenues of

17. Douglas Harink, *Paul among the Postliberals: Pauline Theology beyond Christendom and Modernity* (Grand Rapids: Brazos, 2003), 65.
18. Ibid., 64.

the discussion that need to be considered more closely than they have been to date.

The first has to do with the *extent* to which and the *purpose* for which we undertake a discussion of Paul's concept of sin and death as powers. This study has shown that both Barth and scholars of Pauline apocalyptic eschatology are keenly attuned to the fact that sin and death are no small actors in Romans. Barth, in fact, throughout the whole of the *Church Dogmatics*, unfolds the doctrine of sin with an almost unparalleled breadth and intensity that flows out of the christological concentration governing the whole of his work.[19] The work of Martyn, Meyer, and Gaventa has been seminal in pointing out the fact that Paul, especially in Galatians and Romans, portrays sin and death as powers imprisoning humanity. While this emphasis has proved to be one of the defining features of Pauline apocalyptic scholarship today, it is my conviction that Paul's main purpose for painting sin and death this way is sometimes lost amid the talk of powers in conflict with God. For Barth, as we saw, what is undeniable is that only Christ's death is capable of releasing humanity from enslavement to sin and death. There is no contest or true conflict between God's grace and the power of sin and death. God's grace is so much more powerful than sin and death. Sin "does not exist in any way on the basis of its own independent right, or even in its dreadful reality by its own independent power. . . . It has its power, but it is the stealthy power of impotence."[20] Guided by Käsemann's call to continually focus our work around the question of who Jesus is, I would submit two helpful comments made in passing by Martyn that must be sounded louder in Pauline apocalyptic studies: (1) Paul's apocalyptic picture shows "genuine powers arrayed against God, *yet ultimately subject to God's sovereignty*"; and (2) "[t]he stark reality of [universal] enslavement is shown in the fact that its power has been

19. For an excellent treatment of Barth's doctrine of sin, see Wolf Krötke, *Sin and Nothingness in the Theology of Karl Barth*, trans. Philip G. Ziegler, Studies in Reformed Theology and History NS10 (Princeton: Princeton Theological Seminary, 2005); *Sünde und Nichtiges bei Karl Barth* (Neukirchen-Vluyn: Neukirchener Verlag, 1983).
20. *CD* IV/1, 139 [153].

broken *only by the atoning death of God's Christ . . . even that state of enslavement served God's purpose, for it precluded all thought that there might be some redemptive route other than that of Christ's atoning death.*"[21]

The second area for future clarification concerns the disagreement over the guiding framework within which to understand Paul's apocalyptic theology of justification. This study has shown that Barth chose a forensic framework within which to explicate Paul's apocalyptic theology of justification, not simply because it was the Reformers' choice but, more importantly, because in it he found a way to articulate, in a way the Reformers could not, a historicized theological ontology that made sense of Paul's "in Christ" logic and further enabled that logic to give shape to the various interrelated doctrinal themes surrounding justification. Furthermore, where Barth encountered other images for speaking of Christ's work on our behalf in Paul, such as cosmic, cultic, financial, or military conquest, he found the forensic model best able to incorporate those other images and give them their due weight. Barth felt that all that could be done is to speak only approximately and to choose what is only "relatively the best" way to achieve "systematic reflection on the *pro nobis*."[22] Nevertheless, this study has repeatedly shown that Barth continually sought to incorporate the cosmic-apocalyptic dimensions of Christ's work into his overarching forensic apocalyptic framework.

By contrast, we have found Barth's allies, scholars of Pauline apocalyptic eschatology, operating under cosmic or military conquest frameworks. Käsemann is one prime example of this. Philip Ziegler points out,

> [w]hile vigorously defending the central place of justification in Christian theology, he [Käsemann] fundamentally reconceives the doctrine by shifting the locus of divine salvation away from anthropology and onto cosmology, as the advent of God's righteousness means "God's power reaches out for the world, and the world's salvation lies in its being recaptured for the sovereignty of God."[23]

21. J. Louis Martyn, *Galatians: A New Translation with Introduction and Commentary*, AB 33A (New York: Doubleday, 1997), 373.
22. *CD* IV/1, 274 [301].
23. Philip G. Ziegler, "'Christ Must Reign': Ernst Käsemann and Soteriology in an Apocalyptic Key," in

As Käsemann says,

> For to Paul the doctrine of justification is the heart of the Christian message; it establishes the legitimacy and sets the limits of all varieties and even interpretations of NT teaching. In his view, it is essential that its substance (not its terminology) be preserved. The extent of the variations serves to prevent oversimplifying, restricting, blunting, or misunderstanding the doctrine. Yet the variations, no matter what degree of refraction they may involve, reflect the *one* central concern; they are taken up by the apostle only in so far as they are capable of doing so.[24]

As Ziegler notes, "Käsemann . . . argues that while the juridical and cultic aspects of the reality of salvation are necessary implicates of its cosmological understanding, the converse cannot be said."[25] He upholds Käsemann's "eschatological account of *Christus victor*" for the way it is not only able to account for the power and scope of sin but also "the ever-so-much-greater power and scope of divine grace rampant in Jesus Christ."[26] Finally, Käsemann's apocalyptic soteriology is recommended for the way "it does justice to both the bondage and complicity of humans in Sin, and so includes rather than bypasses the reality of human enmity and guilt. So too, salvation comes upon us as liberation that, precisely because it translates the sinner from one sphere of lordship to another, gives radical evangelical substance to notions of forgiveness, justification, and new life."[27]

Two things about Käsemann's approach are worth highlighting. First, he in no way diminishes the doctrine of justification or its centrality for understanding Paul's apocalyptic eschatology. Second, his chosen framework, an eschatological *Christus victor* model, is, as

Apocalyptic and the Future of Theology: With and beyond J. Louis Martyn, ed. Joshua B. Davis and Douglas Harink (Eugene, OR: Cascade Books, 2012), 202–3.

24. Ernst Käsemann, "Some Thoughts on the Theme 'The Doctrine of Reconciliation in the New Testament,'" in *The Future of Our Religious Past: Essays in Honour of Rudolf Bultmann*, ed. James M. Robinson, trans. Charles E. Carlston and Robert P. Scharlemann (New York: Harper & Row, 1964), 63.
25. Ziegler, "'Christ Must Reign,'" 209–10. Käsemann writes that "[t]he principalities and powers have been dethroned. If this picture is correct, reconciliation in this instance implies an eschatological, even an apocalyptic, phenomenon which is not primarily connected with, and cannot be appropriately conceived by the use of, either juridical or cultic categories." Käsemann, "Some Thoughts on the Theme 'The Doctrine of Reconciliation,'" 55.
26. Ziegler, "'Christ Must Reign,'" 217.
27. Ibid.

Ziegler demonstrates, after the very things that Barth, with his forensic framework, prioritizes. What this proves, therefore, is an idea that neither Barth nor Käsemann seems willing to concede: namely, that given the reality of a shared allegiance to Paul's radical message of justification in Christ, it is indeed possible to work out of either a forensic or a cosmological framework provided one does not ignore nor overcome the other perspective but rather seeks, at every juncture, to incorporate it. Really, this should not surprise us when we consider that Paul himself christologically adapts and modifies both forensic and cosmic patterns of Jewish eschatology in light of the in-breaking action of God in the death and resurrection of Christ. Käsemann and Barth, both pastors, theologians, and exegetes, were themselves fairly consumed with understanding and expounding Paul's apocalyptic gospel of the invading grace of God in Christ. They each found this not perfectly but still profoundly witnessed to in the Protestant doctrine of justification. What we need today is more dialogue between those of us who seek to follow after the likes of Barth and Käsemann and a renewed commitment from all involved neither simply to go "back to" the Reformers, nor to move "beyond Protestantism," but rather to circle again around Paul's polemical and radical message of salvation in Christ alone by offering "ever new attempts to bring out the saving significance of the cross"[28] and resurrection. This study is offered as but one small attempt in that direction.

28. Käsemann, "Saving Significance of the Death of Jesus," 59.

Bibliography

Aune, David E. "Recent Readings of Paul Relating to Justification by Faith." In *Rereading Paul Together: Protestant and Catholic Perspectives on Justification*, edited by David E. Aune, 188–245. Grand Rapids: Baker Academic, 2006.

Barth, Karl. *Christ and Adam: Man and Humanity in Romans 5*. Translated by T. A. Smail. Introduction by Wilhelm Pauck. New York: Harper & Brothers, 1956.

____. *The Christian Life: Church Dogmatics IV, 4 Lecture Fragments*. Translated by Geoffrey W. Bromiley. Grand Rapids: Eerdmans, 1981.

____. *Das christliche Leben: Die kirchliche Dogmatik IV/4. Fragmente aus dem Nachlass. Vorlesungen 1959-1961*. Edited by Anton Dewes and Eberhard Jüngel. Zürich: Theologischer Verlag, 1999.

____. *Christus und Adam nach Römer 5*. Zollikon-Zürich: Evangelischer Verlag, 1952.

____. *The Church Dogmatics*. Edited by Geoffrey W. Bromiley and Thomas F. Torrance. Translated by Geoffrey W. Bromiley et al. 5 vols. in 14 parts. Edinburgh: T&T Clark, 1936–77.

____. "Dank und Reverenz." *EvT* 23, no. 7 (1963): 337–42.

____. *The Epistle to the Romans*. Translated by Edwyn C. Hoskyns. London: Oxford University Press, 1933.

____. *The Göttingen Dogmatics: Instructions in the Christian Religion I*. Translated by Geoffrey W. Bromiley. Grand Rapids: Eerdmans, 1991.

____. *How I Changed My Mind*. Introduction and epilogue by John D. Godsey. Richmond, VA: John Knox, 1966.

____. "The Humanity of God." In *The Humanity of God*, translated by John Newton Thomas, 37–65. Richmond, VA: John Knox, 1960.

____. *Karl Barth-Eduard Thurneysen Briefwechsel. Band 2: 1921-1930.* Edited by Eduard Thurneysen. Zürich: Theologischer Verlag, 1974.

____. *Die kirchliche Dogmatik.* 5 vols. in 14 parts. Zollikon-Zürich: Evangelischer Verlag, 1932–70.

____. *Kurze Erklärung des Römerbriefes*, München: Chr. Kaiser Verlag, 1956.

____. *Der Römerbrief.* Zürich: Evangelischer Verlag, 1967.

____. *Der Römerbrief.* German reprint of 1st edition. Zürich: Evangelischer Verlag, 1963.

____. *Selbstdarstellung*. 1964.

____. *A Shorter Commentary on Romans.* Edited by Maico Michielin. Translated by D. H. van Daleen. Aldershot, UK: Ashgate, 2007.

____. *"Unterricht in der christlichen Religion" 1924, I.* Edited by Hannelotte Reiffen. Zürich: Theologischer Verlag, 1985.

____. *"Unterricht in der christlichen Religion" Teil 3.* Edited by Hinrich Stoevesandt. Zürich: Theologischer Verlag, 2003.

Barth, Karl, and Eduard Thurneysen. *Revolutionary Theology in the Making: Barth-Thurneysen Correspondence, 1914-1925.* Translated by James D. Smart. Richmond, VA: John Knox Press, 1964.

Bayer, Oswald. *Living by Faith: Justification and Sanctification.* Grand Rapids: Eerdmans, 2003.

Beker, J. Christiaan. "The Dilemma of Sin and Death: Equivalent or Disparate Powers?" In *Paul the Apostle: The Triumph of God in Life and Thought*, 213–34. Philadelphia: Fortress Press, 1980.

____. *Paul the Apostle: The Triumph of God in Life and Thought*. Philadelphia: Fortress Press, 1980.

____. *Paul's Apocalyptic Gospel: The Coming Triumph of God.* Philadelphia: Fortress Press, 1982.

____. "Paul's Apocalyptic Theology: Apocalyptic and the Resurrection of Christ." In *Paul the Apostle*, 135–81.

____. "The Scandal of the Cross." In *Paul the Apostle*, 182–212.

____. *The Triumph of God: The Essence of Paul's Thought*. Minneapolis: Fortress Press, 1990.

Billings, J. Todd. *Calvin, Participation and the Gift: The Activity of Believers in Union with Christ*. Oxford: Oxford University Press, 2007.

Bradbury, Rosalene. *Cross Theology: The Classical* Theologia Crucis *and Karl Barth's Modern Theology of the Cross*. Eugene, OR: Pickwick, 2011.

Bultmann, Rudolf. "Karl Barth's *Epistle to the Romans* in Its Second Edition." In *The Beginnings of Dialectic Theology*, vol. 1, edited by James M. Robinson and translated by Keith R. Crim, 100–120. Richmond, VA: John Knox, 1962.

Burnett, Richard E. *Karl Barth's Theological Exegesis: The Hermeneutical Principles of the Römerbrief Period*. Foreword by Bruce McCormack. Grand Rapids: Eerdmans, 2004.

Busch, Eberhard. *The Great Passion: An Introduction to Karl Barth's Theology*. Translated by Geoffrey W. Bromiley. Edited and annotated by Darrell L. Guder and Judith J. Guder. Grand Rapids: Eerdmans, 2004.

____. *Karl Barth: His Life from Letters and Autobiographical Texts*. Translated by John Bowden. Reprint, Eugene, OR: Wipf & Stock, 2005.

____. *Karl Barths Lebenslauf*. München: Christian Kaiser Verlag, 1975.

Calvin, John. *Institutes of the Christian Religion*. Edited by John T. O'Neill. Translated by Ford Lewis Battles. 2 vols. Library of Christian Classics. Reissued, Louisville: Westminster John Knox, 2006.

Canlis, Julie. *Calvin's Ladder: A Spiritual Theology of Ascent and Ascension*. Grand Rapids: Eerdmans, 2010.

Childs, Brevard. "Karl Barth as Interpreter of Scripture." In *Karl Barth and the Future of Theology*, edited by David L. Dickerman, 30–35. New Haven, CT: Yale Divinity School Association, 1969.

Congdon, David W. "Bonhoeffer and Bultmann: Toward an Apocalyptic Rapprochement." *International Journal of Systematic Theology* 15, no. 2 (2013): 172–95.

____. "Eschatologizing Apocalyptic: An Assessment of the Present Conversation on Pauline Apocalyptic." In *Apocalyptic and the Future of Theology: With and beyond J. Louis Martyn*, edited by Joshua B. Davis and Douglas Harink, 118–36. Eugene, OR: Cascade Books, 2012.

____. *The Mission of Demythologizing: Rudolf Bultmann's Dialectical Theology*. Minneapolis: Fortress Press, 2015.

Cousar, Charles B. "Continuity and Discontinuity: Reflections on Romans 5–8." In *Pauline Theology*, vol. 3, *Romans*, edited by David M. Hay and E. Elizabeth Johnson, 196–210. Minneapolis: Fortress Press, 1995.

____. *A Theology of the Cross: The Death of Jesus in the Pauline Letters*. Minneapolis: Fortress Press, 1990.

Dalferth, Ingolf U. "Karl Barth's Eschatological Realism" In *Karl Barth: Centenary Essays*, edited by S. W. Sykes, 14–45. Cambridge: Cambridge University Press, 1989.

de Boer, Martinus C. *The Defeat of Death: Apocalyptic Eschatology in 1 Corinthians 15 and Romans 5*. Sheffield: JSOT, 1988.

____. "Paul and Apocalyptic Eschatology." In *The Origins of Apocalypticism in Judaism and Christianity*, vol. 1 of *The Encyclopedia of Apocalypticism*, edited by John J. Collins, 345–83. New York: Continuum, 1998.

____. "Paul, Theologian of God's Apocalypse." *Interpretation* 56 (2002): 21–33.

Dunn, James D. G. *The Epistle to the Galatians*. Peabody, MA: Hendrickson, 1993.

____. "The New Perspective on Paul." *Bulletin of the John Rylands Library* 65 (1983): 95–122. Reprinted in *Jesus Paul, and the Law: Studies in Mark and Galatians*, 183–214. Louisville: Westminster John Knox, 1990.

____. "The New Perspective: Whence and Whither?" In *The New Perspective on Paul*, 17–22. WUNT 185. Tübingen: Mohr Siebeck, 2005.

____. *Romans 1-8*. Word Biblical Commentary 38A. Waco: Word Books, 1988.

____. *Romans 9-16*. Word Biblical Commentary 38B. Waco: Word Books, 1988.

____. *The Theology of Paul the Apostle*. Grand Rapids: Eerdmans, 1998.

Eastman, Susan. "Whose Apocalypse? The Identity of the Sons of God in Romans 8:19." *Journal of Biblical Literature* 121, no. 2 (2002): 263–77.

Furnish, Victor Paul. "Uncommon Love and the Common God: Christians as Citizens in the Letters of Paul." In *In Search of the Common Good*, edited by Dennis P. McCann and Patrick D. Miller, 58–87. New York: T&T Clark, 2005.

Gaventa, Beverly Roberts. "The Apocalyptic Community." In *Our Mother Saint Paul*, 137–47. Louisville: Westminster John Knox, 2007.

____. "From Toxic Speech to the Redemption of Doxology in Paul's Letter to the Romans." In *The Word Leaps the Gap: Essays on Scripture and Theology in Honor of Richard B. Hays*, edited by J. Ross Wagner, C. Kavin Rowe, and A. Katherine Grieb, 392–408. Grand Rapids: Eerdmans, 2008.

____. "God Handed Them Over." In *Our Mother Saint Paul*, 113–23. Louisville: Westminster John Knox, 2007.

____. "Interpreting the Death of Jesus Apocalyptically: Reconsidering Romans 8:32." In *Jesus and Paul Reconnected: Fresh Pathways into an Old Debate*, edited by Todd D. Still, 125–45. Grand Rapids: Eerdmans, 2007.

____. "Neither Height nor Depth: Discerning the Cosmology of Romans." *Scottish Journal of Theology* 64, no. 3 (2011): 265–78.

____. *Our Mother Saint Paul*. Louisville: Westminster John Knox, 2007.

Gockel, Matthias. *Barth and Schleiermacher on the Doctrine of Election: A Systematic-Theological Comparison*. Oxford: Oxford University Press, 2006.

Harink, Douglas. "Justification: Beyond Protestantism." In *Paul among the Postliberals: Pauline Theology beyond Christendom and Modernity*, 23–65. Grand Rapids: Brazos, 2003.

____. *Paul among the Postliberals: Pauline Theology beyond Christendom and Modernity*. Grand Rapids: Brazos, 2003.

Hays, Richard B. *The Faith of Jesus Christ: The Narrative Substructure of Galatians 3:1–4:11*. Grand Rapids: Eerdmans, 2002.

____. "Πίστις and Pauline Christology: What Is at Stake?" in *Pauline Theology*, vol. 4, *Looking Back, Pressing On*, edited by Elizabeth Johnson and David M. Hay, 714–29. Atlanta: Scholars Press, 1997.

____. "Psalm 143 and the Logic of Romans 3." *Journal of Biblical Literature* 99 (1980): 107–15.

Henry, David P. *The Early Development of the Hermeneutic of Karl Barth as Evidenced by His Appropriation of Romans 5.12–21*. Macon, GA: Mercer University Press, 1985.

Hill, Charles E., and Frank A. James III, eds. *The Glory of the Atonement: Biblical, Historical & Practical Perspectives*. Downers Grove, IL: InterVarsity Press, 2004.

Hirsch, Emmanuel. *Hilfsbuch zum Studium der Dogmatik: Die Dogmatik der Reformatoren und der altevangelischen Lehrer quellmässig belegt und verdeutscht*. Berlin: de Gruyter, 1951.

Hultgren, Arland J. *Paul's Gospel and Mission: The Outlook from His Letters to the Romans*. Philadelphia: Fortress Press, 1985.

Hunsinger, George. "The Mediator of Communion: Karl Barth's Doctrine of the Holy Spirit." In *Disruptive Grace: Studies in the Theology of Karl Barth*, 148–85. Grand Rapids: Eerdmans, 2000.

____. "What Karl Barth Learned from Martin Luther." In *Disruptive Grace: Studies in the Theology of Karl Barth*, 279–304. Grand Rapids: Eerdmans, 2000.

Husbands, Mark, and Daniel J. Treier, eds. *Justification: What's at Stake in the Current Debates*. Downers Grove, IL: InterVarsity Press, 2004.

Jüngel, Eberhard. *God's Being Is in Becoming: The Trinitarian Being of God in the Theology of Karl Barth*. Translated by John Webster. Edinburgh: T&T Clark, 2001.

____. *Justification: The Heart of the Christian Faith. A Theological Study with an Ecumenical Purpose*. Translated by Jeffrey F. Cayzer. Introduction by John Webster. Edinburgh: T&T Clark, 2001.

Kärkkäinen, Veli-Matti. *One with God: Salvation as Deification and Justification*. Collegeville, MN: Liturgical, 2004.

Käsemann, Ernst. "The Beginnings of Christian Theology." In *New Testament Questions of Today*, translated by W. J. Montague, 82–107. London: SCM Press, 1969.

____. *Commentary on Romans*. Edited and translated by Geoffrey W. Bromiley. Grand Rapids: Eerdmans, 1980.

____. "Justification and Salvation History in the Epistle to the Romans." In *Perspectives on Paul*, 60–78.

____. "On Paul's Anthropology." In *Perspectives on Paul*, 1–31.

____. "On the Subject of Primitive Christian Apocalyptic." In *New Testament Questions of Today*, translated by W. J. Montague, 108–37. London: SCM Press, 1969.

____. "Paul and Early Catholicism." In *New Testament Questions of Today*, translated by W. J. Montague, 236–51. London: SCM Press, 1969.

____. *Perspectives on Paul*. Translated by Margaret Kohl. Philadelphia: Fortress Press, 1971.

____. "'The Righteousness of God' in Paul." In *New Testament Questions of Today*, translated by W. J. Montague, 168–82. London: SCM Press, 1969.

____. "The Saving Significance of the Death of Jesus in Paul." In *Perspectives on Paul*, 32–59.

____. "Some Thoughts on the Theme 'The Doctrine of Reconciliation in the New Testament.'" In *The Future of Our Religious Past: Essays in Honour of Rudolf Bultmann*, edited by James M. Robinson and translated by Charles E. Carlston and Robert P. Scharlemann, 49–64. New York: Harper & Row, 1964.

Keck, Leander E. *Paul and His Letters*. 2nd ed. Proclamation Commentaries. Minneapolis: Fortress Press, 1988.

____. *Romans*. Abingdon New Testament Commentary. Nashville: Abingdon, 2005.

____. "What Makes Romans Tick?" In *Romans*, vol. 3 of *Pauline Theology*, edited by David M. Hay and E. Elizabeth Johnson, 3–29. Minneapolis: Fortress Press, 1995.

Kerr, Nathan. *Christ, Apocalyptic, and History: The Politics of Christian Mission*. Eugene, OR: Cascade, 2009.

Kolb, Robert. "Contemporary Lutheran Understandings of the Doctrine of Justification." In *Justification: What's at Stake in the Current Debates?*, edited by Mark Husbands and Daniel J. Treier, 153–76. Downers Grove, IL: InterVarsity Press, 2004.

Krötke, Wolf. *Sin and Nothingness in the Theology of Karl Barth*. Translated by Philip G. Ziegler. Studies in Reformed Theology and History NS10. Princeton: Princeton Theological Seminary Press, 2005.

____. *Sünde und Nichtiges bei Karl Barth*. Neukirchen-Vluyn: Neukichener Verlag, 1983.

Lewis, Scott M. *What Are They Saying about New Testament Apocalyptic?* New York: Paulist Press, 2004.

Lowe, Walter. "Why We Need Apocalyptic." *Scottish Journal of Theology* 63, no. 1 (2010): 41–53.

Luther, Martin. *Lectures on Galatians 1535: Chapters 1-4*. Edited by Jaroslav Pelikan. Luther's Works 26. St. Louis: Concordia Publishing House, 1963.

____. *Lectures on Romans*. Translated by Wilhelm Pauck. Library of Christian Classics. Philadelphia: Westminster John Knox, 1961.

Lutheran World Federation and the Roman Catholic Church. *Joint Declaration on the Doctrine of Justification*. English edition. Grand Rapids: Eerdmans, 2000.

Mannermaa, Tuomo. *Christ Present in Faith: Luther's View of Justification*. Minneapolis: Fortress Press, 2005.

Martyn, J. Louis. "Apocalyptic Antinomies." In *Theological Issues in the Letters of Paul*, 111–23. Nashville: Abingdon, 1997.

____. "The Apocalyptic Gospel in Galatians." *Interpretation* 54, no. 3 (2000): 244–66.

____. "Apocalyptic Rectification." In *Theological Issues in the Letters of Paul*, 87–88. Nashville: Abingdon, 1997.

____. "A Formula for Communal Discord!" In *Theological Issues in the Letters of Paul*, 267–78. Nashville: Abingdon, 1997.

____. *Galatians: A New Translation with Introduction and Commentary*. AB 33A. New York: Doubleday, 1997.

____. "Galatians, An Anti-Judaic Document?" In *Theological Issues in the Letters of Paul*, 77–88.

____. "God's Way of Making Right What Is Wrong." In *Theological Issues in the Letters of Paul*, 141–56.

____. "*Nomos* Plus Genitive in Paul: The History of God's Law." In *Early Christianity and Classical Culture: Comparative Studies in Honor of Abraham J. Malherbe*, edited by J. F. Fitzgerald, Thomas H. Olbricht, and L. Michael White, 575–87. Leiden: Brill, 2003.

____. "Paul and His Jewish-Christian Interpreters." *Union Seminary Quarterly Review* 42 (1988): 1–15.

____. "A Personal Word." In *The Word in the World: Essays in New Testament Exegesis and Theology*, edited by Paul W. Meyer and John T. Carroll, xvii–xxx. Louisville: Westminster John Knox, 2004.

____. *Theological Issues in the Letters of Paul*. Nashville: Abingdon, 1997.

Matlock, Barry. *Unveiling the Apocalyptic Paul: Paul's Interpreters and the Rhetoric of Criticism*. Sheffield: Sheffield Academic Press, 1996.

Mattes, Mark C. *The Role of Justification in Contemporary Theology*. Grand Rapids: Eerdmans, 2004.

McCormack, Bruce L. "Can We Still Speak of 'Justification by Faith'?: An In-House Debate with Apocalyptic Readings of Paul." In *Galatians and Christian Theology: Justification, the Gospel, and Ethics in Paul's Letter*, edited by Mark W. Elliott, Scott J. Hafemann, N. T. Wright, and John Frederick, 159–84. Grand Rapids: Baker Academic, 2014.

____. "Christonomie." In *Karl Barth Handbuch*, edited by Michael Beintker. Tübingen: Mohr Siebeck, forthcoming.

____. "Divine Impassibility or Simply Divine Constancy? Implications of Karl Barth's Later Christology for Debates over Impassibility." In *Divine Impassibility and the Mystery of Human Suffering*, edited by James F. Keating and Thomas Joseph White, OP, 150–86. Grand Rapids: Eerdmans, 2009.

____, ed. *Justification in Perspective: Historical Developments and Contemporary Challenges*. Grand Rapids: Baker Academic, 2006.

____. "*Justitia Aliena*: Karl Barth in Conversation with the Evangelical Doctrine of Imputed Righteousness." In *Justification in Perspective*, 167–96.

____. *Karl Barth's Critically Realistic Dialectical Theology: Its Genesis and Development 1909–1936.* Oxford: Clarendon Press, 2004.

____. "Karl Barth's Historicized Christology: Just How 'Chalcedonian' Is It?" In *Orthodox and Modern: Studies in the Theology of Karl Barth*, 201–33. Grand Rapids: Baker Academic, 2008.

____. "Longing for a New World: On Socialism, Eschatology and Apocalyptic in Barth's Early Dialectical Theology." In *Theologie im Umbruch der Moderne: Karl Barths frühe Dialektische Theologie*, edited by Georg Pfleiderer and Harald Matern, 135–49. Christentum unk Kultur Band 15. Zürich: Theologischer Verlag, 2014.

____. "The Ontological Presuppositions of Barth's Doctrine of Atonement." In *The Glory of the Atonement: Biblical, Historical and Practical Perspectives*, edited by Charles E. Hill and Frank A. James III, 346–66. Downers Grove, IL: InterVarsity Press, 2004.

____. *Orthodox and Modern: Studies in the Theology of Karl Barth*. Grand Rapids: Baker Academic, 2008.

____. "Seek God Where He May Be Found: A Response to Edwin Chr. Van Driel." *Scottish Journal of Theology* 60, no. 1 (2007): 62–79.

____. "The Significance of Karl Barth's Theological Exegesis of Philippians." In *Orthodox and Modern: Studies in the Theology of Karl Barth*, 89–105. Grand Rapids: Baker Academic, 2008.

Meyer, Paul W. "Romans: A Commentary." In *The Word in This World: Essays in New Testament Exegesis and Theology*, edited by John T. Carroll, 149–218. Louisville: Westminster John Knox, 2004.

____. "The Worm at the Core of the Apple: Exegetical Reflections on Romans 7." In *The Conversation Continues: Studies in Paul and John in Honor of J. Louis Martyn*, edited by Robert T. Fortna and Beverly Roberts Gaventa, 62–84. Nashville: Abingdon, 1990.

Michielin, Maico. "Exegesis That Corresponds to God's Activity." In Karl Barth, *A Shorter Commentary on Romans*, edited by Maico Michielin and translated by D. H. van Daleen, vii–xxiii. Aldershot, UK: Ashgate, 2007.

Moltmann, Jürgen. *Theology of Hope: On the Ground and the Implications of a Christian Eschatology*. Translated by James W. Leitch. London: SCM Press, 1967.

Myers, Benjamin. "From Faithfulness to Faith in the Theology of Karl Barth." In *The Faith of Jesus Christ: Exegetical, Biblical and Theological Studies*, edited by Michael F. Bird and Preston M. Sprinkle, 291–308. Carlisle, UK: Paternoster, 2009.

Neder, Adam. *Participation in Christ: An Entry into Karl Barth's Church Dogmatics*. Louisville: Westminster John Knox, 2009.

Rutledge, Fleming. "A Modest Proposal: Apocalyptic Theology." *Generous Orthodoxy Blog*. October 23, 2009. http://ruminations.generousorthodoxy.org/2009/10/modest-proposal-apocalyptic-theology.htm.

Sanders, E. P. *Paul and Palestinian Judaism: A Comparison of Patterns of Religion*. Minneapolis: Fortress Press, 1997.

Schweitzer, Albert. *The Mysticism of Paul the Apostle*. Translated by William Montgomery. Foreword by Jaroslav Pelikan. Baltimore: Johns Hopkins University Press, 1998.

Stendahl, Krister. "The Apostle Paul and the Introspective Conscience of the West," *Harvard Theological Review* 56 (1963): 199–215. Reprinted in *The Writings of St. Paul: Annotated Text and Criticism*, edited by W. A. Meeks. Norton Critical Editions in the History of Ideas. New York: W. W. Norton, 1972.

Sturm, Richard E. "Defining the Word 'Apocalyptic': A Problem in Biblical Criticism." In *Apocalyptic and New Testament: Essays in Honor of J. Louis Martyn*, edited by Joel Marcus and Marion L. Soards, 17–47. Sheffield: JSOT, 1989.

Thurneysen, Eduard. "Die Anfänge." In *Antwort: Karl Barth zum siebzigsten*

Geburtstag, edited by Rudolf Frey, Ernst Wolf, and Ch. Von Kirschbaum, 832. Zürich: Evangelischer Verlag, 1956.

Vielhauer, Philipp. "Introduction [to Apocalypses and Related Subjects]." In *New Testament Apocrypha*, edited by E. Hennecke and W. Schneemelcher, 2.581–607. Philadelphia: Westminster, 1963–65.

Watson, Francis. "The Triune Divine Identity: Reflections on Pauline God-Language, in Disagreement with J. D. G. Dunn." *Journal for the Study of the New Testament* 80 (2000): 99–124.

Webster, John. "Eloquent and Radiant: The Prophetic Office of Christ and the Mission of the Church." In *Barth's Moral Theology: Human Action in Barth's Thought*. Grand Rapids: Eerdmans, 1998.

____. "Karl Barth." In *Reading Romans through the Centuries: From the Early Church to Karl Barth*, edited by Jeffrey P. Greenman and Timothy Larsen, 205–23. Grand Rapids: Brazos, 2005.

____. "Rescuing the Subject: Barth and Postmodern Anthropology." In *Karl Barth: A Future for Postmodern Theology?*, edited by Geoff Thompson and Christiaan Mostert, 46–69. Hindmarsh: Australian Theological Forum, 2000.

Westerholm, Stephen. *Perspectives Old and New on Paul: The "Lutheran" Paul and His Critics.* Grand Rapids: Eerdmans, 2004.

Wharton, James. "Karl Barth as Exegete and His Influence on Biblical Interpretation." *Union Seminary Quarterly Review* 28 (1972): 5–13.

Wrede, William. *Paul.* Translated by Edward Lummis. Preface by J. Estlin Carpenter. Reprint, Eugene, OR: Wipf & Stock, 2001.

Wright, N. T. *The Climax of the Covenant: Christ and the Law in Pauline Theology.* Minneapolis: Fortress Press, 1991.

____. "Justification: The Biblical Basis and Its Relevance for Contemporary Evangelicalism." In *The Great Acquittal: Justification by Faith in Current Christian Thought*, edited by Gavin Reid, 13–37. London: Collins, 1980.

____. *The New Testament and the People of God*. Minneapolis: Fortress Press, 1992.

____. "The Paul of History and the Apostle of Faith." *TB* 29 (1978): 61–88.

____. *Romans*. New Interpreters Bible 101. Nashville: Abingdon, 2002.

____. "Romans and the Theology of Paul." In *Romans*, volume 3 of *Pauline Theology*, edited by D. M. Hay and E. E. Johnson, 30–67. Minneapolis: Fortress Press, 1992.

____. *What Saint Paul Really Said: Was Paul of Tarsus the Real Founder of Christianity?* Grand Rapids: Eerdmans, 1997.

Ziegler, Philip G. "'Christ Must Reign': Ernst Käsemann and Soteriology in an Apocalyptic Key." In *Apocalyptic and the Future of Theology with and beyond J. Louis Martyn*, edited by Joshua B. Davis and Douglas Harink, 200–218. Eugene, OR: Cascade Books, 2012.

Index

CPSIA information can be obtained
at www.ICGtesting.com
Printed in the USA
LVOW04*2022190416
484382LV00010B/86/P

9 781506 410555